EARLY EXPERIENCE, THE
BRAIN, AND CONSCIOUSNESS

EARLY EXPERIENCE, THE BRAIN, AND CONSCIOUSNESS

An Historical and Interdisciplinary Synthesis

Thomas C. Dalton • Victor W. Bergenn

Lawrence Erlbaum Associates
Taylor & Francis Group

New York   London

Lawrence Erlbaum Associates
Taylor & Francis Group
270 Madison Avenue
New York, NY 10016

Lawrence Erlbaum Associates
Taylor & Francis Group
2 Park Square
Milton Park, Abingdon
Oxon OX14 4RN

Printed in the United States of America on acid-free paper
10 9 8 7 6 5 4 3 2 1

International Standard Book Number-13: 978-0-8058-4085-8 (Softcover) 978-0-8058-4084-1 (Hardcover)

Library of Congress Cataloging-in-Publication Data

Dalton, Thomas Carlyle.
      Early experience, the brain, and consciousness : an historical and interdisciplinary synthesis / Thomas C. Dalton, Victor W. Bergenn.
          p. cm.
      Includes bibliographical references and index.
      ISBN 0-8058-4084-2 (cloth : alk. paper) -- ISBN 0-8058-4085-0 (pbk. : alk. paper)
      1. Developmental psychology. 2. Experience. I. Bergenn, Victor W. II. Title.

BF719.6.D35 2007
155.4'13--dc22   2006027106

Visit the Taylor & Francis Web site at
http://www.taylorandfrancis.com

and the LEA Web site at
http://www.erlbaum.com

Contents

Preface

There is a growing interest and demand among developmental scientists and practitioners across disciplines to put the burgeoning knowledge of the brain, mind, and behavior in historical and contemporary contexts. This book shows how different lines of inquiry intersect to afford a more coherent and comprehensive understanding of the relationship between brain development and experience. Historically significant events that contributed to the scientific study of the brain and consciousness are described, and an interdisciplinary body of literature is synthesized regarding what we know about the relationship between early experience and the brain. Recent theories about the relationship between motor and perceptual development are critically assessed in light of neuroscientific evidence. An alternative theory is proposed that the acquisition of behavioral, cognitive, and linguistic functions during early childhood is governed by mechanisms of selection, variation, complexity, and integration characteristic of emergent biological systems.

The neuroscientific revolution has forced developmental scientists to reexamine assumptions about the causes of human behavior. The persistent tendency among psychologists to understand the phenomena of development in terms of nature versus nurture is a dichotomy that has outlived its usefulness as a theoretical construct. Over the last decade, there have been enormous advances in the theories and methods employed by scientists to understand how genetic and environmental factors interact during the processes of human growth and development. Developmental scientists no longer view development as if it could be neatly partitioned along a continuum in which the earliest events reflect largely genetic influences and the later events are shaped by environment and culture. Instead they see individual growth in terms of a reciprocal interaction of biological, behavioral, and cultural events that occur throughout an individual's lifetime. Together over time, these interactions contribute cumulatively to small but important changes in the human phenotype.

Scientific knowledge about the effects of experience on neural growth and brain function has been limited, until recently, to experimental behavioral, electrophysiological, and surgical interventions in nonhuman primates and other animals. These animal studies have been enormously useful in generating knowledge about the probable effects of experience in human neurobehavioral development. Although these studies continue to furnish new insights about brain-behavior relationships, newer, noninvasive techniques have significantly enlarged our understanding of how different regions of the human brain are functionally integrated during development. Functional magnetic resonance imaging (fMRI) now makes it possible to isolate brain regions that show the largest increase in metabolic activity and trace their interaction in response to stimulation. The authors describe what investigators have learned about the development of motor, perceptual, and cognitive skills by experimentally manipulating these processes. Readers find out why information is processed differently by persons with normal and dysfunctional brains and why individuals learn about and experience their world in contrasting ways.

These and other methods for recording brain activity also suggest that consciousness is a tool that infants acquire early on to integrate multiple sensory and motor experiences, communicate, attain a sense of self, and acquire knowledge of other minds. Neither mind nor consciousness are entities confined to cortical or prefrontal regions, but involve the functional integration of neurobiological and neurobehavioral processes that include the whole brain and involve experiential influences at every phase of development.

We have chosen to focus on attention and memory in this book because these mechanisms of consciousness appear to play a crucial role in the perceptual judgments that infants form and the motor strategies they undertake to learn about and change their world. These mechanisms enable the coupling between sensory inputs and motor actions through a series of developmental events needed to gain perceptual access and control of the meaning and significance of situations encountered through personal experience. Attention and memory are complex functional mechanisms that reflect continuous changes in neural, behavioral, and emotional states. The efficacy of attention and memory can be temporarily or even seriously impaired if the normal interaction between brain regions is impeded by persisting states of behavioral redundancy and/or restricted sensory or emotional variability. Evidence from such episodes is presented in the chapters that follow to explain how small deviations from the expected trajectory of neurobehavioral development can compromise the mechanisms that infants rely on to gain conscious access to their world and control of the consequences of their behavior.

This book also features the discoveries of pioneers and contemporary innovators who have made important contributions to our knowledge of the relationship between brain growth and early development. This seminal knowledge has come from several fields, including philosophy, embryology, ethology, neurology, neurobiology, cognitive neuroscience, developmental psychology, and the nascent field of mind and consciousness studies. Experimental research with animals and humans, including individuals with normal and damaged or dysfunctional brains, indicates that the brain is remarkably plastic and resilient, and that the neural mechanisms supporting attention and memory play equally important roles in learning in both humans and animals.

The beliefs that developmental outcomes are strongly influenced by the timing of stimulation and its duration remain controversial. The contention has been that there are critical periods in early development during which sensorimotor functions must be acquired that, if delayed, result in permanent impairment. Nevertheless, researchers are increasingly divided about the effects of early experience in later childhood. Researchers who track the influence of developmental events over time are finding more complex and variable patterns that reduce the probability that adult personality, behavioral traits, or cognitive abilities can be accurately predicted by any one factor or influence occurring in early development. Moreover, children with learning disorders, such as attention deficits or dyslexia, possess compensatory, brain-based strategies to mitigate these deficits. Alternative sites for neural processing provide windows of opportunity for children and adults to acquire new skills long after the earliest formative years. The brain's plasticity, interactivity, and structural redundancy enable individuals to attain sensorimotor integration in different ways that support diverse but comparable modes of learning.

Developmental psychologists who do experimental or clinical work with infants and young children should find this book useful. In addition, this book will be of considerable interest to neurobiologists, cognitive neuroscientists, pediatricians, educators, and parents with infants and young children. We believe that developmental scientists will find this volume appealing because it furnishes to their students the conceptual tools to critically assess and put into historical context scientific knowledge about experience and the brain. Students will become familiar with the latest theories about how development has evolved and will better understand how the sequence of early development is susceptible to variations introduced by the contingencies of experience. They will also learn about the biological processes that contribute to the plasticity of the human brain, and they will be better able to assess the competing arguments about how the brain is organized and becomes integrated through experience.

Chapter 1 addresses several issues regarding the brain and mind from historical and neuroscientific perspectives. Philosophical speculation about the mind and soul dominated the discourse about human nature for centuries until scientists sought more knowledge about the biological foundations of human thought and behavior. The American pragmatists William James and John Dewey decisively contributed to the ascendancy of psychological science by showing how the brain generates thoughts whose value does not require certitude that they represent some indisputable truth about nature or our perceptions of the world. Instead, they believed that the brain and mind evolved to furnish new capabilities to respond effectively to the uncertainties and contingencies of nature that depend less on certain knowledge than on the accumulation of experience.

Developmental psychologists are generally divided on how best to characterize what infants know and how they use their brains to gain knowledge about their world. That is why developmental scientists have increasingly adopted neuroscientific techniques, described in Chapter 1, to better understand the relationship between brain development and the acquisition of motor and cognitive functions. Neurobiologist Gerald Edelman advances a useful theory that brain development can be best explained by processes of Darwinian selection that exploit the enormous diversity of alternative patterns of interaction to satisfy the functional needs of the organism. The uniquely important argument Edelman makes is that the units of selection at different levels of complexity are not single entities, such as molecules, cells, reflexes, or percepts, but dynamic, large-scale patterns of interactions among groups of neurons, which support diverse global mappings. Perception is not limited to isolated objects of sensory input, but is constituted by conscious actions that engage the entire senorimotor apparatus of the organism. Accordingly, Edelman takes the position that knowledge is not representational, but relational and pluralistic—a theory of knowledge that is grounded in the pragmatism of James and Dewey.

Attempts have been rare among developmental scientists to advance general theories of neuropsychological development that address from interdisciplinary standpoints how biological structures, mental processes, and social conduct are interrelated. A general theory should account for phenomena that occur at different levels of complexity and explain how they are combined to produce coherent and integrated behavior. Chapter 2 critically examines the prevailing hierarchical conception of brain function and proposes an alternative, nonhierarchical conception to better reflect the interrelated physical and psychological aspects of emergent processes. We focus on the problem of hierarchy and indicate how the interdependence among physical, physiological, and psychological attributes of sentient organisms contributes to the emergence of consciousness.

To be certain the explanatory gap between neuronal processes and psychological functions remains considerable. We do not pretend to close this gap in understanding how physical and mental events are interrelated. Nevertheless, we believe that the elusive phenomenal dimension of conscious states can be better understood by examining how human sentient capacities and motor skills set the boundaries in which sensory input is converted into gestures and behaviors that possess meaning and significance. We contend that the threshold of consciousness is reached only when there is multimodal stimulation sufficient to sustain intersensory perception. Multimodal stimulation is essential because it furnishes organisms a way to make discriminations involving judgments about equivalence. By equivalence, we do not simply mean the " the same as." Equivalence also entails the sense that one thing may be substituted for another to reach the same judgment or attain the same outcome differently. Unisensory organisms cannot detect and process complex signals and thus do not have the ability to make such comparative judgments. Only organisms that possess a multisensory apparatus are fully capable of discriminating among and integrating multiple sensory inputs into scenes that involve a conscious experience.

Only within the last two decades has it been possible to observe prenatal development in real time. Ultrasound and vibroacoustic stimulation are providing a more detailed picture of how the prenatal brain grows and acquires sensory access, and how fetal behavior becomes differentiated. Chapter 3 examines how prenatal sensation and movement become organized into coherent neurobehavioral states by late term. Chapter 4 describes the multimodal processes through which infants attain sensorimotor integration after birth. These chapters reveal the underlying continuity in the processes through which complex functions become integrated from late term through the first year.

Drawing on evidence from animal stimulation studies, Chapter 5 scrutinizes the conventional theory that motor functionality is attained only after a rapid process of synaptic proliferation and elimination. Instead a more heterogeneous process comes into play involving the recombination of sensory inputs and the strategic deployment of attention and memory that depends less on the absolute numbers of synapses than on their scope and pattern of interaction. Chapter 6 moves this line of inquiry forward to explain why some children derive larger cognitive benefits than other children who undergo similar experiences. The challenges that children with brain-based disorders face in learning from experience are traced to limitations of conscious awareness that appear in the earliest stages of sensory processing, which compromise attention and memory.

Chapter 7 describes how the acquisition of language and recognition of intentional behavior are rooted in motor development. We contend that language use involves the same principles of selection on variation as those entailed in the construction of motor repertoires and gestures. Prelinguistic children possess only a limited understanding of intentional behavior. Only when children use language with gesture to distinguish between desires and beliefs, and when they recognize that other people possess knowledge and beliefs different than their own, do they fully grasp intentional behavior. This chapter critically examines attempts to explain the neural processes underlying language and intentionality, and it advances an alternative theory based on the recursive nature of consciousness.

Chapter 8 addresses the crucial problem of whether attempts to modify the human behavioral phenotype through alterations in individual development and strategies of learning have value in terms of enhancing human powers or threaten to compromise or weaken them. This requires an assessment of the possibilities and limits to genetic and experientially induced changes in the phenotype. Preschool programs, such as Head Start, recognize that learning is affected by diverse biological and experiential factors. That is why attempts to implement educational strategies to attain uniform outcomes run the risk of ignoring significant differences among children in how their brains develop and how they use them to learn. Parents and children need to be better informed about brain development and how neural processes affect learning. This book concludes by proposing interdisciplinary, multisector strategies to increase the use of knowledge of individual neurodevelopmental processes to improve educational outcomes.

ACKNOWLEDGMENTS

The first author would like to express his appreciation to Gerald Edelman, Einar Gall, and several fellows at the Neurosciences Institute in San Diego for their encouragement and stimulating discussions as a visiting fellow since 1999. Special thanks also go to Gilbert Gottlieb, who supported this project from its inception. We also thank Bill Weber for his early support in getting us signed with Lawrence Erlbaum Associates, and for Lori Handelman's patience as our editor.

1

Historical and Contemporary Perspectives in Developmental Neuroscience

Scientific advances in understanding how the brain develops and functions in relation to behavior were made possible by four related transformations that provided new ways to conceptualize the relationships among brain and mind and knowledge and perception. The first involved a transition from a spiritual to a scientific conception of mind. René Descartes' doctrine that the brain and mind are different entities supported a dualistic distinction between the physical and mental that discouraged scientists from trying to understand how neural and psychological processes are related. Only when brain scientists ignored religious doctrine and viewed the mind as physically embodied in the brain did they make progress in identifying the neural determinants of perception and memory.

The second transformation involved a philosophical change in how knowledge is understood in relation to experience, perception, and learning. The American pragmatists William James and John Dewey enabled philosophers to conceive of knowledge about the world in relational rather than representational terms. This has freed philosophers from equating meaning or physical identity with truth by showing that all knowledge is experientially variable and contextual. This epistemological reconstruction of learning and knowledge is slowly changing scientists' theories of how neural processes affect the relationship between perception and behavior.

The third transformation involved a shift from a Newtonian to Maxwellian conception of physical phenomena. A universe governed by the pendular swing between the forces of attraction and repulsion was replaced by a dynamic conception involving less predictable self-organizing interactions between energy and matter. Through his collaboration with infant experimentalist Myrtle McGraw, Dewey outlined how the brain and consciousness could be understood in naturalistic terms, whereby Newtonian physics is replaced with a Maxwellian conception of mind as matter in motion. This shifted the emphasis from a genetically deterministic conception of human development to one stressing the contingencies of growth and experiential variability.

Finally, the fourth transformation showed how a Darwinian conception of natural selection could be used to explain how brain development occurs through selection on variations that involve the behavior of whole populations of neurons. Darwin contributed fundamentally to our knowledge of how the principles of natural selection explain human evolution, but knowledge of how they apply to neurobiological development remained unclear and controversial. Embryologists attempted to discover the genetic principles that accounted for continuity of life forms across species, but little was known about the underlying mechanisms. Neuropsychologist Hebb (1949) acknowledged the role of selection in the formation of cell assemblies through use-dependent reinforcement of synaptic activity. Not until the late 20th century, however, was neuroscientist Edelman (1987) able to show how selection works at multiple levels of biological complexity by enabling the brain to select behavioral and perceptual strategies to respond to the contingencies of experience. The complete implications of these four breakthroughs in understanding the relation between brain growth and behavioral development have yet to be fully appreciated by developmental psychologists.

This chapter is intended to introduce readers to the developmental phenomena discussed in this book, and to provide them with the conceptual tools to better understand the different roles of genes and experience in the evolution and development of the brain, cognition, and behavior. There is little consensus about how genetic and experiential factors interact in the brain through developmental sequences that mold and reshape the human behavioral phenotype. The relationship between growth and development is construed in the broadest theoretical terms to enable a firmer grasp of the underlying complexities involved in these interactions.

This chapter focuses on several questions that are pertinent to framing a general theory of neuropsychological development: 1) How do the forces of nature affect human sentience and our self-perceptions? 2) How does selection act on variability to produce stable but adaptive neuronal structures? 3) How does the brain provide knowledge of the world and support memory and judgments based on value? 4) Is knowledge about the world representational or relational? Historically, philosophers were preoccupied with the epistemological dilemma posed by the last question long before brain science elevated the importance of these other issues for understanding the human mind. Only in the last few decades have fundamental advances occurred in brain science, providing knowledge about perception, attention, and memory and their relationship to behavioral development. Special techniques are described later in this chapter, by which researchers identify the neural and electrophysiological mechanisms involved and the models they employ to simulate the conditions involved when learning occurs.

KNOWLEDGE, PERCEPTION, AND MOTOR CONTROL: REPRESENTATIONAL OR RELATIONAL?

Neuroscientists and developmental psychologists are challenged to understand the relationship between perception and knowledge without collapsing the distinction between them. Individuals differ fundamentally in how and what they perceive and the modes of inference and reasoning they use to extract meaning and gain understanding. Moreover, perception happens quickly, with little awareness of the innumerable sensory inputs that make it a coherent experience. Being aware of something is not the same thing as knowing what it is or knowing how to reproduce it. Knowledge is not simple recognition, but understanding the conditions that change the behavior of things or alter the course of familiar events. The history of the philosophical debate about knowledge gained traction when discussion about mind was grounded in human experience and merged with the scientific study of the brain.

Dualism and Its Repercussions

Philosophers since antiquity have struggled to understand the perceptual, behavioral, and experiential processes that humans use to acquire knowledge of their world that is reliable and valid. The Greek philosopher Plato proposed an analogy of a cave to argue that human perception was indirect and limited to the light and shadows reflected off the walls. Truth was instead embodied in preexisting concepts that represented the form of an idea in its perfection. For many centuries, religion also has furnished an answer to the ultimate question of validity by positing the origin of truth in a deity. But as science advanced, philosophers struggled to reconcile their philosophical theories about the relationship among mind, consciousness, and the human soul and the emerging knowledge about the brain that sometimes strained credulity.

René Descartes' attempt to advance a conception of knowledge that was consistent with theological views of the mind and soul in the 17th century illustrates how this prevented a clear understanding of the role of the brain in the production of knowledge. For nearly 1,500 years preceding Descartes' work, the prevailing view was that the seat of knowledge resided in the ventricular spaces or the empty sinus cavities of the brain (Gross, 1998). This was consistent with church doctrine that the mind and soul were not material substances, and thus could not be corrupted by being located apart from the gray and white matter. Descartes supported this dualism by cleverly proposing that human sensory images are processed through *hollow* optic nerves connecting the eyes to the pineal gland, where the information from each eye is fused into a single upright image. Descartes believed that some ideas, such as unity or God, are innate because their conceptualization requires experientially transcendent rational thought, whereas other, more worldly ideas are shaped by experience (Wade, 1995).

Immanuel Kant completely sidestepped the brain science and soul-based theology of his day by holding that mind consisted of transcendent, *a priori* categories that are not directly accessible to the senses, such as space, time, causality, and motion. This categorical knowledge furnished the ultimate standards of truth and validity. The British empiricists took another tack by according a larger role to human experience. John Locke rejected Cartesian nativism and Kantian transcendentalism, contending instead that human perception and knowledge come from experience. Locke was strongly influenced by Thomas Willis, a 17th-century British neuroanatomist who repudiated ventricular theory in favor of a cerebral, cortically based system of memory and cognition (Finger, 2000; Martensen, 2004). Locke believed that the mind is a blank slate on which ideas are passively inscribed and actively combined through reflection to form complex thoughts. Locke originated the theory that ideas could be associated with one another to enable learning—a theory that led to the formation of the school of "association psychologists" in the 19th century. The behaviorist John Watson revived Locke's conception of mind in the early 20th century by holding that infant brains and behavior are malleable and shaped significantly by environmental influences.

Pragmatism and Relational Knowledge

Nearly two more centuries of the scientific study of the brain ensued before philosophers and psychologists saw a way around dualism to confidently theorize about the relationship between the brain and behavior and perception and knowledge. The American pragmatists James and Dewey played pivotal roles in this epistemological and scientific reconstruction. James and Dewey sought to ground mind and perception in a dynamic view of consciousness that supported a *relational* rather than representational theory of knowledge. James (1981) first likened consciousness to a stream or process that involved volition and a changing focus of attention—a conception that strongly influenced his fellow pragmatist, Dewey. James also argued that events which occur at the fringe or periphery of consciousness influence perception just as pervasively as those occupying the center of vision. Finally, he believed that underlying feelings contribute to perceptual and behavioral differences in conscious emotional states. This is a dynamic and relational theory of knowledge, whereby the concepts we use reflect the different degrees of access we have to our internal states and the amount of control of the surrounding environment.

Dewey (1981) surmounted the methodological dilemmas of mindbody dualism and reductionism that caused many philosophers and psychologists to vacillate between the mental and physical—between equating all psychological processes with cognition and reducing consciousness experience to physiological processes. Dewey also stubbornly resisted the modern trends toward materialism and reductionism in science and logical formalism and epistemological realism in philosophy, which threatened to erase the naturalistic origins of mind. He adopted a psychobiological conception of mind proposed by the "American school" of neurologists led by Clarence L. Herrick, who viewed consciousness as an instrument for motor, cognitive, and emotional integration (Windle, 1979). Dewey took the Darwinian position that the brain evolved in animals to mount more effective functional responses to environmental pressures.

The evolutionary advantage of consciousness is that it enables the organism to discover new values by rendering explicit and in commensurate terms the physical and mental attitudes and desires that influenced past behavior and that will affect the outcome of future events (Dalton, 2002a). As discussed later, Dewey was a naturalist who believed that the brain and mind develop by experiencing, responding to, and mobilizing

the forces of nature. The force of gravity, energy, motion, space, and time
are not simply constants of nature that constrain and limit human behavior, but are tools with which humans master locomotion, increase their
powers of perception, and, ultimately, overcome their terrestrial and
sensorimotor limitations.

Dewey (1981) contended, like James, that consciousness is not a thing,
but a process involving uncertainty and the transformation of indeterminate events into ones subject to human control. Beliefs and intentions
are not about things that possess intrinsic worth or represent knowledge
or truth, but refer to actions performed on things that change their
sequence or relationship to one another and that affect their meaning,
applicability, and efficacy. The capacity to shift attention between foreground and background is essential to balanced perception and judgment.
This feature of consciousness makes mind contextual and dependent on
the meaning and significance attributed to a situation in its entirety.
Judgment grounded in sensorimotor functions is employed to detect and
differentiate among qualitative and quantitative features of situations
involving force, movement, duration, contrast, and balance, among other
elements that affect sentient and energetic states and behavioral capabilities. Consciousness and judgment work in tandem with attitudes and
emotions to enable the determination of whether changes in feelings,
beliefs, behavior, intentions, or meanings make a difference that have
value in situations that satisfy a need or desire.

Building on James' provocative distinction between the focal point and
fringe of consciousness, Dewey described how our perceptions and assessments of situations change as we distance ourselves physically, emotionally, and conceptually (i.e., adopting someone else's perspective, looking at
a situation from a different vantage point). These dimensions of perception furnish depth, breadth, volume, and other quantitative and qualitative features of experience that are vital to our judgment. The processes
through which perception and action are coupled and decoupled depend,
in part, on experiences in early development, whereby reflexive, sensory,
and vestibular systems are engaged differently in response to nearby and
remote events. Distance or proximity influences the weight or value we
place on our perceptions, their urgency, and the time needed to reflect on
memory of related events. This process of deliberation is essential to rational judgment, conceptualization planning and generalization.

As the context changes, so do our perceptions and the judgments that
we make about the *relationship* between the foreground and background
features of conscious experience. Dewey believed that this revolving

process of substitution or replacement of the foreground and background characteristics of phenomenal experience renders our knowledge conditional, contextual, tentative, and approximate. This is because the order and depth of field in which we perceive events and experience them emotionally are forever undergoing changes that alter our basis of comparison. The transient, developmentally dependent, and contextual basis of human perception is vividly illustrated in early infancy (described later), when babies must rely heavily on expectations about natural events that are sometimes violated by novel situations.

A MAXWELLIAN UNIVERSE

As noted before, philosophers of mind employed a mechanistic, Newtonian conception of science that is now outmoded. Descartes, Kant, and Hegel believed that gravitational and energetic forces have predictable outcomes that govern the movement and behavior of all physical phenomena, including biological processes. Descartes (1985) adapted this mechanistic and materialistic conception of the world to explain how physical brain functions operated independently of mental processes. Dewey rejected this mechanistic model that segregated mind from brain. Newtonian physics, which focused on the attractive and repulsive gravitational forces governing the relationships among large objects, failed to account for how the self-generating and form-shaping forces of growth propel and displace biological bodies in space and time through brain-based developmental processes.

Dewey was persuaded by physicist Maxwell's (1892) theory that motion was governed by energetic principles that did not require an initial precipitating collision. Maxwell explained how dynamic systems involving matter in motion interact randomly and yet result in ordered transformations. He ingeniously visualized how each configuration of potential and kinetic energy occupying a phase space could function independently and yet be connected through a shared underlying motion or oscillation. This model helped Maxwell achieve fundamental breakthroughs in explaining how it was possible for a system as a whole to undergo transformation through the interaction of its parts *without* violating entropy and irreversibility (Harman, 1982).

Dewey (1989) believed that these same principles pertaining to matter in motion applied to human perception. Human perception involves a dynamic and continuous reconfiguration of how our bodies are supported by gravity and situated in space and time. Energy is constantly being redistributed to support new perspectives while retaining in memory the potential energy embodied in the feeling of what it is like to have experienced the world from these different vantage points. Dewey believed that this capacity for sensing *proportionality* or keeping things in perspective enables humans to keep track of things despite physical displacement and an ever-changing context. Dewey (1981) theorized how humans who evolved to walk fully erect used their newfound capacity to anticipate remote, unforeseen events beyond their immediate reach or grasp, whose dimensions change as they draw near, imposing different levels of energetic response. Dewey's naturalism provides a way to explain why the phenomenal attributes of first-person experience cannot be reduced to any one sensory quality, but are grounded in features derived from intersensory perceptions that embody cross-modal relationships and variable contexts. We have more to say about this in subsequent chapters.

A DARWINIAN THEORY OF NEURONAL GROUP SELECTION

Gerald Edelman is one of the few neuroscientists who responded to the need to articulate a general theory of neurodevelopment that squarely addresses the tension between certain knowledge and variable experience that has vexed philosophers and psychologists. He also contends, like Dewey, that consciousness can be naturalized by showing how conscious-ness emerges from neuronal processes that provide evolutionary and biological bases of perception and memory (Edelman, 2003). Edelman has gathered compelling scientific evidence to support his contention that dynamic processes of variation, competition, and selection drive brain growth and organize perception. The study of the human mind is contentious because we lack a general theoretical framework with which to understand the genetic and experiential constituents of the brain and mind from a broad evolutionary and developmental perspective. Unlike his contemporaries, Edelman is attempting to develop a general theory capable of explaining how selection, acting on variations at the molecu-lar, cellular, behavioral, and other biological levels, contributes to the development, differentiation, integration, and regulation of diverse but related phenomena that eventuate in consciousness. Edelman's theory challenges the validity of a representational conception of knowledge that splits apart motor and perceptual development.

Selection and Variability

Edelman's seminal discovery that recognition of antigens occurs through *degeneracy* (the capacity of structurally different antibodies to perform the same function) led to the Nobel Prize in 1972. This breakthrough stimulated his additional discovery that cell adhesion molecules (CAMs) contribute to the diversity of neuronal groups by enabling cells to bind together, form borders, and move and change position. CAMs contribute, in early development, to the formation of a primary repertoire of somatically diverse neural structures (Edelman, 1974, 1989). This primary repertoire exhibits an extensive variability of topographical relationships resulting from self-organizing processes of cellular growth. A secondary repertoire of experience-dependent synaptic connections is formed from this primary repertoire through processes of selection that result in multiple configurations of functional neuronal interactions. Developmental neurologists, discussed in Chapter 3, have exploited the clinical implications of this two-tiered conception of the brain for the early diagnosis of brain-based disorders.

Selection Versus Instruction

Controversy persists among neuroscientists as to how the brain contributes to the production of knowledge. Instructional and selectionist theories of development and learning characterize the relationship differently between perception and knowledge. Instructional theory assumes that learning is dependent on the specificity and accuracy of information the brain receives from the environment. This information must either come from the environment or be supplied through molecular or genetic instructions (Quartz & Sejnowski, 1997). Hebb's theory of learning is based on the premise that recurring patterns of cognitive and behavioral response are retained through experiential, information-rich postsynaptic processes. Some cognitive psychologists believe that this information is converted by the brain into algorithms that enable organisms to learn by recognizing and choosing the appropriate response to a given situation. But others contend that the degree of freedom humans possess to mount alternative behavioral responses resists encapsulation in computational rules. Although Hebb's cell assembly theory makes sense of how experience contributes to change in synaptic strength, it does not adequately explain how neuronal groups supporting different behaviors *selectively* interact, changing the scope, composition, and firing patterns of synapses involved. This issue is examined in more detail in Chapter 4.

The theory of neuronal group selection does not assume that the environment is information-rich. Situations are often ambiguous, and information is usually fragmentary and incomplete (i.e., not easily converted into coded instructions). Many groups of neurons with overlapping feature detectors are usually involved in the construction of scenes that are perceived as integral wholes before individual features become apparent. Accordingly, there are many alternative ways to obtain the same perceptual outcome, and the nervous system must possess the flexibility to sample and choose among responses that do not merely duplicate past behavior, but possess adaptive value.

Memory, Reentry, and Consciousness

Perhaps Edelman's (1987) most controversial hypothesis is that memory does not require a central repository of exact replicas of experienced things, but depends on a dynamic process of *categorization*. Categorization results from the perceptual recognition of things that share *similar*, rather than identical, features. The view that memory requires storage of a fixed copy is questionable because there is no direct isomorphic relationship among a physical event, its synaptic effects, and recall. This is so because memory derives from scenes involving spatiotemporally ordered sets of categorizations of familiar and unfamiliar events, only some of which possess a physical or causal connection to that scene. Memory is therefore selective and transformational, rather than redundant and duplicative. The content of what is recalled depends on the basis of comparison, its value, and current informational demands. The same situation also can be remembered, described, and interpreted differently depending on where one focuses in the sequence of prior events or actions. In essence, according to Edelman, what is recalled is an updated or latest version of past events.

Edelman's conception of memory preserves the potential of thought to enlarge the meaning and significance of experience by incorporating dual functions. Memory is a mechanism that maintains a tight coupling between present intentions and future goals. It helps us keep track of where we are in a sequence of ongoing activities necessary to attain intended outcomes. Memory also provides a reservoir of experiences for recall and reflection. Without working memory or the capacity to remember the present, as Edelman characterizes it, we would be unable to know whether we are the agent or recipient of our own experiences. Without long-term memory, we would be unable to distance ourselves from the present and juxtapose events in time. Memory enables us to transcend the physical limitations of embodiment to disengage from present concerns, critically reflect on previous decisions and interests, and imagine a future in which the focus and priority of events change order. Only through memory do we recognize who we are, what we have done, and the kind of person we would like to become.

According to Edelman, perceptual experience is continuously recategorized through mechanisms of *reentry*. Reentrant processes make possible the correlation of sensory stimulation and motor output whose source, locus, and intensity are undergoing continuous change. Widely distributed neuronal groups are bound through synchronous activity controlled by the thalamus to produce scenes that possess integrity, but whose complex features can be differentiated. Recent brain imaging experiments employing binocular rivalry isolated apparent reentrant processes by indicating that conscious perception involves distributed changes in local and global synchrony that include frontal and anterior areas *beyond* the visual system (Srinivassen et al., 1999).

With these theoretical distinctions in hand, Edelman (1989) proposes that primary consciousness is an emergent outcome of recursive memory that enables an organism to discriminate between self and nonself through categorizations that are continually related to the succession of ongoing events. Primary consciousness enables a sense of continuity between actions that take place in spatially distinct, but temporarily related, experiences that involve an embodied self.

PSYCHOLOGICAL THEORIES
OF EARLY DEVELOPMENT

Developmental scientists have been challenged to advance theories of infant perception that avoid the epistemological dualist traps set by their philosophical predecessors. The contemporary debate about infant knowledge can be traced to Jean Piaget and John Gibson, among other pioneering psychologists, who advanced contrasting conceptions of how infants and young children acquire knowledge about their world. Developmental psychologists have been reluctant to fully embrace a neuroscientific conception of the brain, mind, and behavior because of the concern that complex cognitive capabilities will be reduced to neurophysiological processes. This is a legitimate concern, especially in the lingering shadow of Sigmund Freud's ambitious but incomplete attempt in his scientific project to anchor his psychological theory in a neuropsychological framework. It is important at this point to understand why alternative conceptualizations of infant knowledge depend on how the relationship is conceived between infant motor development and perception.

Symbolic Mental Representations

Freud rejected epistemological realism and instead proposed a theory in which dreams furnished the primary contents of conscious experience. Freud asserted that the unconscious generates an inner reality that obeys its own logic of necessity that is unaffected by the events of conscious experience. Subconscious forces that were reflected in idiosyncratic patterns of behavior and represented in dreams propelled infant motor development. The perceptual contents of mental events, Freud (1953a) explained, need not involve actual experiences, but only imagined ones, eliminating the need to confer a separate existence on the objects of consciousness. This led Freud to abandon his early seduction theory in favor of a theory of spontaneous childhood sexuality. Freud tried unsuccessfully to develop a convincing metapsychological theory to explain how nervous energy could be diverted into somatic disturbances that were expressed in inexplicable forms of neuroses originating in childhood. Although Freud (1953b) gave up his *Project for a Scientific Psychology* to establish a functional neurological basis for psychoanalysis, he insisted that there was ample evidence from the interpretation of dreams and phylogeny that human behavior is rooted in instinctive wishes and drives that are expressed unconsciously in individual experience and culture. Freud's theory undermined the claim that nature and mind could be comprehended in the same functional terms—a possibility that Dewey believed was essential to grounding mind in nature and enabling humans to consciously create and embrace different cultural values.

Attunement Theory

Although contemporary psychologists have moved beyond Freudian neuropsychology, the problem of emotional attachment still attracts considerable interest and research. Schore (1994) furnished a detailed neurobiological foundation to support the primacy of emotional affect in constituting individual identity. He believes, for example, that available neurobiological evidence strongly supports Colwyn Trevarthen's theory that infant emotional development depends on the reciprocal detection of affective gestures by infant and mother. Trevarthen (2001) contends that infants possess innate motives and emotions that anticipate the development of communication and intersubjective understanding in the first few months after birth. Thus, the child's capacity to assimilate emotional signals and social information develops prenatally through gene expression and the formation of body-movement-representing systems that eventually enable infants to imitate the actions of others.

There are undeniable rhythms and recurring patterns involved in the sequences of early development, even before birth. But brain activity before birth shows little coherence, and endogenous movements are spontaneous, displaying little organization until late term, when a pattern of alternation between writhing and fidgety movement appears (Hadders-Algra & Forssberg, 2001). There also is considerable evidence that prenatal development is influenced by external stimulation, and that the extent and nature of this exposure affect infants' subsequent potential to attain neurobehavioral integration (Lecanuet et al., 1995). These issues regarding the relationship between events occurring during pre- and postnatal development are discussed in more detail in Chapter 3.

Trevarthen (2001) argues that infants are born with the ability to sense meaning by anticipating the goals of others' actions. He also believes that infants possess an early capacity to sympathize, which facilitates attunement with their mothers or other caregivers. This attunement is first evidenced in the synchrony that newborns attain in patterns of erect locomotion and coordination. However, this controversial claim is not well supported by the scientific literature on motor development. The pioneering studies of locomotion by Myrtle McGraw (Dalton, 1998) and many contemporary researchers (see Thelen, 2001) demonstrate that balance and synchrony are not the *cause*, but the *result* of infant attainment of erect locomotion. Infants employ many different strategies in their attempts to overcome gravitational and perceptual constraints to walking independently. Erect locomotion is a skill that must be mastered through several preliminary stages that are punctuated by awkwardness and setbacks. Although mothers may be able to anticipate a child's moods or affective states, motor development requires stimulation and self-initiated experiences involving instability and the lack of support. Motor development and emotional development are unlikely to develop in a synchronous fashion because newborns lack the physical foundation to sustain a stable and predictable affective state (Dalton, 2000).

Stage Theories of Maturation and Cognition

Piaget adopted a position similar to Dewey and McGraw's that infant cognitive development emerges from their sensorimotor development.

He also stressed, as did Dewey, that practical knowledge does not come from knowing what something is, but knowing how (i.e., operations) to reproduce it under different circumstances and understanding the variable causal relationships involved. But Piaget differed from their perspective in crucial ways.

First, Piaget measured infant and child cognitive development according to how closely they approximated or conformed to modes of reasoning dictated by standards of formal logic, such as identity and contradiction. Accordingly, he believed that children eventually transcend their dependency on motor-based reasoning to comprehend abstract relationships and ideas. It should be noted, however, that in his later work, Piaget adopted a problem-centered approach to infant learning, which put more emphasis on the transformational rather than reproductive nature of inquiry and the ability to understand equivalence (see Beilin, 1994).

Second, Piaget (1928) divided judgment into separate cognitive stages involving age-sensitive levels of awareness (i.e., egocentric vs. allocentric) and different modes of reasoning (i.e., preoperational and operational, circular reasoning) that contemporary researchers now claim to occur much sooner than predicted by Piaget's theory. Third, Piaget argued that infants lack a concept of object permanence, and that this accounts for their misperception of occluded objects as nonexistent. This has fueled a long-running debate as to whether this phenomenon represents a deficient object concept, a motor deficiency, or simply confuses permanence with other spatial attributes, such as unity, continuity, or identity, which guide infant tracking of temporarily disappearing objects.

Arnold Gesell is also well known for having proposed a stage theory based on the presumption that infants must undergo neurobiological and neurobehavioral maturation before they are ready to learn (Gesell & Thompson, 1934). Gesell gave more weight to genetics than experience in early brain development, when infants are first acquiring locomotor capabilities governed by subcortical regions. Gesell believed that the process by which behavioral traits attain greater complexity occurs solely through mechanisms of reciprocal enervation and inhibition at the subcortical level. There is no cortical involvement, and that is why Gesell did not concur with McGraw that these attainments entail deliberate or purposeful control. Experience plays a more prominent role later on in contributing to perceptual and skill development, after motor control is attained and cortex is functioning. Thus, Gesell was unable to conceive of motor and perceptual development as concurrent, rather than sequentially separate phenomena (Dalton, 2002b).

Ecological Perception

James and Eleanor Gibson adopted an ecological theory of perception that emphasizes the active, exploratory nature of infant learning. They believed that the supposed gulf between the knower and known could be bridged by showing that, through activity, infants extract the use afforded by objects that then defines their meaning. J. Gibson (1950) rejected the ideas that information is statically possessed by genes or located in the environment. Instead a dynamic informational relationship existed between the organism and environment through optic flow, whereby perception acquires depth and perspective. Perhaps J. Gibson's most original idea was that the senses are integrated at birth, thus enabling infants to detect *amodal relationships* (i.e., shared general properties of intersensory perception, such as rhythm or synchrony). Only later do infants distinguish percepts provided by different sensory modalities. Contemporary researchers have criticized as nativist J. Gibson's position that *amodal* relationships are invariant, but they need not be so. Amodal perception may be an emergent property of spontaneous brain electrical activity that enables newborns to detect temporal relations through synaptic resonance. Nevertheless, J. Gibson clung to an ontological realism, claiming that the environment possesses structure and thus is capable of providing the categories needed to understand our world.

Representation and Imitation

Developmental psychologist Spelke and her colleagues (2002) contend, contrary to Piaget, that infants possess innate concepts of continuity and solidity that organize their perceptions from birth. Spelke argues that infants have the ability to represent and infer the continuous existence of moving objects that are temporarily occluded. Kellman and Arterberry (1998) distance themselves further from Piaget's assertion of the primacy of sensorimotor control by arguing that "perception of objects, surfaces and events does not depend on motoric experiences, such as reaching or locomoting, simply because the relevant perceptual abilities can be demonstrated before directed reaching and crawling begin" (p. 260). Nevertheless, there is a substantial difference between being able to follow and anticipate the movements of things and knowing why objects behave the way they do. Perception and cognition are two different capabilities that are sometimes conflated in studies of infant knowledge—a controversy that is examined in subsequent chapters.

Meltzoff and Moore (1998) adopt a slightly different perspective. They propose that, "The young infant is not a purely sensorimotor being but a representational one. Although sensorimotor development is essential to infants, preverbal cognition neither reduces to, nor is wholly dependent upon, such development" (p. 224). They argue that, "the capacity for representation is the initial state from which development proceeds" (Meltzoff & Moore, 1998, p. 227). According to these researchers, infants possess an innate concept of identity based on spatiotemporal criteria of place and trajectory (a Newtonian conception) that enables them to keep track of objects in their perceptual field. Meltzoff argues that infants' knowledge of identity is best illustrated by their capacity, in the first few months, to imitate the actions of another person. In a recent fMRI brain-imaging study of a child imitating the body gestures and actions of another person, Meltzoff and his colleagues (Chaminade, Meltzoff, & Decety, 2005) determined that only visuospatial (i.e., occipital-temporal and parietal) regions were activated, not motor areas. This finding, however, is at odds with research indicating that mirror neurons in the premotor area are activated also when monkeys (and humans) watch conspecifics executing goal-directed intentional actions (Rizzolatti, Fadiga, Fogassi & Gallesse, 2002). Meltzoff's theory is examined in more detail in Chapter 7.

Self-Produced Locomotion and Dynamic Systems Theory

Other contemporary developmental psychologists differ sharply with these theories that subordinate motor development to early emotional development or visual control, preferring a neo-Gibsonian perspective. Campos et al. (2000) and Anderson et al. (2004) indicate that there are multiple sources of sensory input (i.e., visual, somatosensory, and vestibular) that provide information about self-motion relative to physical features of objects that move in the environment. These redundant sensory systems provide different frames of reference that enable the coupling between and neural remapping of optical flow and postural control. Thelen and Smith (1998) propose a dynamical system theory, which views behavior and perceptual categorization as continuously interacting events that are task-specific and governed by the history of previous acts of knowing. They contend that infants do not possess innate concepts. Instead, they believe that infants acquire flexible categories from sensory- and motor-based actions involving processes of global mapping, as proposed by Edelman (1987). These alternative motor theories of infant perception are given closer inspection in Chapter 6.

Intersensory Perception

One other theoretical orientation with Gibsonian roots, but that offers a distinctive perspective regarding the integration of motor and cognitive development, is the theory of intersensory perception. As its leading exponents, Lickliter and Bahrick (2000) build on available scientific knowledge that animal and human sensory capabilities develop in specific sequences involving tactile, vestibular, and chemical, then auditory and visual modalities. Accordingly, each sensory modality may acquire a different stimulation history, which in turn affects the salience of and attentiveness to sensory information during postnatal development. Their research demonstrates that the increasingly multimodal nature of stimulation following birth amplifies the amodal attributes of concurrently or redundantly presented information—a phenomenon discussed in Chapter 5. The infant brain may be particularly responsive to multimodal input because different receptive fields require coincident activation for initial alignment. For these reasons, Lickliter and Bahrick contend that sensory integration at birth gradually gives way to differentiation and the capacity to detect contingent or arbitrary relationships driven by unimodal inputs.

BRAIN-BASED METHODS FOR STUDYING EARLY PERCEPTUAL AND MOTOR DEVELOPMENT

Developmental scientists have increasingly turned to neuroscience to find evidence to support their different theories of perceptual and motor development. This is a significant trend that enables us to empirically scrutinize assumptions about whether infants possess foundational knowledge at birth, or whether perceptual categories and concepts emerge from experiential events involving the interaction of brain and behavior. Several methods have been employed in contemporary studies.

This section focuses on recent modeling, electrophysiological, and imaging methods used to detect neural correlates of behavioral and perceptual processes (chaps. 4 and 5 examine how methods of special stimulation have been used to identify functional relationships among brain regions involved in attention, memory, and related neuropsychological mechanisms). Scientists employ devices that measure electrical or metabolic brain activity to understand how the brain organizes itself and communicates information through signaling or synaptic firing processes. Brain plasticity also can be modeled to discover the rules and values that govern perception, learning, and memory by using computer-simulated training or stimulation regimes. Finally, brain-based devices that move freely within the environment have been constructed to discover how the brain, perception, and behavior become organized and integrated through experience.

A crucial difficulty that confronts both neuroscientists and psychologists employing these different methods is that it is not self-evident at what level of biological complexity to look for mechanisms, which contribute in a causal way to specific psychological functions, such as perception, attention, memory, or learning. This issue remains controversial today largely because scientists who study brain activity have adopted competing assumptions about what their methods tell us about the structure and function of the brain, which are essentially disputed. This discussion is intended to clarify what those assumptions are, identify their theoretical implications, and examine the merits and deficiencies of these different ways of understanding the brain and behavior. This analysis provides the reader with the tools needed to assess the comparative strengths and weaknesses of these alternative methods to decipher the role of experience in the developing brain.

Brain Imaging: EEG, MEG, and Evoked Potentials

Electroencephalography (EEG) uses electrodes positioned on the scalp to detect changes in spontaneous electrical field activity in the brain. Magnetoencephalography (MEG) detects changes in magnetic fields that accompany electrical activity in the brain and obtains higher resolution images than EEG. EEG is also used to identify changes in waveforms or evoked potentials that occur in response to stimulation. Using EEG to obtain event-related changes in the brain's electrical responses to stimulation is a particularly useful method for recording infants' reactions to surprise or unexpected events because it clearly reveals peaks and troughs in visual attention that correspond to the discrimination between novel and familiar events. EEG and MEG are particularly sensitive to changes in coherence or the synchronous activity of large populations of neurons, but these shared wave properties do not convey information about the neural source or origin of this electrical activity. Consequently, source models must be constructed that reflect theoretical judgments about the probable locus of activity (Revonsuo, 2001; Taylor, 2001).

Although EEG and MEG enable measurement of dynamic, large-scale macroscopic activity, these methods are not capable of detecting local networks that may be obscured by global activity. Moreover, many local networks may be inactive due to inhibitory neuromodulation, and thus do not reach the threshold of detectable activity. Nevertheless, they can strongly influence the timing of observed patterns of synchrony. Although numerous EEG studies suggest that human cognitive mechanisms, such as attention and memory, exhibit characteristic frequency ranges, these mechanisms are active simultaneously and may interact in ways that would not be apparent from their specific electrical or magnetic waveforms.

Longitudinal Studies of EEG Coherence: What Do They Measure?

Most developmental psychologists are unaware that pioneering infant experimentalist Myrtle McGraw collaborated with J. R. Smith, a pioneer in the use of EEG, to measure the development of brain electrical activity during the first year (Dalton, 1998). According to Bell (1998), Smith was the first scientist to "relate behavioral development to the ontogeny of the EEG." Smith (1938) detected synchronous slow *delta* wave brain activity in the somatic motor area in neonates. He speculated that this indicated the waning influence of a phylogenetically older pacemaker in the cerebellum governing equilibrium before the onset of cortical control. Smith (1941) eventually identified a central occipital *alpha* rhythm between 3 and 4 months that he believed signaled the loss of Babinski and Moro reflexes and the emergence of reaching, which he considered to be indicative of the onset of cortical control.

Smith (1939) also detected a curious dramatic increase in the number, amplitude, and frequency, within the first 3 months, of somatic motor waves, particularly in the postcentral area. When he increased the distance of the electrodes, the rhythmic waves rarely registered simultaneously, suggesting that the locus of brain waves shifted subtly from one site to another in the premotor cortex. Smith's studies suggested the possibility that, in the absence of a well-developed cortex, cerebral rhythms provide the balance infants need in early development to exercise judgment despite undergoing continuously destabilizing growth and change.

Researchers conducted a series of subsequent studies of EEG potentials during the first year in the decades following Smith's initial work on McGraw's project. What is important to notice about these studies, summarized by Marshall, Bar-Haim, and Fox (2002), is that infant experimentalists are no longer employing EEG as a device to measure the relationship between brain states and motor behavior. Instead, EEG and ERPs are used nearly exclusively to measure visual processes involved in perception, attention, and other *cognitive* behaviors. This emphasis neglects the fundamentally interactive relationship between brain and behavior—perception and action.

Fortunately, a new line of inquiry is emerging that shows promise in explaining how cortex and subcortical regions are linked through oscillatory interactions. For example, by combining EEG and electromyographs (EMG), which measure motor potentials, Salenius and Hari (2003) found that electrical rhythms in the motor cortex interact with spinal motorneurons producing an increase in corticomuscular coherence. The coherence of EEG and EMG signals is not confined to the motor cortex, but also includes the premotor area, supplementary motor area, thalamus, and subthalamic nucleus. This is an important finding that coherence is sustained through the interaction of different brain regions whose electrical properties diverge in the absence of interaction.

Two additional findings from this study were also significant. First, when subjects' attention was divided, coherence decreased, indicating that corticomuscular coherence depends on the level of attention directed to the task. Salenius and Hari (2003) also found that coherence was a product of the co-action of motor cortex and spinal motorneurons. In other words, coherence was sustained despite the alternation between the two sources of electrical activity. These results suggest that a sensory feedback loop (the central premise of instructionist models of the brain) is not necessary to sustain corticomuscular coherence.

Thatcher's Longitudinal EEG Study of the Frontal Lobes

Perhaps the most ambitious attempt to measure changes in EEG coherence occurring in the first two decades of child development was mounted by Thatcher (1997). This seminal work documenting the cyclical pattern by which synaptic connections are forged across the entire frontal lobe broke new ground, with compelling evidence supporting a general theory of neurodevelopment. Fischer and Rose (1994) and Fischer and Bidell (1998) rely heavily on Thatcher's findings to specify the neural correlates of motor and cognitive milestones proposed by Piaget.

Thatcher theorizes that the driving force behind the cyclical process of frontal lobe development is a "traveling wave of nerve growth factor" that originates in the left hemisphere lateral cortex and rotates clockwise. Approximately every 4 years, these cycles undergo phase transitions, whereby the formation and differentiation of short-range connections are replaced by the formation of long-range connections and their integration with short-range connections formed previously. But clearly there are other mechanisms besides neural growth that contribute to brain development, such as the thalamus, through which a plenitude of reciprocal connections are formed between cortical and subcortical regions (Faggin, Nguyen, & Nicolelis, 1997).

Thatcher (1997) also proposes that the leading edge of traveling waves produces a surplus of synaptic connections, whereas the trailing edge results in the elimination or pruning of excess connections. Undoubtedly, nerve growth factor plays an important role in synaptogenesis, but Thatcher does not specify how experience affects brain electrical activity and contributes to processes of synaptic reorganization. Developmental changes in the level of cortical EEG coherence could be explained by several alternative mechanisms, such as the amount of axonal sprouting, the extent of myelination (when axons are secured in a protective sheath that stabilizes transmission), the level of neurmodulation, the strength of postsynaptic response, or the differential temporal response properties of neuron groups. That is why Thatcher (1997) appropriately concedes that, "EEG coherence cannot distinguish between these various possibilities" (p. 91). For reasons that I examine in subsequent chapters, brain development is complex, nonlinear, interactive, variable, and strongly experience-dependent. Neuropsychological development involves more than a series of sequentially invariable frontal lobe interactions.

PET and fMRI Studies

Brain imaging that is based on changes in regional blood flow has also become a popular method employed by neuroscientists to establish the cognitive significance of functional relationships among brain regions. Blood flow is assumed to be indicative of brain metabolic activity, and thus a measure of the task-related involvement of corresponding regions. Positron emission tomography (PET) obtains scans of images created by the coincident behavior of unstable radioactive isotopes that are injected into the bloodstream. PET has high resolution, but individual scanning sessions are restricted to prescribed exposure limits. Consequently, data from different subjects must be combined through techniques that normalize for differences in head size, shape, and incidental movement.

Functional magnetic resonance imaging (fMRI) is a noninvasive technique and does not require intersubject averaging. Unlike PET, images can be obtained more rapidly before shifts in regional blood flow have been completed. Brain activity occurs in milliseconds, whereas blood flow takes up to 13 seconds or more to measure. We are already several steps away from the initial activation, so those areas indicating the strongest activity may not be the same ones at the onset. This presents problems for the subtraction technique of analysis. This technique assumes that regions exhibiting weaker activation do not play a causal role in the performance of a task, and thus can be subtracted from the total number of regions to reveal areas of strongest and, therefore, significant activation. If differences in task performance are measured by the strength of the earliest interactions, then how do we decide which components are functionally indispensable, especially if the ones that occur later are not measured? (See Frith & Friston, 1997, for an excellent methodological assessment.)

These same considerations apply to the measurement challenges involved in determining whether transformations in infant perceptual or cognitive capacity are governed by maturation of neural structures, or reflect changes in the strength of connections between widely distributed neuronal groups. When brain-imaging techniques are better adapted to the problems of accuracy posed by movement, it may be possible to address this issue through longitudinal studies of infants. Clearly, as different regions of an infant's brain become connected, the pattern of interaction will change over time.

Neuroimaging studies based on subtraction methods of analysis (i.e., regions exhibiting small or weak changes in blood flow are eliminated) have led many scientists to believe (as do those conducting single-cell electrical studies) that neurons and receptive fields are regionally and functionally specialized to perform cognitively separable roles. Nevertheless, these assumptions are controversial largely because brain functions interact, receptive fields overlap, and different structures have been found to perform similar functions (Edelman & Gally, 2001). Consequently, neuroscientists have developed new methods to better capture the interactive nature and contextual basis of conscious brain processes first proposed by Dewey. For example, Tononi, Edelman, and Sporns (1998) proposed a useful theory to understand how the brain balances the competing demands for coherence through integration while maintaining the flexibility needed to support complexity. They indicate how clusters of neuronal groups can interact more strongly within a larger ensemble of temporally connected but weakly interacting groups. This is typified by the act of attending to a particular feature of a larger scene that temporarily relegates the broader context to the periphery of consciousness involving neurons that are only weakly activated (Tononi & Edelman, 1998).

Drawing on this research, neurobiologist McIntosh (2000) outlined theoretical considerations and proposed methods to more accurately measure the highly distributed and interconnected nature of the functioning brain that is usually depicted but often ignored in subsequent analysis of brain imaging data. McIntosh makes an important distinction between functional and effective connectivity that is neglected in most fMRI studies. Two brain regions may exhibit a functional correlation but not specify how this correlation comes about. Effective connectivity accounts for the mutual or intervening influences that one region has on another. More important, McIntosh contends that neural context is an intervening factor consisting of a pattern of spatiotemporal interaction that makes a specific brain response unique. This is an emergent property of neuronal processes that is dependent on the temporal order of appearance of widely distributed but convergent sensory inputs.

Computer Simulation: Instructed Modular Networks

Another method that has gained popularity among cognitive scientists is the use of neural networks to simulate the conditions in which neural systems are organized, acquire cognitive functions, and learn and adapt to new situations. Feed-forward networks have become a preferred method of modeling the brain. This network model is based on the assumption of hierarchy, or that sensory inputs are processed from lower units to higher ones through a system of weights that enable the model to sustain a pattern of activation appropriate to the tasks that it is attempting to learn. Feed-forward models also assume that the brain possesses systems for the detection of error or the discrepancy between input and output. When an error occurs, a message is returned to lower level processing mechanisms through backpropogation, which enables them to adjust their connection weights.

The rationale for error detection is threefold. First, the brain must receive instruction from the environment regarding the physical features or behaviors to be matched. Elman et al. (1996) and his co-authors appear to share Gibson's belief that the environment is information-rich, by saying that, "considerably more structure is latent in the environment than one might have guessed" (p. 99). But this assumes that the stimulus properties remain the same or identical from one moment to the next. This also ignores the contextual nature of experience described before, which can change considerably task demands.

Second, although learning depends on the perception of discrepant events, the converse of discrepancy is not identity or equivalence. Discrepant events indicate that they are at odds with or vary from expectations. As such, discrepancy is a psychological attribute of perception, not an epistemic condition of the truth of the thing perceived. Instructionist networks seem to confuse this distinction between perceptual and truth status by assuming that learning entails the physical matching of input patterns. The problem of ambiguous input signals is sidestepped by providing a set of weights that will give the right or correct response to novelty based on differences in physical properties.

Third, attempts to circumvent this problem of physical equivalence have been mounted by creating hidden units, which furnish internal representations that allow networks to treat similar inputs differently and thus change output. However, this element of flexibility does not really approximate the ability to learn how to learn because that would require the ability to change the underlying network architecture. Generative network structures possess the virtue over static ones that more computational power is made available to learn complex tasks. But generative networks have not overcome a dependency on a representational logic, which imposes arbitrary structural and epistemic limitations on learning (Shultz & Mareschal, 1997).

Finally, practitioners of connectionist modeling (Elman et al., 1997) claim that this approach is uniquely suited to explain the phenomena of early development. They claim that a primary virtue is that no assumptions about innateness are required. But this assertion is belied by their uncritical acceptance of the view that infants possess at birth the capacity to employ causal inferences in their spatial-temporal reasoning about fundamental physical phenomena, such as movement, gravity, and object relationships. They also suppose that brain modularity and domain-specificity are not present at the outset, but emerge from experience and the demands on specific mechanisms to process, store, and access information. Their contention is that the key to understanding brain dysfunction is likely to be traced to breakdowns in domain-specific functions. Yet there is contrary evidence that brain-based disorders occur because functionally related, but widely distributed, neuron groups fail to reach the threshold of interaction needed to sustain motor and perceptual integration.

Self-Generating Networks

Neuroscientists who are dissatisfied with these and other limitations of instructional computational models have attempted to build more flexibility into neural modeling by more closely approximating the plastic, self-generating powers of neural networks. Drawing on long-range, but differential, connectivity of spike-timing-dependent plasticity, Izhikevich, Gally, and Edelman (2004) demonstrated that a network can be generated that consists of several interacting neuronal groups that exceed the number of individual neurons or synapses, thus creating an enormous memory capacity.

Through this simulation, Izhikevich et al. (2004) found that the timing of spikes to postsynaptic targets not only affected their strength or weights, but also influenced with whom the neuronal groups will be firing. This allowed the same neuron groups or subgroups to be apportioned differently depending on the timing of arrival of the signal. This temporal approach differs fundamentally from feed-forward models, Izhikevich (2003) contends, because the stimulus perturbs ongoing intrinsic activity. Consequently, the same stimulus does not evoke a recurring response pattern each time, but can recruit a different random subset of polychronous groups. What is peculiar and significant about this dynamic is that signal timing contributed to different relationships between inhibitory and excitatory neurons and their respective weights without introducing these weights as externally generated values. This model allows presynaptic inhibitory neurons to fire first, thus initiating a delay in potentiation and, thus, facilitating a differential response from neuronal subgroups.

This model also seems better able to explain how neurons and synapses grow, how they are distributed, how they interact, and how long they survive. These developmental attributes of the brain were demonstrated by experimentally perturbing the networks in two different ways (Izhikevich et al., 2004). First, when all synaptic weights were shuffled, the number of groups dropped from 900 to 80, indicating that a majority of groups in the model were activity-dependent whose persistence depended on temporal firing. The model also simulated synaptic turnover by perturbing synaptic weights every 10 milliseconds, thus resetting all synaptic weights to zero at least once. This simulated the reduction of synapses through dendritic attrition and then permitted regrowth and synaptic repotentiation.

This self-generative model also successfully simulated the growth and alteration of the response properties of receptive fields. Merzenich et al. (1984) first discovered that competitive, experience-dependent processes shape the boundaries between the response properties of cortical neurons. However, Merzenich and colleagues also found more recently that the development of receptive fields in auditory cortex is misaligned through distortion of normal auditory input (Nagarajan et al., 1999). When incongruent patterns of spiking input simulated this auditory distortion, Izhikevich et al. (2004) found that this discordant signal accelerated the dissolution of the neuron groups constituting the receptive field. This outcome showed that binding of sensory cortexes depends on spike timing, and that neurons, which are incapable of filtering signals through temporal processing, cannot sustain the interneuronal communication needed to bind sensory information into coherent frequencies.

Brain-Based Devices (BBDs)

One of the most daunting challenges confronting neuroscientists is to somehow approximate the conditions of an experiencing brain without imposing limitations that interfere with or predispose it toward a specific perceptual or behavioral outcome. The modelers of neural networks, discussed earlier, must make assumptions about system architecture and behavior that fall well short of mimicking neuroanatomically realistic behavior. The sensory and motor processes involved in real brains are capable of interacting flexibly in response to situations that present complex perceptual challenges. BBDs are designed with these challenges in mind. They are freely moving machines that possess simulated neuronal structures and processes and whose behavior can be displayed and modeled in real time. Research fellows at the Neurosciences Institute (NSI) in San Diego have produced and tested several iterations of devices, such as Darwin, a BBD that was originated by Gerald Edelman and George Reeke (Reeke et al., 1993).

Darwin VII is a recent generation of Institute-constructed BBDs (Krichmar & Edelman, 2003). It possesses several attributes that make BBDs useful and compelling devices for simulating the conditions in which motor and perceptual development occur during infancy. Darwin is equipped with intersensory capabilities. It has grippers that detect electrical conductivity and grasp and taste objects. It has whiskers that enable it to feel its way along walls in the dark and to discriminate different textures. And Darwin "sees" with a video camera that pans left and right, and it has two microphones that detect sound.

Darwin VIII has several computer-simulated densely and reciprocally or reentrantly interconnected cortical appendages analogous to the primary visual cortex, infertemporal cortex, and motor cortex. Importantly, Darwin X possesses a hippocampus capable of episodic memory and a value system that approximates the processes of neuromodulation. This brain function enables Darwin X to remember a previous sequence of movement, to recognize objects based on previous contact, and to develop associations between sensory stimuli. While Darwin VII and X are given certain value preferences, such as light versus darkness and vertical lines rather than blobs, they must discriminate among objects that vary in size, shape, and texture. The weight that is given to a particular situation or element of a situation depends on its experiential history and extent of perceptual coherence. The NSI staff has employed BBDs to test theories of how sensory modalities are bound through movement to form coherent images from scenes that initially exhibit ambiguous and sometimes conflicting intersensory relationships.

By focusing on the multiple factors that shape perceptual categorization, BBDs challenge information-processing theories, which assume that the structural attributes of objects are compared to stored representations, and that all members of a category are characterized by singly necessary and jointly sufficient defining features. Instead, BBD researchers suggest that self-generated movements contribute to temporal feature correlations that facilitate perceptual recognition.

In a particularly intriguing recent experiment, Seth et al. (2004) showed that after Darwin VII received only a minimal degree of innately specified behavior, consisting of tracking toward auditory and visual stimuli and attaching a positive value to sound, it was eventually able to select stimuli closest to the sound source. After repeated runs, Darwin VIII was able to recall the association between visual and auditory stimuli and make contact with the preferred object *without* hearing the sound in advance of the tracking behavior. The BBD responded reliably to targets, which appeared within 20 degrees of the center, despite distractors and differences in object size and scale.

During this experiment, Darwin VIII was disabled to mimic a lesion by cutting all interareal reentrant connections between brain regions, which had the effect of transforming the simulated nervous system into a feed-forward model of visual processing (Seth et al., 2004). In this instance, synchrony was not observed, nor was absence of reentry compensated by synaptic plasticity. Outputs in cortical visual areas V2 and V4 were amplified, but did not reach coherence or synchrony. This showed that no one of the specialized brain area was sufficient for binding features of visual objects. These and other outputs of a real world-behaving device strongly supports the notion that early perceptual categorization depends on the salience of intersensory signals afforded by the contingencies of movement.

METHODS FOR STUDYING INFANT MOTOR
CONTROL AND PERCEPTION

Infants possess powers of discrimination that extend well beyond those available to BBDs. The fact that infants cannot tell us what they are seeing, hearing, touching, or tasting does not prevent experimental researchers from determining what they know by employing reliable methods based on infants' predictable alternative reactions to movement, familiar and novel events, surprise, and violations of their expectations. Developmental scientists can draw reasonable inferences about infant sensory capabilities by observing how infants behave in response to these different situations. For example, infants tend to look longer at novel events than ones in which they have become familiar or habituated. Similarly, infants show a preference for attending to the more complex of two novel stimuli. Infants are able to learn simple associations between two events through conditioning, and they can learn through operant conditioning that their own actions have consequences. After repeated exposure to an object moving across a monitor, infants will tend to move their eyes in advance of the direction the object is heading, anticipating its arrival. When an object fails to reach the expected destination, infants show surprise and often look back to an earlier point in the trajectory to see what happened, indicating a violation of expectancy. The experimental results of employing these techniques to study infant perception are described in more detail in subsequent chapters.

Although many more illustrations could be provided, what should be noticed about these methods of determining infant perceptual capacities is that they depend on the cues provided by infants' own motor behavior. Looking, seeing, hearing, and feeling are behaviors from which inferences are drawn about what exactly an infant perceives when it is touching or noticing something or attending to a movement or sound. Although infants may sit passively when they are exposed to stimuli, they must still sustain a stable posture by coordinating the movements of head, neck, and back with eye saccades and be able to switch from focal to peripheral events as required by the experimental conditions. In other words, movement is an intrinsic and ineradicable element of each and every act of sensory perception. There are important reasons for making this assertion that have a bearing on how mechanisms of consciousness are defined, their role in learning, and their singular contribution to the integration of motor and perceptual development. Developmental scientists have yet to construct a theory of neuropsychological development, discussed next, that is capable of explaining how complex mental processes emerge from these fundamental constituents of infant behavior.

2

Toward a General Theory
of Neuropsychological
Development

The processes that contribute to the formation of the brain, the organization of behavior, and the emergence of mind and consciousness are complex and commonly believed to be embedded in different levels of organization (Revonsuo, 2000: Shaw & McEachern, 2001). Higher level functions like perception are dependent on but not reducible to lower level events involving gene transcription, the development of protein molecules, and transmitter release. Outputs at one level can, but do not necessarily, produce complementary changes at other levels because events occurring at each level operate within specific boundaries, which limit the interaction of the entities involved (Tononi & Edelman, 1998).

A daunting challenge facing contemporary neurobiologists and psychologists is to explain the mechanisms by which events occurring at lower levels of biological complexity contribute to the emergence of events at higher levels even though higher levels are not reducible to these lower level events. A general theory of neurodevelopment is needed that resolves fundamental questions about the sequence and boundaries of complex neuronal interactions by showing how perception and motor development interact, engaging the whole brain. This knowledge is also crucial to understanding how conscious experience is uniquely individual and embodied, and yet capable of supporting beliefs that can be communicated, shared, and intersubjectively understood (Barresi & Moore, 1996). In this chapter, we defend our conten-tion that knowledge about consciousness is crucial to further advances in understanding why infants and children perceive and experience the world differently. Asserting that

31

infants possess consciousness as newborns or within the first 3 months of birth is controversial and requires empirical support. Accordingly, a primary goal of this book is to establish an empirically verifiable conception of consciousness that contributes fundamentally to understanding the causes of individual differences in behavioral and perceptual development.

A NONHIERARCHICAL CONCEPTION OF DEVELOPMENT AND EMERGENCE

Emergence is a phenomenon of biological growth involving the interaction between and recombination of separate entities into structures capable of performing new functions. Organisms that are undergoing growth processes perhaps epitomize emergence because they acquire new perceptual, behavioral, and cognitive functions through development that are not possessed at birth. The facts that motor control requires coordination and that sensory modalities do not come online all at once, but take time to produce coherent perceptions, indicate that experience is essential to their complete development and integration. As organisms develop, they are increasingly exposed to contingencies of nature that require them to enlarge their capacity to anticipate, predict, and control events beyond immediate individual sensory and physical contact. In this way, organisms acquire new powers that emerge from the integration of previously uncoordinated actions in response to new experiences.

Sensory Access, Dimensionality, and Signaling

There are at least two ways to understand emergence that have a bearing on the relative weight accorded to genes and experience in developmental processes. According to Cariani (1997), a fixed set of primitives can be recombined in new ways to form emergent structures. Novel DNA sequences can be produced by recombination of preexisting nucleotides, condons, and condon sequences. Clearly structural and functional variety can be generated from a small set of genetic sequences. But recombinant emergence cannot easily produce new primitives that effectively enlarge the *dimensionality* of the organism as a whole. This condition can be met through structural alteration—when a new sensor is added that increases the capacity of the organism to detect some new property or quality of the environment. For example, multimodal stimuli that are presented redundantly enable infants to acquire amodal percepts that contribute to perceptual integration by expanding the dimensionality or modes of sensory access they have to their world. As described in Chapter 7, the dimensions in which thoughts and beliefs are communicated and comprehended can also be enormously expanded through processes of semantic emergence, whereby words acquire more than one sense and use within different syntactic constructions.

There are different theories about how signals can be transmitted and processed that affect knowledge about neurobiological pathways through which new structures and functions are likely to emerge. Cognitive neuroscientists who see brain development primarily occurring through genetically determined structures tend to view signal processing in segments. Accordingly, sensory inputs are encoded by different neurons that are connected to different receptors. Different values of these sensations are encoded in discharge rates. The coherence of the system is channel and rate dependent. That is, neurons that fire together wire together in recurring and predictable patterns of discharge that represent the spatial and temporal attributes of the stimulus. Any changes that involve rewiring must preserve this channel identity and these firing patterns. Significantly, these conditions for the preservation of dedicated functions are rarely, if ever, satisfied when compensatory or alternative connections are forged after brain injuries that nevertheless produce similar functional outcomes.

A temporal pattern of processing would appear to overcome these cumbersome and rigid features of rate- and channel-dependent systems. Temporal processing also more closely approximates the conditions that facilitate memory and retrieval, such as timing, sequential recall, amodal recognition, and semantic and contextual variation. Unlike channel coding, which forces a signal into a predesignated frequency, temporal coding allows neurons to fire in staggered and variable sequences. The intervals between spikes (and their amplitude and frequency) can consequently be spread out over larger populations of neurons, producing a combination of synchronous and asynchronous firing patterns. There are two types of temporal processing networks: time-delay networks and timing networks. Time-delay networks convert incoming signals with different time patterns into spatial, channel-coded output patterns. This reflects the dubious assumption that all stimulus signals are converted by cortex into spatially analyzable patterns. Timing networks view cortical neurons as coincidence detectors, rather than rate integrators. This enables neurons to differentially process the same temporal signals and correlate stimulus attributes according to their time of arrival. Point-to-point wiring is no longer necessary, allowing time-based signals to be broadcast widely throughout large neuron populations in reverberating

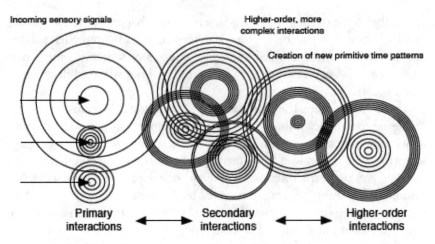

Incoming sensory signals   Higher-order, more
                                                      complex interactions

                                              Creation of new primitive time patterns

Primary   Secondary   Higher-order
interactions   interactions   interactions

FIGURE 2.1   A time-coded broadcast model for asynchronous global integration. In time-coded systems, multidimensional signals can be conveyed through time patterns that are transmitted asynchronously through neuronal groups. Stimuli with multiple time patterns can be sent on the same lines and interspersed or interleaved with other patterns. Synchrony across transmission lines is not required, and delays in signal processing facilitate the integration of patterns arriving at different times. This broadcast model has the virtues of facilitating the reciprocal coupling between neuronal groups possessing different degrees of complexity, making possible the creation of new patterns of interaction that expand the dimensionality of the system as a whole. "Emergence of a New Signal Primitive in Neural Systems," by P. Cariani, 1987 Intellectica, 25 (2) pp. 65–143, Figure 7. Copyright 1997 by Reprinted with permission.

synchronous and asynchronous overlapping waves, as illustrated in Figure 2.1. In this scheme, lower level representations of stimulus attributes are not discarded, as is assumed in hierarchical models, but are reactivated and recombined to form new memories.

Causal Efficacy and Nonreduction

The concept of emergence is controversial because it affects how we understand the relationship between the senses and the causal relationship among and between physical and nonphysical processes that produce complex systems. *Emergence* conventionally has been defined as involving the production of higher order phenomena from lower level processes but are not themselves reducible to lower level processes. Complex physical systems are emergent if their higher level properties are not identical to any parts of the lower level taken in isolation, nor do they result from a simple summation of properties of the lower level parts of the system. Scientists who believe it is possible for mental phenomena to emerge from complex physical or biological systems, such as brains, but which are not reducible to neural processes, prefer emergence defined in this way. The philosophical notion of supervenience is pertinent to understanding the empirical and logical implications of this idea. The principle of supervenience holds that

1. No two objects can differ in their mental properties without differing in their physical properties.
2. A single object cannot change its mental properties without changing its physical properties.
3. If, at a given time t, a single object has two different subsets of mental properties, it must have two different subsets of physical properties.

The first condition is consistent with neuroscientific views that individual differences in perceptual or cognitive processes reflect underlying differences in brain connectivity and processing. Overwhelming evidence that individual mental development involves extensive growth and reorganization of brain functions supports the second condition. There is ample evidence from lesion studies supporting the third condition that brain injuries impair some neural processes while sparing others, which assumes a compensatory role in partially restoring neuropsychological functions.

These principles justify the belief that only physical things, such as brains, are capable of being causal agents, but they do not account completely for the psychological states that are generated. In this sense, lower level neural processes are necessary, but not sufficient, to explain higher level emergent phenomena involving perception, memory, or a sense of self. There are circumstances that may help account for this explanatory deficiency, although they may force us to drop a hierarchical conception of brain function, and thus revise the conditions in which supervenience is applicable.

Open Systems, Experiential Variability, and Causal Indeterminacy

Biological organisms are open systems that bear a thermodynamic relationship to the environment and typically spend part of the time in a far-from-equilibrium state. As such, the unity and integrity of an organism at any given time depends on the process of thermodynamic exchange, which renders the whole organism in continuous transition from unstable to stable states to the next. In complex biological systems undergoing change or state transitions, some constituent parts may work to restore equilibrium while others may not, thus undermining the assumption that lower level processes co-vary in a direction that produces consistent causal consequences. For example, the expansion and depletion of synaptic connections can occur concurrently in the same brain region. Developmental psychologists have documented inconsistencies or regressions in infant motor development that may be indicative of these differential processes of brain growth involving the piecemeal and overlapping integration of postural, sensory, and motor systems (McGraw, 1935; Touwen, 1976).

Neural systems appear to violate this condition of internal relational consistency because stimulation from the environment is an *external relationship* that contributes to variability observed in how individual brains process sensory inputs. More significant, brain organization is plastic or experience dependent. Experience induces changes in dendrite growth and synaptic connections, alters the boundaries between receptive fields, and effects changes in the level of neuromodulation, among other functions, that modify brain structures and functions throughout the life of an organism. If the brain is dependent in part, on stimulation that varies from one experience to the next for each individual, and if different structures can perform the same functions, then causal *indeterminacy* is introduced. (Causal indeterminacy should not be confused with the absence of causality. It simply means that alternative structures possess equivalent causal force and their exact role depends on their relationship to other components of mechanisms with which they interact.) This complicates, but does not eliminate, judgments about how different brain functions contribute to variations in the psychological processes that constitute human experience.

The degenerative nature of neuronal group structures requires the adoption of a weaker version of global supervenience that reflects the capacity of the brain to provide alternative biological mechanisms to attain similar functional psychological outcomes. This version of supervenience acknowledges the importance of intra- and cross-brain variability in contributing to significant differences in individual neuropsychological responses to similar experiences. Strong versions of global supervenience propose a condition of strict entailment between mental phenomena and their neurophysiological underpinnings. The argument goes that mental phenomena depend on physical causes that are invariant despite profound differences in individual experience because physical events are governed by principles of closure and finality. Accordingly, mental phenomena that appear to possess inexplicably extrinsic properties ultimately can be explained by (or reduced to) mechanisms intrinsic to the functioning of the brain. Although closure is essential to a naturalistic explanation of conscious experience, it may not be possible to pinpoint precisely which factors possess causal force due to the extensive reciprocal interactions among brain regions. The belief may be mistaken that a recurring pattern of causal relationships among neurons involved in brain function will be discovered that is capable of explaining the tremendous variability in individual conscious experience. Degeneracy introduces considerable intrabrain variability in neuronal group interactions, and experience adds an element of extrinsic contingency that complicates analyses that insist on causal sufficiency (Edelman, 2003, 2006).

Functional Boundaries

This leads to a third issue regarding whether the temporal and spatial boundaries that separate inputs and outputs of neural processes, occurring at different levels of complexity and possessing different degrees of plasticity, unambiguously correspond to the boundaries between one psychological function and another that they support (Shaw & McEachern, 2001). Boundary drawing typically reflects a spatial bias, which stipulates that entities or functions should be self-contained. We reason by analogy that if physical, three-dimensional objects have edges that establish the limits of their mass and extension in space, then biological functions, which occupy space that contains cells and tissue, must possess similar characteristics. Digestion is conventionally designated as a function of the stomach, but food processing continues through the intestine and then involves the liver, where the molecular by-products of fat and sugar—metabolism—are further filtered and released into the bloodstream. At what point in the process should we declare the function of digestion to have been completed?

The same question can be posed about the brain and perception. Asking when perception begins or ends depends not only on how we define it, but also is determined by judgments about which sensory processes are involved in this psychological function. Of course, from a developmental perspective, this judgment is governed by knowledge of which brain functions are capable of adequately supporting sensory processing. The fact that infants acquire visual acuity early on has led some researchers to focus nearly exclusively on visual perception. But other researchers contend that vision is but one of many sensory modalities that must be sufficiently integrated with motor control before perception yields reliable categorizations. Vision is a motor skill that requires mastery of eye movement in coordination with head movement and vestibular and postural control. Accordingly, some neuroscientists argue that the first acts of perception involve categories formed from self-generated patterns of movement and postural variation that are subsequently employed to extract form from motion and to discriminate among separate features of stationary objects and scenes.

Complexity, Ambiguity, and Degeneracy

There are numerous reasons that hierarchical conceptions of brain function encounter difficulty in providing an adequate account of the biological complexity involved. We know that the firing properties of individual neurons play a significant role in understanding long-term potentiation, and that some sensory receptors are sensitive to certain kinds of input. We know that neurotransmitters affect the behavior of many neurons through modulation of pre- and postsynaptic signals. We also know that perceptual recognition may not occur until interacting groups of neurons reach a threshold of coherence through synchronous firing. But the problem persists that we do not yet know which of these events are the proximate cause of the psychological function we are trying to explain (McIntosh, 2000). This difficulty is no more vividly illustrated than by the endless disputes regarding how many distinct visual cortical areas there are and what information is processed at each level. This task is complicated by the fact that the extrastriate cortex through which the visual cortex traverses is connected with numerous cortical areas.

Many neuroscientists believe that perception and memory represent reality and that brain states provide static, veridical images, rather than constructed scenes. This is the position that Koch (2004) takes on consciousness, contending that, "what you experience at any given point in time is static (with motion painted onto the snapshot), even if the stimulus is changing" (p. 268). If perception consisted of series of snapshots, motion would no longer be integral to experience. This happens in individuals with a rare brain disorder involving motion blindness who are unable to detect accurately the movement, direction, and speed of objects that appear frozen in time.

Koch's assertion that consciousness is possible without movement is profoundly mistaken. Motion permeates every aspect of nature, including our own behavior. Eye saccades are movements that aid visual discrimination, and head movements help to detect and locate sound. In fact, without self-motion, humans would be unable to obtain the physical and psychological distance needed to gain a new perspective on an ever-changing and uncertain world. This mistake of uncritically equating the characteristics of normal consciousness with abnormal cases can be avoided by acknowledging the multimodal, intersensory, and dynamic basis of human perceptual experience.

Purves and Lotto's (2003) research on vision has dealt a devastating blow to the hierarchical view that image features are detected and processed through successively more complex stages of the visual pathway until a percept is formed. This view assumes that the stimulus is information rich and that visual receptive fields are sufficiently differentiated and selectively sensitive to form a representation, which can furnish an unambiguous concept. But Purves and Lotto (2003) found that most perceptual information is ambiguous and dependent on its relationship to the context or scene within which it appears. Accordingly, visual processing depends largely on probabilistic judgments about spatial relationships that are strongly influenced by illumination, angle of vision, and other pertinent postural and behavioral factors affecting percepts.

Purves and Lotto (2003) believe that the degenerate nature of the relationship between visual neurons and stimulus properties explains this distinctive attribute of vision, contending that the "pattern of activity of any neuron or subset of neurons in the visual brain . . . can be associated with many different percepts" (p. 178). They observe further that, "Just as the outcome of a single cell to a given stimulus is ambiguous (since it can be activated the same way by many different stimulus attributes and contextual settings), so too is the activity of any subset of all the responding neurons" (p. 178). Consequently, the visual percept that is seen by the observer can only be predicted, according to Purves and Lotto, "by knowing the activity at that moment of *all* the neurons in the visual brain" (p. 178). The authors clearly grasp the ontogenetic implications of this perspective by saying that the visual system has been constructed to serve "historical rather than logical goals," whereby visual percepts are formed on the basis of experiential probabilities.

CONSCIOUSNESS AND REDUCTIONISM

Purvis and Lotto's (2003) model depicting the events involved in the formation of percepts is consistent with the broad perspective proposed by Edelman (1987). Perception does not require the sequential transfer of information from lower to higher order regions or vice versa. Instead, information can be transmitted in the brain through a temporally staggered, reciprocally coordinated process of reentry. This takes some of the mystery out of the idea that consciousness is causally dependent on so-called lower level processes and yet not reducible to brain function. Consciousness is not needed much of the time because humans rely on automatic responses that have been learned and internalized as habits (Tassi & Muset, 2001). Only when confronted with perceptual ambiguity and uncertainty of motor response do brain regions interact differently, reaching a threshold of consciousness that contributes to recognition. This is not a matter of the all-or-none involvement of cortical structures because cortex is involved in some degree in most behaviors through processes of perceptual categorization. Instead, this book describes how consciousness emerges through developmental processes that enlarge or contract the scope and frequency of interactions between neuronal groups.

Stated briefly, consciousness emerges through the expansion of neural processes beyond the boundaries in which communication and exchange of information can take place in an orderly fashion without effortful attention. In physical terms, consciousness arises when neural systems reach a state of disorder involving divergent or incongruent signals. In this instance, competing sensory inputs produce complex signals that must be reintegrated. Consciousness coincides with momentary discrepancies in the source and duration of sensory information that must be filtered or bound together to make sense. Binding occurs only if there are sufficiently variable or degenerately recurrent circuits available that provide alternative means to map and assign an appropriate categorization. Successful binding restores order temporarily by reducing the sensory load to a smaller and more manageable subset of neuronal groups. It is precisely the inability, experienced by persons with autism or attention deficit disorders, to control the conditions involving the growth or expansion and contraction of neural processes supporting consciousness that makes these afflictions disorders of reentry and degeneracy.

In subsequent chapters, we describe why sensory and motor processes are not functionally segmented, but develop concurrently and frequently overlap. There is a reciprocal relationship between brain and behavior. Neural growth processes create new pathways for the transmission of excitatory and inhibitory electrical impulses that enable movements to become more precise and better coordinated with one another. Through the synchronous firing of synapses across neuronal groups, complex movements are transformed into gestures and correlated with sensory input to form topographic maps that generate categories and support concepts.

This problem of designating boundaries challenges whether distinctions that are drawn between higher and lower brain functions are justified and whether particular brain structures can be separately correlated with complex psychological functions, such as consciousness. One argument is that theories of emergence resist reductionism by denying that higher level phenomena can be explained by lower level mechanisms. Accordingly, it is claimed that emergent events are epiphenomenal; that is, they are simply nonphysical, residual side effects, like the brief afterglow of a light that has been turned off. It does not possess functional significance and is irrelevant to the workings of light bulbs.

To circumvent the possibility that consciousness is eliminable, a different claim is made that, precisely because consciousness is an emergent phenomena, it possesses a special energetic efficacy or force that is fed back through the brain, altering the neuronal processes that gave rise to it (Penrose, 1994). But this argument assumes that consciousness possesses a special gravitational energy that behaves differently from all known physical forces of nature. This proposition not only remains unproved, but one that would appear to treat consciousness as if it were a basic force of nature, rather than a state of awareness possessed only by living organisms.

There is a third position which holds that emergent phenomena, such as consciousness, are caused by neural mechanisms, which themselves emerge from physical processes (Edelman, 2003, 2004). Nevertheless, the possibility is rejected that consciousness exerts independent causal influence on the brain. Instead, consciousness makes possible the perception of countless qualitative differences in sensory discriminations (described later) that constitute individual perception and memory. Edelman (2006) contends that qualia are the discriminations afforded by various core states that support consciousness. Each core state is capable of differentiating into a new state of integration almost instantaneously. Qualia space is a complex, multidimensional space that can produce different experiences. While qualia space entails phenomenal discriminations, there is no one-to-one correspondence between the physical (i.e., spatial or temporal) dimensions of complexity and the psychological dimensions of qualia space (Seth et al., 2006). According to Edelman (2006), core states do not cause qualia but rather faithfully entail particular combinations of qualia that constitute unique and private experiences. This conception of consciousness maintains a boundary between physical and nonphysical events. It allows conscious access to memory and discrimination among the different sensory and motor sources of experience. Yet consciousness does not cause the ensuing physical changes in brain states or functions. Experiencing a feeling and being able to report what it is like to possess that feeling are not the causes but the results of underlying neural processes. Consciousness does, however, enable changes in activity through intentional goal-directed behaviors, which involve energetic events that do produce physical changes in the brain.

Consciousness is closely linked to a behavioral process that makes qualitative process that enables individuals to keep track of what they are doing and to discriminate among changing facets of these experiences. It does so by making the qualitative differences in sentient states generated by the brain accessible through motor-based mechanisms of attention, memory, and judgment. But access by itself is not sufficient to enable perception to occur. Sentient states must be differentiated and communicated through intersubjective modes of categorization, conceptualization, and generalization. From this perspective, intentional actions do not acquire epistemic status as reasons (i.e., causes of) for behavior simply because they involve self-reference for the conditions for their satisfaction, as Searle (2004) contends (see chap. 7). More important, the meaning of actions taken to attain satisfaction must relate to beliefs about their appropriateness and efficacy in order for them to be intersubjectively understood as being fulfilled (Dalton, 2005). This does not deny that intentionality entails a first-person ontological status in the sense that only I am capable of possessing my thoughts and expressing them overtly in action. But what I do not possess is complete control over the meaning attributed to the actions I take and/or the outcomes or consequences of fulfilling my desires. In this regard, infants' dependency on second- and third-person interpretations of their desires affords early experience in understanding intentional behavior (Barresi & Moore, 1996; Metzinger & Gallese, 2003). In fact, there are good policy reasons for maintaining this intersubjective condition of consciousness. Persons with brain disorders are subject to delusions that are defeasable from a third-person perspective, and thus can be prevented from acting on them because they will result in harm rather than benefit.

RENDERING SENTIENT STATES ACCESSIBLE

Our contention is that consciousness renders sentient states and experiences accessible through intersensory perception and motor control. Intersensory perception does not represent the primary attributes of sensations in a physical sense, but reflects amodal, secondary qualities of percepts in the phenomenal sense that they are attributes of an embodied brain embedded in the world (Lewkowitz, 1994; Lickliter & Bahrick, 2000; Stein, Meredith, & Wallace, 1994). That is why intersensory perceptions are typically experienced as implicit, intangible qualities, rather than explicit reproducible sensations. The sense of self is an emergent property of sentient organisms. An embodied self possesses behavioral flexibility, multisensory access to the world; can distinguish between endogenous and external stimulation; and possesses the capacity to adopt alternative frames of reference. Sentience is a feeling or sensation, for example, of one's own body in motion or rest, or in a state of balance or imbalance, of calmness or agitation, and so forth. These states are communicated to the brain through proprioceptive mechanisms. Sentience involves awareness of physically engendered feelings closely associated with gravity, such as height, depth, width, volume, height, and movement. It also includes awareness of physiological behaviors, such as breathing, digesting, crying, and coughing, as well as functional ones, such as looking, noticing, reacting, believing, and so forth. These latter forms of sentience are not perceptions, but the behaviors involved in perceiving that engage the self. Finally, sentience involves specific phenomenal states, such as the feelings of pain, fear, desire, satisfaction, fulfillment, and other similar states involving intentional states or goals.

Small changes in any of the physical and physiological mechanisms or the phenomenal attributes of an embodied self can alter our self-awareness, self-attributions, and conceptions of ourselves as possessing physical and mental unity, integrity, and the feeling of control of our thoughts and actions. The argument advanced in this book is that infants develop a coherent and stable conception of self by sometimes undergoing opposing feelings of what it is like to experience different states of existence. These feeling states include motor stability and instability, perceptual consistency and inconsistency, emotional stability and conflict and the sense of fulfillment or lack of fulfillment, and other forms of incongruity among desire, intention, and outcome. Only when one or more of these different dimensions of sentient behavior become severely impaired through brain dysfunctions are children unable, without extensive compensatory stimulation, to attain a level of conscious control necessary to sustain a centered and coherent conception of themselves as intentional agents (Stein, Brailowsky, & Will 1995).

SELF-CONSCIOUSNESS AND INTERSUBJECTIVE UNDERSTANDING

It is important to distinguish between two levels of consciousness in terms of their different neural status and functional role in development. Higher order self-consciousness is not a direct extension of primary consciousness. This is so, as Edelman (2004) argues, because higher order consciousness required additional neuroanatomical and neurobiological changes in human evolution before emerging to become an important psychological feature of the phenotype. Edelman (1989, 2004) hypothesizes that primary and higher order consciousness are made possible through the emergence of semantic capabilities and language. Gesture and the need to discriminate and express sentient states occur before language. These are traits of primary consciousness common to many animals and infants alike who must be aware of their needs and communicate them nonverbally to others (Seth, Baars, & Edelman, 2005).

But a spoken language requires physical changes not only in the larynx, but also in the brain. The growth of novel subcortical structures and the development of prefrontal cortical inhibition significantly expanded the conceptual power of existing reentrant connections, making possible syntax (a linguistic form of sequencing events), semantics, planning, and foresight. The capacity to keep track of sequential processes through procedural memory, characteristic of primary consciousness, also is carried forward in the development of the hippocampus and episodic memory characteristic of higher order consciousness. These changes enormously expanded the human capacity to reflect, plan generalize, speculate, theorize, discover new values, and imagine a different world.

The capacities to be aware of one's own bodily and mental states and to reflect on them constitute important milestones in the infant's acquisition of a sense of self. But this does not exhaust the capabilities that humans possess to express and share feelings, communicate ideas, interpret one another's intentions and beliefs, anticipate behavior, and cooperate to attain mutual goals. These are not simply extensions of self-recognition, but involve the attainment of an important psychological ability whereby 4-year-olds are able to read other minds.

Knowledge of other minds involves the realization that people differ in their beliefs and intentions and are capable of being deceived and of holding false beliefs. There are neurobiological and behavioral requisites to mind reading, described in this book, whose impairment can weaken or seriously undermine the capacity to communicate with, understand, and respond appropriately to the actions of other people. Prefrontal cortex and basal ganglia must be functionally connected, focal attention must be stable, and there must be good functional connections between anterior cingulate cortex and prefrontal areas involved in the recognition of emotions (Casey, Durston & Fossella, 2001; Posner & Rothbart, 1998).

Neuroscientists Chris and Uta Frith (1999) found that self-directed deliberation and the attribution of intentions to other minds is nested in a cluster of closely interacting brain regions. These regions include the inferior frontal regions; the superior temporal sulcus, which processes actions and goals; and the anterior cingulate and medial frontal regions, which enable recognition of one's own mental and emotional states. They contend that consciousness is made possible by the fact that we use our analysis of someone else's behavior, in conjunction with reference to our own mental states, to make inferences about the intentions of other persons and their emotions. They also assert that our ability to mentalize "evolved largely from the dorsal *action* system rather than the ventral object identification system" (p. 1694).

Only when children express themselves within communities, where differences in belief are acknowledged, is it possible for them to be released from the solitude of private thoughts and desires to experience what it is like to reflect on the nature of one's own identity and as others view it. Childhood marks the passage through which instrumental judgments based on dimly understood physiological states and emotive feelings are transformed into expressive acts that draw on personal reflection, interpersonal interaction, and recognition to render explicit the shared values on which these preconscious judgments are based.

Knowledge about individual brain states and neural functions underlying behavior provides information that is vital to the attribution of intentions, the expression of emotion, and the ascription of responsibility. That is why 2-year-olds do not fully understand the moral consequences of their conduct, although they are quite capable of understanding rules and rule-governed behavior because the multiple brain regions involved are not sufficiently connected to make such judgments possible. These mitigating considerations apply to children with autism, whose capacity to form and recognize intentions and to express sympathy and show empathy are severely impaired because of the absence of sufficient interactions among these brain functions that underlie these psychological capacities. Before attaining these more sophisticated stages of self-understanding, infants undergo concentrated and intense periods of prenatal and postnatal neurobiological and neurobehavioral growth, described in the next two chapters, which contribute to eventual individual differences in neuropsychological responses to experience.

3

Prenatal Patterns of Neural Growth and Behavior

Early human development involves the emergence of motor and perceptual capacities that eventually become integrated. The conceptual distinction between growth and development is important because each plays distinctive and sometimes contrasting roles in the processes of neurobehavioral and psychobiological integration. Scientific opinion has changed dramatically in the last few decades regarding how the relationship between pre- and postnatal growth and development is understood in genetic, behavioral, and experiential terms. The doctrine that our body and brains are genetically preformed dominated embryological theory until the late 19th century, when experience was accorded a larger role. Well into the 20th century, physicians viewed infants as if they were governed solely by involuntary reflexes equivalent to persons with neural disorders, until the brain and cortex attained complete maturation. Only when it became evident that individual differences in brain, behavior, and cognition could not be explained by genetic factors alone did scientists acknowledge the experience-dependent nature of early development.

MODULARITY AND SPECIALIZATION

As noted before, developmental scientists are divided about how best to characterize the processes and sequence of behavioral and perceptual growth and integration. Some contend that behavior and perception are governed by separate genetically controlled neural events, which contribute to the observed discontinuities (or dissociations) in motor control and cognition occurring in early development (Baron-Cohen, 1999;

Fodor, 1983). Accordingly, from birth infants are believed to possess perceptual skills that exceed the motor skills needed for their effective utilization. From this perspective, infants attain their cognitive potential by simply receiving appropriate experiences involving the exercise of sensorimotor processes needed to execute cognitively demanding (i.e., memory and attention) tasks.

A contrary view holds that sensory processes initially exhibit a high degree of multimodal integration, but subsequently become differentiated through motor experiences. Developmental scientists who adopt this alternative position (i.e., Johnson, 2000a; Karmiloff-Smith, 1998) believe that modularity emerges at later stages of experience-dependent development, when specialization takes hold. These developmental theorists believe that the timing of skill acquisition varies according to when cortex is actively involved in the construction of motor skills. But these contrasting conceptualizations of motor and perceptual development represent opposite ends of a continuum of modular conceptions of the brain. However, neither view conveys completely the versatility of the brain and its capacity to produce functionally equivalent alternative behavioral and perceptual strategies throughout development that do not depend on the involvement of any one functionally exclusive component.

COMPLEXITY AND INTEGRATION

The challenge of motor and perceptual development confronting growing organisms could be better expressed in terms of how the demands for integration and complexity are reconciled over time to enable flexible forms of adaptive response to experiential contingencies. As Figure 3.1 illustrates, behavioral and cognitive development could be conceived in terms of different phases involving alternative or opposing states of motor and perceptual integration and complexity. This scheme better accounts for the differences in the rates and patterns of brain growth that occur in the first 2 years of infant development. From late term through the first 3 months of life, infants experience explosive synaptic growth in primary sensory cortexes that make them particularly sensitive to multimodal intersensory stimulation. Nevertheless, intrabrain connectivity and topographic complexity are extremely limited, and infants possess only rudimentary motor integration and control. In the course of early development, infants undergo a seesaw process, whereby motor and perceptual abilities advance and regress, and sometimes appear to be dissociated, until a plateau is reached that supports simultaneous states of high integration

1 Low Integration Low Complexity	2 Low Integration Moderate Complexity
3 Moderate Integration Moderate Complexity	4 High Integration High Complexity

FIGURE 3.1   Matrix depicting relationship between complexity and integration during early development.

and cognitive complexity. This S-shaped trajectory of infant development, depicted in Figure 3.2, is not completely consistent with the well-documented patterns of neuron depletion and synaptic attrition occurring during the first 14 months of infancy, as basic motor skills are attained during a period of rapid synaptogenesis that begins before birth. However, this trajectory is indicative of the cyclical alternation in cortical development from highly differentiated to highly integrated intracortical connections, documented by Thatcher (1997), that occurs during the first 5 years of development.

There is a dynamic, nonlinear relationship between integration and complexity that affects perceptual categorization. The human brain must possess sufficient functional diversity to sustain a high degree of interaction between different neuronal groups. But functionally specific or segregated neurons must also attain a high level of coherence or synchrony for information to be effectively shared and distributed among the cluster as a whole. Whether these two requirements are met depends on the degree of complexity sustained by the entire functional cluster. According to Tononi and Edelman (1998), complexity measures the amount of information that is integrated within a neural system. Complex neural systems are ones that are neither randomly connected nor redundantly and repetitively wired, as

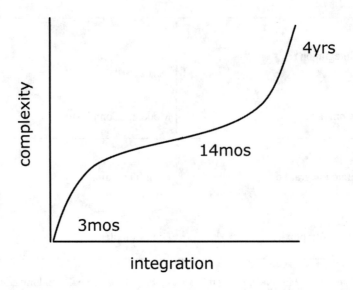

FIGURE 3.2   Graph depicting relationship between complexity and integration
from 3 months to 4 years.

depicted in Figure 3.3. In random systems (Figure 3.3A), firing patterns
are isolated, connections are incomplete, and there is no synchrony.
Consequently, information in randomly connected systems lacks coherence
and meaning. Redundant systems (Figure 3.3B) involve duplicate patterns
of highly segregated, modular groups. Synapses fire in repetitive sequences
that produce a high degree of synchrony, but little temporal variability.
Redundant systems produce predictable and uniform responses to familiar
stimuli, but do not generate diverse approaches needed to respond creatively to novelty. Complex systems that exhibit effective connectivity
(Figure 3.3C) are ones that possess a high degree of degeneracy and recursion, striking a balance between short- and long-range connections,
between segregation and integration, and between synchronization and
temporal variation. These attributes increase the likelihood of a match
between stimulus events and a topographic mapping, which enables the
assimilation of novel information that enlarges categorization.

   Edelman's (1987) theory of brain development shows promise in explaining how these competing demands for complexity and integration are reconciled through processes of neuronal group selection. But developmental

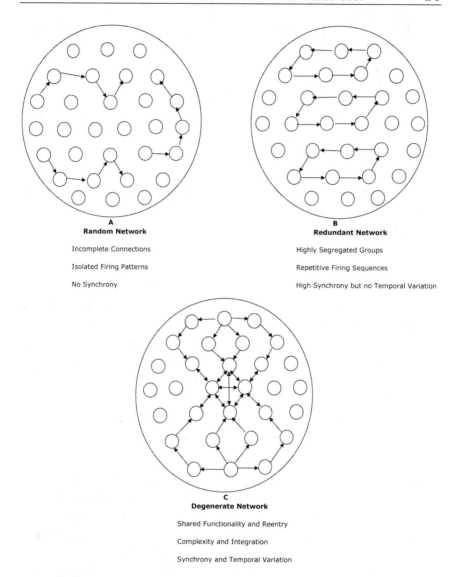

FIGURE 3.3   Networks with different configuration of complexity and integration. Random, redundant, and degenerate networks are illustrated.

neurologists who employ Edelman's theory of neuronal group selection (TNGS) in empirical studies have restricted their investigations to the construction of motor repertoires. This neglects the important roles that reentrant processes play in sensory interaction, mapping, and categorization, which contribute to motor and perceptual integration. This chapter assesses available evidence regarding how spontaneous and experience-dependent events occurring prenatally contribute to coherent behaviors in late term, eventuating in sensorimotor integration after birth.

The discussion in this chapter focuses on the transitions in state that infants undergo to examine the relationships among brain electrical activity, prenatal movement, behavioral state, and temperament. Chapter 4 examines the relationship between the early phases of postnatal, sensory, and motor development and the development of perception. Together these chapters describe how the patterns of neurobehavioral and sensory development that emerge before birth appear to depend on a combination of spontaneous movements and sensory stimulation that give way to organized and integrated forms of locomotion after birth. The capacity of prenatal infants to attain smooth transitions between sleep and wake cycles before birth, their ability to solve the challenge of balance posed by gravitational constraints after birth, and their flexibility in adopting alternative frames of reference each contributes significantly to the exact trajectory by which they attain a high degree of both neurobehavioral and neuropsychological complexity and integration. A significant factor contributing to differences in the pace and trajectory of infant development is the onset and rate of cortical development.

NEURAL GROWTH AND THE DEVELOPMENT OF CORTEX

Neuroscientists speculate that changes in the pattern of human development originated in structural changes in the brain that accelerated the rate and extended the phases of neural growth and behavioral differentiation. Vastly increased the interneuronal connections available to support complex behavior (Finlay & Darlington, 1995; McKinney & McNamara, 1991; Purves, 1988). Edelman (1987) contends that morphoregulatory genes influence the timing of the expression of cell adhesion molecules, which form neuronal groups that are capable of altering phenotypic traits during development. Neural growth factors may also instigate metabolically driven waves of synaptic growth and dendritic branching. This facilitates the formation of short- and long-range cortical connections essential to motor and cognitive development (Purves, 1988; Thatcher, 1997). Moreover, neurotransmitters, such as GABA, which normally inhibit synaptic firing, actually perform a growth-promoting role during early development (Lagercrantz & Herlenius, 2001). Thus, neurotransmitters carry out alternative functions that are genetically expressed at different stages in development.

Recent evidence from PET scans taken for clinical reasons indicates that infants' cerebral glucose metabolic rate is 1.8% higher than adults for the first 2 years and continues to surpass adult rates until 10 years of age (Chugani, 1996). The highest metabolic rates occurring in the first 2 years closely correspond to the period of time when synapses undergo overproduction and subsequent pruning and/or reorganization to support stable forms of behavior. This is also a time during which brain electrical activity shows increased coherence within and across cortical regions, which is needed to support mechanisms of attention and memory (Bell & Fox 1994; Fischer & Bidell, 1998; Thatcher, 1997). The upshot is that the brain contributes to the early tempo or rate of growth, whereas development depends on the timing within which genetic and experiential factors interact. Taken together, these facts indicate that early brain development is sensitive to changes in the rate and tempo of growth that contribute to the extensive variability in subsequent stages of behavioral and cognitive development.

Infant experimentalist Myrtle McGraw (1946) saw development as a continuous process of interaction between neuroanatomical structures and physiological functions, involving the construction, dissolution, and reintegration of the brain and behavior into more varied and complex patterns. Development involves functional differentiation and specialization. Growth determines the rate that energy is transformed to affect size and complexity (i.e., degree of functional specificity) from birth to old age. Differences in energy input and the rate or velocity of growth introduce elements of indeterminacy in development that, McGraw believed, make possible the modification of the sequence through which neuromuscular functions are combined to form a pattern of behavior (McGraw, 1935). She attempted to demonstrate that brain growth furnishes the energy and resources that enable infants to deliberately control the pace and sequence of their development.

McGraw was one of the first developmental psychologists to assert that cortical influences begin to appear at the onset of motor development. However, this is not a statement supporting maturation as is commonly supposed, but a hypothesis about the dynamics in which brain and behavior become integrated. The maturational perspective holds that the cortex becomes functional only after the connections between frontal and prefrontal areas and other regions are well underway. The point at which these regions show minimal functionality is believed to occur within the first year while many more years of prefrontal development are required before more extensive capabilities emerge. As Segalowitz (1994) cogently argues, McGraw was on the verge of formulating a neuropsychologically sophisticated theory. But it slipped from her grasp because credible scientific knowledge of the brain and experience was not available to support her behavioral findings.

However, as Johnson (2000b) observes, persuasive evidence of infant cognitive capacities well before the end of the first year strongly challenges the maturational assumption. He contends that, "It is erroneous to assume that regions of the cortex which are slowest to show anatomical changes during postnatal development are necessarily those that are last to have functional activity" (p. 126). This assumption that cortical development is an all-or-nothing phenomenon is misleading, as Johnson (1994) shows elsewhere, because connections are already being forged, for example, between cortex and subcortical regions during the first *three* months that govern eye saccades.

In fact, as Finlay (2005) points out, there is no evidence that cortex "switches on postnatally." Cortex is already electrophysiologically active even before birth. The extent to which cortex becomes functionally active appears to depend on experience and subcortical developmental processes. Although higher order associative cortex may be primed to function, it cannot do so until afferent or sensory input pathways are made available through the thalamus. In addition, neurons that are sensitive to particular features, such as edges or faces, are not concentrated in specific regions, but are found in widely distributed areas and overlap with neurons in receptive fields possessing multimodal sensitivity. This means that several areas of the brain involving different functions contribute simultaneously and in parallel to perceptual processing, rather than in a stagelike manner dominated by cortex. In this way, the processing of visual space involves "coordinate transformations" (Finlay, 2005) that cut across the visual stream, involving body-centered neurons, head and saccade neurons, and ones having to do with self-motion.

These demonstrable variations in growth and neural connectivity, according to Benes (1997), may also account for the peculiar counterrevolutionary patterns of gyral development, myelination, and neurotransmitter release during early development. For example, unlike earlier mammalian forms, Benes found that the orbital frontal and cingulate gyri are the last to appear in early human development, "making it untenable to conclude . . . that the ontongeny of gyral patterns is a replay of vertebrate evolution" (p. 217). In addition, contrary to the view that prefrontal areas are the last to undergo myelination, Benes found that the areas implicated in late neuronal migration and myelination processes (when axons are enclosed in sheaths that speed transmission) are the more primitive cingulate regions. Finally, some neurotransmitters, such as glutamate, are released in the visual cortex, Benes (1997) contends, "before their corticostriatal counterparts projecting to the caudate nucleus" are completed. This is yet another example, according to Benes, "of developmental change occurring in a descending direction" (p. 225). Accordingly, there is considerable alternation in neuronal development between cortical and subcortical regions of the brain—a phenomenon that was the focal point of McGraw's studies.

THE CONSTRUCTION OF PRIMARY
AND SECONDARY REPERTOIRES

The view that both motor and sensory systems are products of selection from the differential growth among an enormously variable and diverse number of neuronal groups is a notion whose implications for perception and cognition have yet to be fully appreciated. Many prominent developmental scientists find Edelman's TNGS compelling, although they often reveal an incomplete understanding of its central notions of recognition and categorization. As noted before, Thelen (2000), a developmental psychologist, has incorporated TNGS into a dynamic systems theory in her infant studies of motor development that closely approximates Edelman's theoretical intentions even though neglecting to specify underlying neural mechanisms. (Her work is discussed in more detail in chap. 4). While concurring that TNGS best explains pre- and postnatal neuromotor development, Minja Hadders-Algra (2000a, 2000b) and Hadders-Algra and Hans Forssberg (2001), nevertheless, fail to acknowledge that sensory perception is intimately connected to motor control. It is difficult to see how perception can take place in the absence of motor control because sensation involves energetic motions that must be bound together in maps that furnish percepts.

Edelman's central concepts and theories regarding the formation of repertoires and maps underpinning perception and categorization remain badly misunderstood. This is so primarily for two reasons. First, there is a widespread but mistaken belief that primary and secondary repertoires correspond to neuroanatomically distinct areas of the brain and nervous system whose formation occurs at separate times during development. However,

Edelman (1987) defines a *repertoire* as widely dispersed interactions among neuronal groups that cut across neuroanatomical boundaries which overlap over time. Second, a key tenet of selective neural systems, essentially obscured, is that neuronal groups are formed to facilitate the processes of recognition and categorization, which engage both motor and sensory systems. These constitute critical elements in any attempt to understand how behavior and perception become fully integrated during development.

Defining Recognition

It is important, at this point, to carefully delineate Edelman's conception of *recognition* in order to fully appreciate its role in experience-dependent, selection-based biological systems. Edelman (1987) states that recognition occurs when a neuronal group in the primary repertoire "responds with characteristic electrical output and chemical change more or less specifically to an input consisting of a particular spatiotemporal configuration of signals," resulting in a "match between that group and the signal configuration" (p. 47). According to Edelman, recognition can only take place if the primary repertoire is sufficiently large and diverse enough to ensure that for each signal at least one matching element can be found. This does not mean that matches are perfect in some isomorphic sense, but only that a specific neuronal group maintains fidelity in subsequent retransmission of the signal through reentrant processes. Recognition essentially involves the capability to distinguish two different but closely related events within a small margin of error. Of course experience-dependent neural systems must be able to recognize previously unencountered inputs that allow them to generalize beyond current experience. This problem of balancing range and specificity is solved by degenerate systems: They possess abundant diversity while overlapping sufficiently to provide functionally equivalent, but nonidentical, responses to inputs that involve both familiar and unfamiliar events. This is a naturalized epistemology in which a theory of knowledge is grounded in how the brain works (Edelman, 2006).

Primary Variability: Gestures and Postures

Edelman's theory of neuronal group selection proposes that the assembly of primary repertoires occurs through dynamic processes involving the distribution, positioning, and modulatory regulation of neurons within stable but flexible boundaries. These events begin in neurogenesis and continue throughout pre- and postnatal development. Cell adhesion molecules help establish the boundaries among different tissues by regulating cell motion and form, thus controlling the timing of gene expression. This morphoregulatory process is not redundant, but produces a diversity of regional patterns of cellular interactions and connectivity. Primary repertoires are not confined to neuroanatomically distinct regions. Instead they consist of large populations of neurons that can be separated by long distances and segregated into groups whose synapses possess shared signaling (i.e., excitatory or inhibitory) and response properties (i.e. receptivity to electrical frequencies). These motor and sensory repertoires must possess enough diversity or variability to ensure the probability that familiar movements and gestures are recognized in new contexts.

Exemplars of degenerate systems include the visual and somatosensory regions whose receptive field boundaries are plastic and easily reorganized, when compromised, to perform alternative functional roles. As discussed shortly, the basic postures that organisms adopt to gain access to their surrounding world constitute the behavioral expression of primary and secondary repertoires. As such, they provide individuals with different frames of reference toward the world and alternative gestures with which to categorize and use objects, express desires, and satisfy individual needs. The patterns of motor gestures and sensory processes that constitute primary and secondary repertoires undergo moderate change during later development and then significant alteration at later stages of the aging process.

Secondary Variability Through Reentry

Secondary repertoires emerge through experience-dependent competitive processes, whereby expanding populations of large neuronal groups are eventually confined and differentiated into smaller interacting clusters involving extensive recursion or reentry. Reentrant processes are made possible, in part, by the reciprocal cortico-cortical connections and those between cortex and subcortex that are routed through the thalamus. But reentry is also a functional expression of intersensory systems, which overlap and provide multimodal access to the world. Reentry gives the brain enormous power to generate global maps capable of correlating features, drawing inferences, establishing equivalence, and generalizing based on shared attributes. As illustrated later, the initial construction of secondary repertoires appears to be concentrated during the first months, when the brain is both expectant and dependent on experience to form stable, short-distance synaptic connections. During this time, multimodal

sensory inputs furnish amodal stimulation that infants utilize to categorize their world.

PRENATAL STATE TRANSITIONS

Let us examine how the construction of primary repertoires occurs
prenatally before the onset of rapid synaptogenesis at near term. The functional assessment of prenatal brains and nervous systems has improved
considerably with the widespread use of ultrasound. Developmental neurologist Prechtl (1997) pioneered this technique, and he and Nijhuis
(1995, 2003) subsequently identified the patterns of movement and sleep
that are used to assess neurological function before and after birth. These
efforts were mounted in order to identify the point at which behavioral,
physiological, and neurological events coalesce into recognizable, recurring states that now appear to begin between 26 and 32 weeks. The fetus
is very active from 7 to 20 weeks, performing a series of random, mostly
separate and distinct movements that begin with the extension and flexion of head and spine (James, Pillai, & Smoleniec, 1995). There is also
extensive variability in general movements, described later, which
involve the conjunction of separate movements that are repeated in a
more controlled fashion after birth. Fetal motility appears to be an ontogenetic adaptation that facilitates the development of the musculoskele-
tal system (Oppenheim, 1988). But movement also increases the stock of
alternative bodily gestures by which the infant can express sentient states
and combine them into complex forms of behavior and perceptual frames
of reference (Edelman, 1987).

Physiological and Behavioral States

Prenatal development is dynamic, rather than static. The fetus undergoes
continuous transitions in state, each of which actively contributes to the
construction of recurring and recognizable forms of behavior. Four categories, 1F through 4F, have been adopted and widely accepted, which
define alternative states of physiological and behavioral activity that
occur before birth (see Figure 3.4). 1F Quiet Sleep (QS) is characterized
as a quiescent state that is regularly interrupted by brief gross body movements, mostly startles. There are no eye movements, and fetal heart rate
is stable. 2F Active Sleep (AS) involves frequent and periodic gross body
movements, mostly stretches. Eye movements are present, and there are

	Fetal Behavioral States	
1F	Quiet Sleep (non REM)	Occasional gross body movement Eye movement absent Stable Fetal Heart Rate Pattern (FHRP)
2F	Active Sleep (REM)	Frequent gross body movement Eye movements Wider oscillation of FHRP with frequent accelerations
3F	Quiet Awake	Gross body movements absent Eye movements FHRP stable with wider oscillations but no accelerations
4F	Active Awake	Vigorous continuous movement with trunk rotations Eye movements FHRP unstable with large accelerations

FIGURE 3.4   Alternating fetal behavioral states that appear during the third trimester (rapid eye movement [rem], stable fetal heart rate pattern [SFHRP].

frequent heart rate accelerations during movement. In 3F Quiet Awake (QA), gross body movements are absent, but eye movements are present. Fetal heart rate is stable with no accelerations. In contrast, 4F Active Awake (AA) involves continuous activity (mainly trunk rotations); eye movements are present, and heart accelerations are long lasting. 1F and 2 F correspond to periods of quiet and active sleep, respectively, with 2F eye movement associated with REM sleep. 3F and 4F correspond, respectively, to quiet awake and active awake periods. These quiet and active periods alternate in cycles from 24 to 32 weeks. From 32 to 36 weeks, the periods of coincidence of body, eye movement, and heart rate increase dramatically until a cessation of activity and quiet sleep returns near term.

There has been much debate and uncertainty about the underlying neural events that may account for these early cyclical behavioral patterns and their eventual consolidation into coherent states. Some scientists argue that prenatal behavior is regulated by circadian rhythms

(Mirmiran & Kok, 1991; Peirano et al., 2003). This seems implausible because fetuses are incapable of visual discrimination, and thus are unable to distinguish between light and dark. Others contend (Borbely, 1982) that this cycle is governed by a homeostatic mechanism closely associated with EEG delta wave activity. But the alternation between active and quiet sleep cannot be explained on the basis of delta wave activity alone.

Another theory holds that the sleep-wake cycle is simply a reflexive behavior controlled by the brain stem (Joseph, 2000). Most of the movements within the fetus' capabilities until the 32nd week obviously do not require cortical involvement. But it seems unlikely that the brain stem alone can account, during late term, for the increased coherence and synchrony of behavior and physiology that is accompanied by the higher proportion of time devoted to REM sleep—events that are indicative of cortical function (James et al., 1995).

Spontaneous Electrical and Motor Activity

Neuroscientists record prenatal patterns of brain electrical activity to better understand the mechanisms governing neurobehavioral development before and after birth. In the absence of direct sensory stimulation, the fetal brain relies on spontaneous electrical and motor activity to furnish the stimulation needed to develop functional neuronal networks. Functional networks can be formed in the absence of extensive synaptic connections through bursts of oscillatory brain waves. GABA, a neurotransmitter that controls neuronal processes of inhibition, facilitates the interneuronal transmission of these oscillatory signals by promoting the growth of excitatory receptors and, only later on, does it advance inhibitory processes through presynaptic neuromodulation (Ben-Ari, 2001). Immature neurons in the neocortex are coupled through dendrodendritic gap junctions, which provide a conduit for horizontal propagation of activity. Gap junctions enable immature cortex to be linked in extensive networks that allow slow wave electrical activity to spread over long distances (Peinado, 2000, 2001). These networks may be capable of organizing themselves into polychronous groups (see chaps. 1 and 5) that generate persistent time-locked firing patterns with delta wave oscillations characteristic of prenatal sleep states (Izhikevich et al., 2003). MEG recordings indicate that spontaneous fetal cerebral activity shifts from a discontinuous pattern before 36 weeks to a mostly continuous pattern after 36 weeks, involving alternating bursts of low-frequency waves and intervals of relative silence (Preissl et al., 2004; Rose & Eswaran, 2004). In addition, eye movements, gross body movements, and mouthing exhibit increased coordination and synchronization between 34 and 38 weeks during F1 quiet sleep (D'Elia et al., 2001).

TRANSITIONS IN POSTNATAL MOVEMENT

Writhing and Fidgety General Movements

Developmental neurologists using ultrasound have documented the first signs of organized and recurring activity involved in the construction of primary behavioral repertoires. From about 6 or 7 weeks postconception to about 28 weeks, the fetus generates spontaneous but sporadic movements of the extremities. The earliest general movements (GMs) occur in the absence of complete functionality of the spinal reflex system (at 8 weeks) and thereafter exhibit considerable intra- and interindividual variation. These movements include such things as startles, hiccups, isolated arm and leg movements, head rotation, hand-face contact, yawning, and so forth. Near the end of term, from 36 to 38 weeks, the fetus undergoes a transition from writhing GMs involving variable movements of the whole body to fidgety ones limited to smaller amplitude but accelerated movements of neck, trunk, and limbs in all directions. Fidgety GMs involve joint activation of antagonistic flexor and extensor muscles. Writhing and fidgety GMs recur during the first 6 to 8 weeks of infancy (Hadders-Algra & Forssberg, 2001). These behaviors process that enable the motor system to recalibrate to the forces of extrauterine gravitation (Touwen, 1998).

The most important attributes of GMs are their fluency, variability, and complexity. Fetuses that show a delayed transition between writhing and fidgety movements, or who exhibit minimal variation in the amount or quality of fidgety movements, are likely to have brain damage. This outcome is indicated during early infancy by the persistence of stereotyped postures, redundant limb movements, poor head balance, and related problems. Deficits in postural control are also good indicators of more severe neuromotor dysfunctions, such as cerebral palsy. Hadders-Algra and Forrsberg (2001) theorize that severe motor impairments are indicative of a breakdown of direction-specific postures governed by central program generators. Consequently, infants are unable to retrieve and adequately process sensory information needed to establish a secondary repertoire underlying the precisely timed and coordinated movements involved in locomotor development.

General Movements: Direction Specific
or Experience Dependent?

Although Hadders-Algra and Forrsberg (2001) stress that variation pervades every aspect of early motor development (i.e., in the emergence, performance, and duration of developmental phases), they are unable to account for how networks are selected to sustain behavioral flexibility. It is not evident that a central program generator alone governs spinal activity. Prechtl (1997) observes that the crucial indicator possessing diagnostic significance is not the quantity, direction, or reflexivity of GMs, but their quality or smoothness. This qualitative factor becomes more important in the transition from writhing to fidgety movements near term, when the fetus displays small but elegant sweeping movements of the arms, hands, and legs. Cortico-spinal fibers have been found in the human fetus as early as 16 weeks and are likely to generate synaptic input to lower body segments from that point onward (Okado & Kojima, 1994). The quality of fidgety movements is therefore possibly modulated by cranial, corticospinal structures, whose disruption, according to Prechtl (1997) can lead to "transient or consistently poor repertoire GMs" (p. 8).

Moreover, O'Donovan (1999) suggests that neural mechanisms governing spontaneous activity in spinal networks are locally distributed, not global, and are activity dependent. Spontaneous activity exhibits network properties involving recurrent connectivity, depolarization, overexpression of glutamate, a neurotransmitter controlling the firing of excitatory neurons, and GABA depression. When combined these processes together contribute to periods of activity and quiescence. It seems more plausible that spinal assemblies are *directionally heterogeneous*, and that the antagonistic relationship between flexion and extension contributes to the observed lack of control over different methods of propulsion.

The selection of a specific posture appears to require alternative combinations of movements to sustain different levels of behavioral control that do not exhibit a uniform direction.

These same considerations regarding the contingencies of movement and sensory stimulation apply to the construction of secondary repertoires. As McGraw (1943) and Touwen (1976) noted, early infancy is characterized by considerable inconsistency in motor and sensory development. This is indicative of the overlap or co-occurrence of contrasting phases of sensorimotor skill development that often involve regression to more labor-intensive forms of movement or more rudimentary methods of retrieval of visual or auditory stimuli. These alternating phases mark the continuous expansion and contraction of the neural networks supporting movement and sensation. Resolving these inconsistencies is not simply a matter of reorganizing generalized motor networks into smaller ones controlling goal-directed behavior, as Hadders-Algra and Forrsberg (2001) argue. Infants actually learn how the same outcome can be attained with different amounts of effort and energy, involving different combinations of sensory processes. In essence, infants are learning lessons in categorization and equivalence. By conceiving early sensorimotor development in terms of the overlap between primary and secondary repertoires, we avoid positing separate stages, whereby a phase dominated by gene expression ends and an experience-dependent one begins. Instead, infants are acquiring *relational knowledge* about how the control of movement (involving a combination of innate involuntary reflexes and deliberate movement) affects differently their attempts to propel themselves in the desired direction.

Directionality is not established in advance through genetic instructions, but emerges through experience. This is well illustrated by experimental perturbations designed to alter infant postures in the sitting position. At 3 to 4 months, infants show no direction-specific preferences in their attempts to sit up, but instead exhibit extensive variability. Only when they are assisted through training is this variation considerably reduced and a preference shown for specific postural responses (Hadders-Algra, Brogan, & Forrsberg, 1996). Researchers have been able to effectuate changes in the sequence of postural response by placing infants on a rotating platform in a sitting position. The introduction of angular momentum contributes to changes in the way infants handle forward and backward translations by increasing antagonist activity through co-activation of head and neck and by changing the temporal order of leg action in relation to head movement (Hadders-Algra et al., 1996). Experiential input can clearly alter how infants respond to changes in trajectory and direction of their own movements.

BEHAVIORAL STATES AND ATTENTION

The Sequence of Early Sensory Development

Perhaps one of the most controversial areas of research in early development involves whether prenatal infants are capable of discriminating between and among different forms of stimulation. This is important for understanding the emergence of consciousness. Discriminations at this stage may be influenced by level of arousal, behavioral state and by the degree of sensory organization. There is good evidence indicating that the human senses develop in a sequence that begins before birth. Each sensory modality acquires its own developmental history and effects differently perceptual responsiveness in interaction with other senses near term and after birth (see Lecanuet and Schaal, 1996; Lickliter & Bahrick, 2000). The intensity and amount of simulation, as described here, can interact with states of arousal and activity to affect perceptual capacities. Of course, arousal is not the same thing as awareness, and infants must acquire considerably more control over their behavior before they can deploy attention in a coordinated, self-aware manner.

The somatosensory and vestibular systems develop in close conjunction because both involve sensitivity to pressure transmitted from maternal motion (Lecanuet & Schaal, 1996). Tactile receptors are highly developed by 11 weeks and are more densely packed than adults on the face, palms, hands, and soles of the feet. These receptors appear on the arms and legs by 15 weeks. The vestibular apparatus is morphologically mature by 14 weeks, and by the 5th month the fetus starts to orient itself in utero. The fetus develops a sense of taste by 13 weeks and exhibits a heightened sense of smell by about 6 months. The amniotic fluid becomes increasingly permeable, allowing penetration of maternal dietary odors that the fetus detects by tasting or gulping the fluid. Between 18 and 20 weeks, the human cochlea becomes functional, and efferent innervation of outer hair cells takes place. The inner ear and its afferent and efferent synaptic connections are completed by 32 weeks. The middle ear, which develops later as a mechanism for amplification of sound, does not appear to be necessary for prenatal hearing.

The Effect of Stimulation on Prenatal State

Developmental scientists have conducted numerous experiments to identify sounds that are potentially detectable by the fetus. By using hydrophones, researchers have been able to distinguish among maternal background noise, sounds emitted by the fetus, and sounds produced externally. An important recurring finding is that external sounds that possess long wavelengths with low frequencies (or low-pitched oscillations) are detectable by the fetus. This is a significant finding for two important reasons. First, fetuses may be particularly sensitive to low frequency sound because they are able to feel it as well as hear it. This is a form of intersensory redundancy that may facilitate the discrimination of sounds on the basis of timbre. This characteristic perceptual response to low-frequency sound was elicited in an interesting habituation study. A French-speaking woman repeatedly uttered two syllables, ba and bi, and then reversed the order to bi and ba (Lecanuet et al., 1993). The fetuses were able to discriminate between the two stimuli based on the intensity difference between the ba and bi. In another study, near-term fetuses were tested to determine whether they could distinguish between a target rhyme that was recited each day for 4 weeks and a control rhyme. Only the target rhyme elicited a decrease in fetal heart rate. Exposure to specific speech sounds can affect subsequent fetal reactions to those sounds. Thus, by the third trimester, fetuses appear to recognize recurrent maternal speech sounds (DeCasper et al., 1994).

Second, concurrently presented stimuli (i.e., bimodal stimulation) may contribute to the early development of attention by enabling the fetus to control the degree of physiological arousal and behavioral reaction. This capacity to suspend activity may be an important precondition to the subsequent ability to shift attention, which emerges in the first year after birth. As noted before, fetuses undergo spontaneous transitions in state, from quiet to active sleep that govern their initial response to induced stimulation. A change of state is more likely to occur when there is congruence between stimulus properties and the level of ongoing intrinsic neural activity. Accordingly, preterm fetuses are more likely to respond to and show a preference for stimuli that complement or coincide with its level of activity or arousal than stimuli that are incongruent with existing state (Lickliter & Bahrick, 2000).

Nevertheless, researchers have encountered difficulty establishing this condition of congruency as illustrated by the seeming lack of a consistent relationship among fetal behavioral state, heart rate, and patterns of habituation to different stimuli. This problem of measurement is compounded by the lack of consensus on how to compare the effects of different sources of sensory stimulation (van Heteren et al., 2001). In an experiment in which late-term fetuses were exposed to separately administered vibroacoustic and light stimulation, fetal heart response (FHR) to vibroacoustic stimulation did not appear closely connected to any behavioral state, as FHR and fetal movements (FM) increased regardless of state. In contrast, fetal response to light simulation was accentuated in the quiet wakeful state (F3) compared with F1 or F2. However, this finding does not necessarily mean that light is a better predictor of fetal state than vibroacoustic stimulation. Rather, it simply means that the strength of light as a stimulus depends on the fetal state when it is introduced, and that low-intensity sound is more likely to result in change of state regardless of initial state (Kiuchi et al., 2000).

Discrimination Through Bimodal Stimulation

Only recently have researchers attempted to determine whether fetuses are capable of differentiating between stimuli that are presented bimodally. Kisilevsky, Fearon, and Muir (1998) contend that, because vibroacoustic stimulation is multimodal (it possesses both higher frequency airborne sound and lower frequency tactile vibration), sound and vibration are coupled during presentation and thus co-vary. This has precluded the possibility of measuring separately the effects of sound and vibration at different thresholds. Kisilevsky and colleagues employed three different kinds of vibroacoustic devices that enabled them to administer stimulation that varied in terms of texture, sound frequency, and tactile pressure. Using habituation techniques, they found that two of the body massagers provoked generalized defensive responses (as distinguished from startles), indicating that fetuses are sensitive to disparities in frequency and pressure delivered by particular vibroacoustic devices. Only by using the third device, which allowed independent control of pressure and sound, were researchers able to determine that a less intense stimulus, modulated by the composition of the vibrating surface, elicited an attenuated orienting response involving decreased heart rate and body movements. Kisilevsky et al. (1998) concluded that this fetal response is indicative of attentiveness.

Studies such as these indicate that near term fetal response to vibroacoustic stimulation is complex and likely to be influenced by behavioral state and reflect the general level of neurological development (D'Elia Pighetti, Moccia & Santangelo, 2005). The development of eye movement prenatally may be a particularly sensitive indicator of central nervous system (CNS) functionality and cortical involvement. The visual system is the most complex of sensory modalities whose development is highly dependent on experience. Adequate visual perception is not assured, however, by the content of stimulation alone, but depends crucially on the access to the world that is furnished by eye movements. Eye movements play a conspicuous role prenatally that is not visual, but vestibular, by enabling fetuses to adjust to growth-related alterations in body mass, posture and vibroacoustic stimulation (Berthoz, 2000; Morokuma et al., 2004). Vestibular stabilization of gaze enables the control of body movement involved in the habituation to vibroacoustic stimulation (Morokuma et al., 2004). It may be reasonable to suppose that increased eye movement near term, especially in REM sleep, is also indicative of the functioning of the locus coeruleus, the pons, and reticular formation.

BEHAVIORAL STATES AND TEMPERAMENT

Temperament and Cortical Development

Temperament is considered a significant factor that influences the capacity of fetuses and infants to smoothly transition from one state to another. Kagan (1994), among others, has persuasively argued that temperament is under some genetic control, predisposing newborns to adopt recurring forms of behavior and affective reactions in their social interactions during early development. Two types of children predominate: (a) shy, inhibited, and fearful; and (b) outgoing, uninhibited, and fearless children. Kagan (1994) believes that the roots of temperament lie in neurochemical and physiological processes that commence before birth, when neurotransmitters become active and when stress (either maternal, biobehavioral, or environmental) can seriously alter affective reactions. We need not examine the research supporting his theory in detail here.

What is important from our perspective is that viewing infant behavior from the point of view of temperament focuses one-sidedly on the reactive rather on both active and reactive capacities of fetuses and infants, and thus neglects the crucial reciprocal relationship between these two kinds of postural orientations in neurobehavioral development (Touwen, 1998). Moreover, the capacity to control state of arousal may be more directly governed by level of brain development and thalamo-cortical activation than by temperament.

Fetal State Concordance and Regulatory Control

Many developmental scientists believe that the ability to control a state of arousal before birth governs subsequent patterns of attention and reactivity to stimulation and stress. To test this hypothesis, DiPietro et al. (2002) conducted a controlled experiment to determine whether there is a significant relationship between near term patterns of spontaneous activity and subsequent postnatal arousal from sleep in response to visual and auditory stimulation. DiPietro et al. (2002) only measured the concordance between behavior and heart rate, although eye movement is normally also considered essential to establishing concordance. As noted before, eye movement patterns in 2F may be indicative of the level of cortical development. The authors found that fetuses who exhibited higher state concordance prenatally showed, after birth, less irritability and strain, longer periods of attention and alertness, and better visual tracking than fetuses who had not attained high states of concordance before birth.

However, there are several weaknesses with this study that call these findings into question. First, although near term fetuses tend to spend a majority of time in 1F (quiet sleep), and thus exhibit state concurrence, there continues to be significant alternation between 1F and 2F (active sleep) during this time (Nijhuis, 1995). This alternation may reflect increased activity in the thalamus and reticular formation, whereby fetuses gain increased access to alternative sources of endogenous sensory information needed to remold writhing movements into qualitatively distinct fidgety gestures, which contribute to the differentiation of motor control after birth.

Second, if there is considerable variability in prenatal cortical development, then the lack of concordance does not necessarily signify a temperamental trait, but a lack of neurobehavioral consistency. In this regard, Groome et al. (1997) found that the percentage of time spent by fetuses in any given state who had inconsistent state profiles overall was identical to those fetuses with relatively predictable and consistent state control. Nor did the time spent in an indeterminate or transitional state appreciably affect the ability of fetuses with unpredictable alternations in state to return to a previous state at different points in time. It seems plausible that inhibitory cortical mechanisms, which serve to limit the duration of and transitions between states, may not be appear to be as fully developed in those fetuses with state profile inconsistencies than those with consistent profiles (Groome et al., 1997).

A third issue is that fetuses in either 1F or 2F may receive different levels of reticular activation, which affect their level of arousal and ability to process sensory information. Using heart rate response as a surrogate for CNS arousal, Groome et al. (1999) found that, when exposed to a low-intensity speech sound, heart rate decelerations in fetuses occurred more often in 1F quiet sleep (QP) than in 2F active sleep (AS). In contrast, the heart rate response in 2F (AS) was more variable and exhibited a greater magnitude of deceleration than in 1F. The authors interpreted this to mean that arousal in AS involved more widespread reticular activation of brain structures that include the hypothalamus, amygdale, and cingulate cortex. In contrast, these brain regions are relatively inactive during QS, allowing an increase in activity of subcortical limbic structures. If degree of arousal is a surrogate measure for temperament, we should expect a more consistent pattern of heart rate response than is apparent in 2F. It would seem more plausible that the level of arousal is governed by differences in the scope of CNS involvement during sleep and waking states, and that heart rate response in one state will not reliably predict response in a different state.

CONCLUSION

The patterns of movement and sensory stimulation involved in the mastery of different postures before birth underscore the continuous and interrelated nature of the brain and behavior during development. Spontaneous movement plays an important role in fetal development. The phases in which fetuses undergo quantitative and qualitative change in their patterns of movement appear to closely parallel processes of brain development. The transition from writhing to fidgety movements appears to be indicative of the onset of cortical inhibition, perhaps facilitated by cortical connections to the basal ganglia. Fetuses differ significantly in their level of arousal to sensory stimulation, and some argue that this is a function of neurochemistry and temperament. But there is also evidence that infant sensory processes become functional at different times during early development; consequently, each sensory modality acquires it own unique and sometimes discordant, stimulation history.

Patterns of action and reaction are interdependent. Transitions in state can be triggered by spontaneous brain activity, behavioral or physiological reactions to stimulation, or a combination of both. Fetuses who exhibit inconsistencies in transition from one behavioral state to another (i.e., arousal rather than quiet sleep when a stimulus is withdrawn) may be more indicative of the level of cortical inhibition or reflect incompatible sensory inputs than signify a temperamental inability to vary response. Inconsistency should therefore not be construed as symptomatic of disorder or dysfunction, but viewed as indicative of the range of variability that fetuses must possess to construct viable and adaptable primary repertoires of behavior. The thalamocortical system may play a crucial role in determining how efferent and afferent sources of stimulation are distributed in the brain to affect the balance of action and reaction. As we see next, there is an essential continuity in the transition from pre- to postnatal development involving the interdependence of primary and secondary repertoires in sensorimotor integration.

4

Postnatal Sensorimotor Integration

As noted in the previous chapter, sustained rates of rapid and prolonged growth contribute to differentiation and functional complexity. Stimulation occurs prenatally through spontaneous electrical activity as a result of the diversity of general movements (i.e., writhing and fidgety) and through exogenous stimulation. General movements recur in the first 6 weeks after birth before undergoing substantial reorganization and eventual integration. The recurrence of writhing and fidgety movements may reflect the fleeting influence of preterm brain electrical activity whose signal strengths change during the course of synaptogenesis. Experience also plays a vital role in the development of motor and perceptual skills by providing the sensory inputs needed to organize synapses into networks capable of organized and reentrant interactions.

Developmental scientists seek to understand three related processes that occur during the first few months of infant development that contribute decisively to later perceptual and cognitive development. The first involves how sensory processes are functionally differentiated and then become integrated. The second phenomenon deals with how sensory inputs are bound to form coherent percepts. Finally, a third developmental phenomenon involves how sensory input and locomotion are combined to enable infants to attain different frames of reference on their world. As becomes apparent in subsequent chapters, these processes are temporally interrelated, and thus are extremely sensitive to disruptions in growth that is evidenced in autistic disorders. Incorrectly timed growth and insufficiently differentiated signal pathways produce neuronal assemblies that are unable to extract amodal signals needed for perceptual discrimination.

INTERSENSORY REDUNDANCY AND
PERCEPTUAL INTEGRATION

The mechanisms and experiential processes that contribute to sensory organization and discrimination are interdependent. The morphological and functional characteristics of synaptic organization and potentiation are strongly influenced by experience-expectant and experience-dependent developmental events. However, the experience-expectant development of the visual striate cortex may not depend solely on the timing, amount, and duration of visual stimulation, but may also require some level of complementary auditory or tactile stimulation to amplify the detection of and discrimination among different sensory signals. Intersensory redundancy fulfills the need for comparison and equivalence. It does so by enhancing the prospects of recognition or matching based on distinctive amodal qualities of different combinations of sensory inputs. Judgments about equivalence are made on the basis of shared attributes and relative differences, rather than according to whether some stimulus features are perceived to be identical.

Infant Capabilities

As described before, sensory development follows an overlapping sequence involving tactile ⇨ vestibular ⇨ chemical ⇨ auditory ⇨ and visual modalities. Each sensory modality acquires its own developmental history and affects differently the level of arousal because the amount of sensory interaction increases near term and after birth (see Lecanuet & Schaal, 1996; Lickliter & Bahrick, 2000). Although the exact scope of prenatal intersensory capabilities requires further scientific investigation, there is mounting evidence that infants possess from birth the capability to detect information that is not specific to a particular sensory modality, but conveyed by more than one sense. In other words, infants recognize amodal qualities, such as rate, rhythm, or intensity, when information is presented concurrently or redundantly across two or more sensory modalities. This ability to perceive relationships between sensory modalities on the basis of shared qualities has been documented in several experimental studies reviewed by Bahrick, Flom, & Lickliter (2002). For example, 4-week-old infants can detect temporal synchrony, and at 7 weeks they can detect amodal composition. Infants within the first year are able to notice the relationship between faces and voices and between facial movements and speech. They can also extract amodal information expressing emotion from the combination of visual and acoustic elements of speech, and they can keep track of the composition and impact of objects according to the tempo and rhythm of their movements. The duration of infant memory and capacity for recognition appear then to depend on the temporally distributed and multimodal nature of intersensory stimulation.

Experimental studies conducted by Lewkowitz (1994), Bahrick (1992), Bahrick (1994), and Bahrick and Pickens (1994) show that bimodal stimulation has greater perceptual salience than unimodal stimulation. Bimodal stimulation exploit the co-variation of two sensory processes involved in amodal recognition. In this way, amodal or redundant stimulus properties become foreground, whereas other modality specific features are relegated to the background, such as color, pattern, pitch, or timbre, which are arbitrary and only contingently related qualities. Intersensory redundancy appears to have a multiplicative effect, Stein and Meredith (1993) contend, as the neural consequences of pairing two stimuli from different modalities exceed those expected to occur by adding the impact of each cue delivered separately. Only after considerable motor development and contextually variable perceptual experiences do infants possess sufficiently rich categories to differentiate between elements that are only contingently associated with a particular object or event and those that cut across categories.

Unlike normal children, children with autism experience severe difficulties integrating multiple sensory inputs, especially visual, auditory, and tactile inputs. Autistic children process intersensory inputs as if they were incongruent rather than complementary signals. Autistic children combat these sensory processing disorders by indulging in some combination of self-stimulating and self-injurious behaviors to reduce the level of uncertainty regarding the unexpected intensity of sensory contact. But these repetitive behaviors also unwittingly furnish amodal stimulation, whose rhythms have a calming effect. Nevertheless, these self-distracting behaviors limit learning and the occasions for social and emotional interaction.

Occupational therapies have been developed that provide multisensory substitutes for self-produced stimulation. Sensory integration, a technique pioneered by Ayers (1972), engages children in active sensory and motor challenges involving multimodal sources of stimulation. By using special equipment designed to facilitate balance and motor control in the completion of tasks intended to furnish vestibular and vibratory stimulation, autistic children are able to decrease their level of arousal and increase the degree to which they attend to learning situations. Sensory integration alone is not purported to produce gains in cognitive achievement.

Instead, it is designed to remove neurobehavioral obstacles that prevent learning (Schneck, 2001).

Multimodal Receptive Fields

There is also increasing neuroscientific evidence challenging the position that most neurons are functionally prespecified, and that multimodal receptive fields play only a limited role. The conventional wisdom is that occipital and somatosensory cortexes are unimodal and are thus sensitive only to modality specific stimulation (Thesen et al., 2004). However, somatosensory neurons have been identified in ERP studies as being involved in multisensory synthesis of different factors that include time, space, and content (Calvert & Thesen, 2004). The superior colliculus, an undisputed multisensory region that is sensitive to motion and guides response to the source and location of visual and auditory stimuli, plays an essential role in the development of eye saccades during early infancy. According to Wallace and Stein (2000), cortex is already involved with the superior colliculus in 3- to 4-month-old infants. In addition, several regions of the superior and inferior parietal lobes and intraparietal sulcus appear involved in the detection and integration of multisensory cues based on common spatial location. The superior temporal sulcus, which is believed to possess neurons dedicated to face recognition, is involved in the integration of audiovisual speech based on shared phonetic features. These regions are either active at birth or become active within the first year.

Brain-imaging studies of adults have shown that vision and touch reciprocally modulate one another. Bimodal stimulation activates the lingual gyrus, normally considered to be an exclusively unimodal visual area (Macaluso et al., 2000). In an ERP study, Taylor, Kennett, and Haggard (2002) found that viewing an arm that is being touched resulted in increased modulation in the somatosensory cortex. Conversely, attending to touch has a greater modulating effect on judgments of simultaneity of visual and tactile stimuli than when vision is attended to alone (Spence, Shore, & Klein, 2001).

Binding and Coherence

The cross-modal nature of sensory perception raises important questions about how and when sensory processes are bound together to form coherent and unified perceptions. The issue of binding is controversial because opposing theories differ fundamentally as to whether perceptual binding is primarily a top-down or bottom-up phenomenon. Top-down theories contend that parietal, temporal, and prefrontal cortexes must be involved for binding to occur. Bottom-up theories emphasize the sequential perspective that stimuli are processed in stages, resulting in the recombination and integration of more primitive features into coherent perceptions. It is also likely that there is a reciprocal interaction between bottom-up and top-down processes. The studies described before indicate that the brain is capable of resolving discrepancies between sensory modalities through instantaneous re-mappings that do not depend on sequential reprocessing or higher level transformations, which impose a common frame of reference (Avillac et al., 2005).

Feature binding emerges in the first month after birth in the absence of a fully developed visual system and before higher level functions become active. In a series of experiments using a habituation procedure, Taga et al. (2002) compared the ability of 1-, 2-, 3-, and 4-month-olds to discriminate changes in the conjunction of a familiar shape and color in two objects. Interestingly, 1-month-olds were able to discriminate a change in the conjunction of features, suggesting that perceptual binding was occurring. However, 2-month-olds had great difficulty with the simultaneous representation of two objects. Infants at this age are at a disadvantage because of a temporary inability to disengage from an object and shift attention. By 3 months infants were again successful, but by 4 months their performance declined. This decline appears to coincide with a decrease in repetitive saccades contributing to a failure to detect changes in the conjunction of features. Taga et al. (2002) argue that the appearance, disappearance, and reappearance of perceptual binding may be due, in part, to the way looking behaviors are organized at each age. These changing infant perceptual capabilities may also as well as reflect changes in the locus of cortical and subcortical connections. This early sequence through which binding occurs is also consistent with the primary contention of the previous chapter that an increase in complexity of a skill is followed by temporary decreases in sensorimotor integration.

A DYNAMIC SYSTEM FOR SENSORIMOTOR CONTROL

Perceptual categorization during infancy depends on more than just broad intersensory input; it requires, from the onset, the capacity to move and change postures. In fact, postural control depends crucially on the interaction of several sensory inputs from vestibular, visual, and somatosensory receptors. Postural control is seriously impaired if one of these sensory cues is modified or disabled because this disrupts the coordinate sensorimotor transformations that must occur across the whole body involving rotational and translational movements. Posture does not consist of distinct and rigid statuesque poses that are supported by the spinal column, but involves the continuous redistribution of forces through bodies that possess segmental independence, allowing flexible movement and interaction. A simple feedback model is incapable of representing the complexity of sensorimotor interactions that are essentially multimodal and intersegmentally coupled through multiple input and output loops, as shown in Figure 4.1. This is a dynamic system that is capable of carrying out feature detection and correlation simultaneously. The system undergoes continuous alteration by the sampling of different sensory sheets, and its input-output correlations are changed by motion or behavior. Subcortical structures that include the hippocampus, cerebellum, and basal ganglia (not shown) play an important role in sequencing events and switching output in accord with alterations in posture.

Infants are confronted with a vexing challenge of properly integrating sensory information under changing postural conditions. Postural instabilities associated with crawling, reaching, and head turning involve the temporary misalignment of visual and tactile receptive fields that must be recalibrated at each level of locomotor attainment. Recent studies indicate that visual and tactile receptive fields use different frames of reference (Avillac et al., 2005). Visual receptive fields can be either eye or head centered, whereas tactile receptive fields are strictly head centered. Thus, changes in eye position associated with trunk rotation affect the accuracy of judgments about distance and trajectory of impending impact because there is a misalignment between tactile and visual information. Infants lack the ability to shift their attention sufficiently to attain congruency in receptive fields needed to rectify posture-dependent information. Instead of imposing a common frame of reference, visual receptive fields may undergo a partial shift in the direction of a head-centered frame of reference to reconcile posture-related discrepancies.

In normal children, transformations posture are often automatic and anticipatory or preemptive in nature, in which vestibular and kinesthetic inputs play a dominant role in response to displacement of the body (Mergner & Rosemeier, 1998; Roberts, 1995). Feature extractors operating through the proprioceptive system work in conjunction with visual, vestibular, and mechanoreceptors for balance to perform a recognition function. As we see in Chapter 7, language expands pattern recognition by

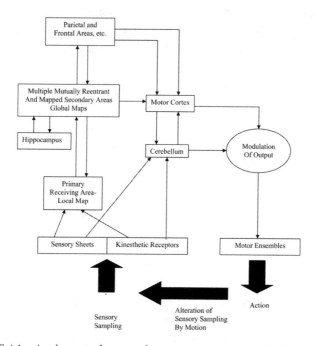

FIGURE 4.1   A schematic diagram of some components contributing to a global mapping. The essential components are (1) sensory sheets tied to separate motor ensembles capable of disjunctive sampling, such as the retina in the eyes linked to the oculomotor system, or receptors for light touch or kinesthesia linked to fingers, hand or arm; (2) a local mapping of the sensory sheets to appropriate primary receiving areas, themselves forming local maps; (3) a profusion of mapped secondary areas for each modality to carry out various submodal responses to disjunctive samples—these secondary areas are linked in turn to mapped motor areas; (4) extensive reentrant connections among various maps of each order, with ultimate reentry back to the primary local map of maintenance of spatiotemporal continuity; (5) subcortical areas (e.g., hippocampus, cerebellum, basal ganglia) or ordering sequential events or switching output; and (6) appropriate postural or orienting changes via the output of the global mapping to alter the position and sampling of sensory components of the motor ensemble. Movement of sensory sheets can thereby lead to feature correlation during the time when these same sheets are carrying out feature detection. A given global mapping can consist of varying contributions by each of the different components and involves input–output correlation. It is therefore a dynamic structure that is altered as the sampling by different sensory sheets and its input–output correlations are changed by motion or behavior. Each alteration can alter neuronal group selection within the components. Notice that a global mapping constitutes a distributed system. From *Remembered Present*, 1990, by Gerald Edelman. Copyright 1990 by Basic Books. Reprinted with permission.

converting perceptual information regarding the movement and displacement of bodies in space into syntactic relationships between subjects and objects that involve changes in tense, meaning, and significance.

Perceptual Distortions in Microgravity

Human physiological sensitivity to gravitational forces plays a fundamental role in the postural orientations that humans adopt and the displacements they experience by acting in and on their terrestrial environment. Gravity strongly biases movement by requiring humans to adopt postures that sustain balance in the midst of destabilizing activities. Gravitational biases are clearly evident in the behavioral and perceptual adjustments to the microgravity environment of outer space (Correia, 1998). Astronauts have reported several unusual effects of microgravity that underscore the important role of balance in human judgment. Many of the perceptual and behavioral distortions that astronauts experience in weightlessness are similar to the challenges of balance that infants and toddlers experience during their locomotor development.

One of the most disorienting effects of zero gravity is the general inability to determine whether the body is vertical. In the absence of vestibular and ground tactile input during weightlessness, external visual cues can be highly misleading as to the relationship between the body and external objects. This is because the perception of the vertical is the result of multisensory compromise. The brain's attempt to work out a frame of reference in zero gravity is thwarted by a lack of a basis of comparison (Berthoz, 2000). For example, although a spacecraft in orbit is undergoing a free fall back to earth, astronauts do not perceive a sense of acceleration. Instead they sense that the floor of the spacecraft is approaching the body—a common sensation that occurs when an elevator is decelerating (Pozzo et al., 1998). Only when astronauts make foot contact with the cabin floor are they able to overcome these forms of perceptual distortion. Interestingly, astronauts tend to flex their legs and lean backward before initiating forward, whole-body reaching movements. In doing so, they are attempting to overcome the effects of imbalance and loss of control over the direction of force by lowering the center of gravity. This is precisely what happens when babies first attempt to crawl. Their attempt to push forward by adopting a crouched position actually propels them backward before they learn how to modulate the force exerted by knees and hands.

Egocentric and Allocentric Perspectives

To counter the distortions of microgravity, astronauts rely primarily on a personal or egocentric frame of reference—a perspective that is characteristic of infancy—whereby all objects and events external to the body are interpreted relative to personal space. That infants adopt this stance is perfectly normal given their limited visual fixation and mobility and their inability to clearly discriminate between endogenous and exogenous sensation. Reaching and grasping behavior within the first 6 months, however, quickly extends body-centered perceptions. The sensory consequences of this behavior are significant because the sense of touch is localized at the point of contact with objects beyond the body, thus changing the point of reference. Babies are highly dependent on touch (through fingers, feet, and mouths) as well as vision to gain experience of how size, form, shape, and texture co-vary as they move toward and away from objects within their grasp. These recurring episodes involve the construction of global maps that consist of small but distinct differences in the number, interaction among, and configuration of neuronal groups. These global maps furnish categories that facilitate the detection of novel features within familiar contexts.

An allocentric frame of reference—one involving multiple perspectives that are contextual and task oriented—is attained only after babies undergo a prolonged series of postural adjustments, each of which presents a different combination of gravitational challenges and developmental relationships between sensory and motor functions. In responding to this series of challenges of balance, infants gradually overcome the physical limitations imposed by finding different ways to combine sensorimotor functions in integrated forms of thought and action. In contrast, autistic children never achieve multistable frames of reference because they lack secure intersensory grounding comparable to what it is like to experience weightlessness. Perhaps that is why some autistic children adopt elaborate but repetitive behavioral rituals and routines, described before, because these movements provide an orderly and grounded stream of amodal stimulation that their poorly integrated sensory systems are incapable of providing.

POSTURAL DIFFERENTIATION AND SENSORIMOTOR INTEGRATION

A noteworthy feature of the sequence of infant sensorimotor development is that the stabilization of posture moves from a head-centered fulcrum to the hips and feet. As infants master erect locomotion, they eventually return to a head-centered frame of reference, in which vision assumes a dominant role. There also is substantial variability of postures and methods of propulsion both within and between individuals that is indicative of secondary variability (Siegler, 2002). This progressive downward and then upward coupling of motor repertoires and sensory receptors is mediated by the thalamus and reticular formation. Global maps constructed through reentry furnish different categorizations of objects and events under alternative frames of reference.

Stabilization of Gaze

Postural control commences at 3 months when babies sit up and are able to hold their heads in a stable position. This is a considerable accomplishment because babies must gain control over gravitational forces by modulating co-activated flexor and extensor muscles necessary to prevent tipping over, especially when reaching. Postural control alternates between the neck and trunk, enabling infants to experience rotation and translational movements that become pronounced in rolling from supine to prone positions and vice versa. The capacity to stabilize the direction of gaze constitutes a crucial intersection in the relationship between balance and attention. Success in recognizing an object or event depends, in part, on whether babies who sit up can control their own movement sufficiently to allow them to fixate on a target. This ability takes experience to master, and body sway detracts from visual fixation until that point when head and neck remain on an even plane despite incidental body motion. Three-month-old infants who are exposed to rotating objects are able to recognize them as the same object when reexposed from different fames of reference. This is comparable to the kinds of mobile experiences they obtain, when placed in or moved through different environments by caregivers (Kraebel & Gerhardstein, 2006).

Although sensitive to movement, infants only gradually acquire the ability to keep track of objects as they move toward and away from their visual fields. Infants as young as 3 to 4 months are able to anticipate the trajectory of moving objects, but they are not good at identifying whether an object is the same object that moves in different directions and at different speeds (Haith, Hazen, & Goodman, 1988). Interestingly, sensory neurons that remain active in working memory during delay periods in match-to-sample tasks are the same ones that are activated when the stimulus is present. The maintenance of neural activity for up to 18 seconds could provide infants working memory without a change in synaptic strength (Ungerleider, 1995). Moreover, infants can accurately relocate objects in the dark, for example, by repeating eye saccades used to attend to the same objects when they are visually accessible. Parietal neurons appear to shift their receptive fields in advance of eye movement, anticipating when in the saccade eye contact will be made with the object (Krekelberg, Kubischik, Hoffman & Bremmer, 2003). Nevertheless, infants experience difficulty relating or matching characteristic movements of objects to specific features that account for those movements. These examples suggest that establishing the functional equivalence between movement and form is a fundamental requisite to higher order generalizations involving the recognition of factors that play a causally relevant role in constituting an object.

Prone Locomotion

There is considerable variability in the development of crawling that may contribute to experience-dependent differences in perception. Although most babies roll first from a supine to a prone posture, a considerable number deviate from this pattern and roll first from a prone to a supine position. Infants who master this latter pattern first may crawl sooner because they have learned how to push themselves up from the floor, a preliminary movement essential to a crawling posture. Crawling often progresses in stages involving belly crawling with arms and legs hands and knees and then hands and feet, but there are also many exceptions. Some children skip belly crawling, some shuffle in a sitting position, while others skip crawling altogether. However, infants who rely on belly crawling for a longer time experience delay in learning how to combine reaching with crawling to attain visuomotor control. Babies who sleep consistently in the prone position crawl sooner than babies who consistently sleep in the supine position because they obtain more experience raising themselves up with hands and feet. Interestingly, a considerable number of babies who are prone sleepers also skip crawling completely. Nevertheless, these babies experience more difficulties and delays in mastering erect locomotion because they have missed the experience of synchronous movement of arms and legs in prone progression and the coordination of reaching (Davis & Moon 1998).

Erect Locomotion

The coupling among vision, postural control, and perception is strengthened substantially with the development of erect locomotion. Increased demands are placed on vision to provide information about surface conditions, potential obstacles, heading and course, distance, and speed that require continual updating, remapping, and behavioral readjustment (Anderson et al., 2004). Movement of the eyes, head, trunk, arms, and legs cannot be too tightly coupled and synchronous without sacrificing flexibility and the need to maintain a wide-angle, global perspective. There must be a good division of labor between different sensory processes that function concurrently. Signals must be retrieved and furnish information. About what is going on at the periphery of the visual field, allowing visual attention to be focused on the most salient and timely events in the locomotor pathway. The speed and reliability of vestibular and tactile sensory receptors make it possible to conduct cognitively demanding activities while walking because motor control is easily relegated to subconscious mechanisms of postural control and proprioception. But multitasking should not be construed as evidence that perception and motion are separable or divisible processes. There is always some degree of movement involved in perceiving and thinking. Even when at rest, postural forces that sustain thought are dynamic rather than static. We hold onto our ideas and sustain a train of thought by ignoring distractions and controlling movements that threaten to derail the train of thought by some new focus of attention.

The development of walking erect vividly illustrates how gravitational forces are eventually mastered by shifting the center of postural control from the feet back up the proprioceptive chain to visual centers. Toddlers who experience assisted standing and, thereafter, stand independently rely extensively on feet and legs to maintain this postural stance (Woollacott et al., 1998). The challenge of balance in the initial stages of walking is mastered by a corset strategy, whereby toddlers maintain a wide stance with tightly interlocked leg and trunk muscles. Stabilization of stance soon moves from the feet to the hips, which provide a more stable frame of reference. At this point, vision does not play a significant role in postural adjustments to counteract sway. By 2 1/2 years, however, noticeable differences in posture begin to emerge that appear to be triggered by the experience of sitting up and rising to a standing position. Sitting down and standing up provide opportunities to alter the synergy or proportionate amount of energy and force exerted by feet, legs, and trunk. By employing these strategies, infants modify the sequence in which the appendages are recruited, enabling them to break free from a corset strategy. Accordingly, the frame of reference for postural control shifts from hip stabilization to head stabilization and visual control.

However, as children reach preschool age and attain more evenly propor-
tioned bodies, increased reliance is placed on proprioception while
dependence on vision is decreased (Hadders-Algra, 2001).

CONCLUSION: THE INTEGRAL NATURE OF PRIMARY AND SECONDARY REPERTOIRES IN POSTNATAL PERCEPTUAL DEVELOPMENT

The essential point to grasp in this chapter is that perception in a terrestrial environment after birth is always relative to movement and the base
of support. Perceptual knowledge is not defined solely by the direction of
gaze or visual input, but depends on the relationship between posture that
furnishes the ground, the spatial position of the object in view, intersensory judgment, and proprioceptive feedback. All four variables and their
interrelationship undergo change as a result of growth and changes in
mobility. The early stages of perceptual categorization reflect the limitations of mapping associated with a restricted range of movement and postures. The perceptual access that toddlers possess in the early stages of
prone and erect locomotion increases substantially in later stages through
enhanced cortical connectivity, increased mobility, and the capacity to
adopt alternative postures that support comparative judgments.
Accordingly, perceptual development involves a continuous increase in
complexity and sensorimotor integration punctuated by variability and
inconsistency, rather than by discontinuity and abrupt change.

Early perceptual knowledge is not modular. It does not depend alone on
unimodal inputs, a gravitational constant, or fixed postural relationships,
but involves their co-variation with sensory and motor processes. Infants
must master the transition from the microgravitational forces of intrauter-
ine life to postnatal gravitational pressures that impinge on their early motor
development. Physical growth contributes to the continuity and reliability
of perception by providing a proportionately reconfigured body whose center of gravity can provide alternative grounds. Movement expands the scope
of perception by increasing the probability of exposure to new contingencies
that produce small but significant changes (i.e., in terms of amodal qualities)
in the existing configuration of intersensory relationships. Growth and
movement contribute together to maximum variability, degeneracy and
complexity of motor synergies, and flexibility of receptive fields. Reentry
facilitates the construction of global maps involving feature detection and
correlation based on experiential selection of those repertoires of movement
and sensation that produce maximum coherence and integration.

Infants' capacity to differentiate between separate objects and events, discussed in more detail in Chapter 6), depends on their effectiveness in adopting postures that afford different frames of reference. Infants perceive an object or event as possessing continuity only when they are able to see that size and form remain constant despite undergoing changes in location or position relative to their own standpoint. Constancy is not established by the unimodal detection of a single recurring feature of something, but by whether access afforded by two or more senses is concordant rather than discrepant. Degenerate systems involving overlapping neuron groups furnish parallel but disjunctive mappings that are exquisitely equipped for extracting form from motion and establishing boundaries that remain consistent and continuous despite changes in the position or movement of objects or as a result of differences in sensory access afforded by changes in posture.

No single network of cortical neurons is capable of providing a comprehensive image of an object in view because perception depends on frame of reference. Discrimination between familiar and unfamiliar events requires time and the opportunity to reexperience them from different perspectives, whereby previously unnoticed novel elements are assimilated through processes of remapping and recategorization through memory. The advances in learning that take place in early development reflect infants' increased attention to local features and details. Previously constructed global maps are reorganized to reflect the numerous changes in prior categorizations induced by new experiences (Quinn, 2002). The essence of learning does not consist in duplicating what infants already know, but by expanding the applicability of their categories and concepts to include new instances. Neural networks capable of flexibly recombining sensory inputs and correlating them with changes in posture and movement are more likely to reveal whether the innumerable contingencies that shape individual experience enlarge self-understanding. What we need to find out next is what forms of stimulation are likely to influence individual development and in what ways they contribute to the reorganization of the brain.

5

Experience and the Reorganization of the Brain: Animal and Infant Studies

Until the mid-20th century, most scientists believed that primarily genetic processes governed brain development. Only in the last few decades has it become clear that the brain is genetically underdetermined and experience is essential to brain development and learning. If genes are incapable of furnishing the instructions necessary for the complete development of a fully functional brain, then the brain must rely on cues from its environment. Pioneering neuropsychologist Hebb (1949) provided a theoretical framework that enabled subsequent researchers to make sense out of how experience becomes a resource for synaptic modification and change. His theory stresses that synaptic processes are highly plastic and use-dependent, and that learning and memory involve physical alterations in the firing and wiring of neurons. Indeed there is considerable evidence from animal studies that stimulation produces significant but temporary changes in dendrite branching and synapse and spine growth, among other effects, although scientists remain uncertain how these changes affect the underlying neuropsychological mechanisms involved in learning and memory.

Neuroscientists have different conceptions about how the brain grows and attains functionality. These include the beliefs that the brain is genetically hard wired, that neurons possess a special affinity for peripheral targets, and that brain function is either driven by the death and elimination of extraneous neurons or by a process of growth and reorganization. An alternative view holds that functional specificity is achieved through competition and selection of repertoires among widely distributed but interconnected and functionally interchangeable neuronal groups.

A theory that has become a popular amalgam of these different perspectives holds that neurons become functionally active through competitive processes involving overgrowth and eventual pruning by selective elimination. This is referred to as the *proliferation and selective elimination theory* (Lichtman, 2001). This theory gained widespread support following Hubel and Weisel's discovery that experience plays a critical role in eliminating excess neurons in the visual cortex and properly orienting them to assume a columnar configuration. According to this theory, neurons are overproduced during early development and then decline in number as they vie for limited sites of functional specificity. Synapses also proliferate on dendrites and then many are retracted. The ones that survive have done so, according to Hebbian theory, by establishing a coincident and synchronous pattern of firing between pre- and postsynaptic terminals. This firing pattern recurs through repetition of experience and is maintained over time by postsynaptic feedback.

The proliferation and selective elimination theory provides a plausible account for how organisms reconcile the need for growth and plasticity with the demands for functional specificity and stability. But it is based on at least two questionable assumptions that will be challenged in this chapter. One assumption is that learning requires the restriction and segregation of sensory input to enable control of motor output. But it is not evident that neurons are dedicated to fulfilling only one unique function. The proliferation and elimination theory also assumes that memory is a function of synapse survival. Accordingly, it is presumed that surviving synapses undergo physical changes that ensure the indelibility of stored information. Once a fact is learned it cannot be unlearned or forgotten, and memories that are retained are considered to be lasting representations of objects and events perceived at the moment they are experienced.

Despite the popularity of this replica theory of neural development, however, we need to examine alternative theories about how the brain and behavior form reciprocal bonds that are dynamic yet stable. Given the enormous numbers of neurons and the magnitude of potential network connections they sustain, it is not evident that brain function and behavior depend primarily on the overproduction and elimination of neurons and synapses. Infants acquire numerous sensorimotor skills when synapse production is at its peak, not nadir. Skills subsequently undergo continued refinement during the period of synapse decline and elimination (Bruer,

1997). More important, mastery of motor skills during later infancy depends, in part, on processes of remapping involving the reintegration of movements underlying separate behaviors into more complex patterns of behavior. Although Hebb's cell assembly theory makes sense of how alterations in firing patterns account for changes in synaptic strength, it does not adequately explain how neuronal groups supporting different behaviors selectively interact, changing the scope, composition, and participation of synapses. Two key issues for the theory of neuronal group selection and a central concern of other perspectives are: (a) What factors account for differences in how the brain responds to stimulation and the capacity to vary the scope and level of responses over time? (b) What neuropsychological mechanisms are involved, and why do individuals differ in their capacity to utilize these mechanisms to consciously control their behavior and learn from experience? This chapter examines the evidence from studies involving stimulation of normal and brain-lesioned animals pertinent to these issues and assesses how this evidence relates to pioneering studies of infant stimulation in the 1930s. The next chapter addresses these questions in more detail from the perspective of more recent experimental studies of normal infants and those with brain-based learning disorders.

The historical pathways that led to a neuroscientific understanding of differences in the capacity to learn are worth reviewing. The debate about the relative weight accorded to genetic or experiential factors came to a head in the 1930s and 1940s, when Gesell and McGraw conducted pathbreaking experiments to resolve this debate. Unfortunately for McGraw, the outcome was not decisive largely because her findings were misinterpreted and her theory was mistaken as maturationist. Only recently, when new details about her collaboration with the philosopher John Dewey and neuroanatomist George Coghill surfaced, prompting a reassessment of her work, has it become evident that McGraw proposed a novel theory of brain-behavior relationships that enables contemporary researchers to better understand infant development from a comparative psychological and neuroscientific point of view (Dalton & Bergenn, 1995; Dalton & Bergenn, 1996). McGraw adopted a surprisingly modern perspective—that experience forges connections among neural structures through temporally variable processes of growth, which account for the uniqueness of individual development. Much evidence has accumulated from subsequent animal studies supporting her contention that early, enriched experience can make a difference in children's capacity to learn.

HISTORICAL ROOTS OF CONTEMPORARY THEORIES
OF EXPERIENCE AND BRAIN DEVELOPMENT

The study of how the brain is affected by stimulation is an evolving field. It contributes profoundly to our knowledge of neural plasticity and the mechanisms that make possible individual growth and development and that contribute to learning and recovery from brain injury or mitigation of dysfunction. Five theories have emerged that are worth highlighting in terms of their relevance to contemporary studies of early experience. These theories differ more in terms of emphasis accorded to specific factors that are ultimately interrelated. Until a few decades ago, the consensus among brain scientists was that the brain is hard wired and neuronal connections are predesignated to perform fixed functions. This perspective seemed reasonable largely because there was little evidence of neuroanatomical change after adulthood, and there was no convincing direct evidence of neural plasticity or axon regrowth after injury.

However, in the 1930s, neuroembryologist Weiss (1965) found contrary evidence that the growth of motor neurons is more random than previously thought, and that neurons appeared to be tuned to particular resonances of muscle fibers that they innervated. He argued that neurons are guided to their appropriate targets by peripheral activity, and synapses are coupled through resonance. Weiss anticipated the Hebbian model that functional specificity appears governed by the complex but recurring relationship between pre- and postsynaptic neurons. Weiss' student, Robert Sperry, lent added support to Weiss' notion of neural plasticity. Sperry (1943) severed the optic nerve of newts and rotated it 180 degrees. When the nerve regenerated, it grew back to the same location even though this inverted the newt's visual perception. This suggested that synaptic connections are formed selectively according to chemical signals that designate the appropriate targets. The problem with this theory is that neurons do not appear to have unique connections and may grow axons and dendrites into regions that are not functionally related.

Alternative ways of understanding neurodevelopment emerged in the late 1940s. Neurobiologists Hamburger and Levi-Montalcini (1949) discovered that neuronal cell death is a naturally occurring phenomenon in early development, and that these so-called regressive events may account for the processes that result in functional neuronal specification. They speculated that neurons that eventually die fail to receive adequate afferent inputs. This led to the view that neurons are initially overproduced through nerve growth factor and subsequently compete for limited synaptic targets.

When afferent input is restricted experimentally, there is considerable cell death, thus supporting this contention. However, Pittman and Oppenheim (1979) found that a drug-induced activity blockade significantly increased cell survival, indicating that cell death appeared governed not by postsynaptic activity, but by the amount of neuromuscular interaction made possible by presynaptic acetylcholine (ACh) receptors. Oppenheim (1988) contends that cell death through regression plays a crucial role in enabling the early nervous system to undergo ontogenetic adaptations, involving the formation of transient connections that are reorganized through behavioral experience. In her studies of brain growth and the development of behavior, McGraw (1935) found evidence of periodic behavioral regressions during infancy that may be indicative of neuron loss and reorganization, although she attributed this phenomenon to the selective onset of cortical inhibition.

Purves (1988, 1994) proposes a neurotrophic theory, which emphasizes growth gains rather than losses. Purves finds the theory of neuronal regression lacking in that it only accounts for neuron survival. What needs explaining, according to Purves, is how axon and dendrite growth contribute to the expansion and increased connectivity among neurons within the brain as a whole. Purves finds mounting evidence that suggests nerve growth factor sets in motion an interactive loop between pre- and postsynaptic terminals, whereby neurons are informed about their state of innervation and targets are informed about their success in attracting and maintaining innervation. Purves argues that neural growth is primarily progressive rather than regressive. Although competition among inputs is extensive, the net reduction of inputs occurs only negligibly when there is an absence of synchrony in synaptic firing patterns. Purves contends that this process of competitive reorganization is not governed by Darwinian selection (and elimination), but by growth processes that govern the size, shape, and morphology of the brain.

Finally, as discussed before, Edelman's theory of neuronal group selection is derived from the principle of Darwinian selection. But Edelman's theory does not rely exclusively on a proliferation and elimination model of neuronal development, as commonly argued by (Lewis, 2005) to explain how selection works. Edelman acknowledges that neurons are physically eliminated during the formation of a primary repertoire, when the form-shaping processes of growth face finite, neuroanatomical limits. Synapses are eliminated as a consequence of the absence of experience-expectant stimulation. But the essence of TNGS is that competition demands selectivity. There must always be sufficient variation to enable alternative solutions to the same problem. Elimination, unlike temporary exclusion, would appear to reduce the degree of flexibility and choice, rather than enlarge it. Edelman (1987) stresses that neurons possess heterosynaptic inputs ensuring that there are multiple alternative pathways of stimulation that affect the strength of the connections formed between neuronal groups. The strength of group interactions does not depend solely on the physical elimination of dendrites or synapses and survival of others. Instead, neuronal groups are the product of transient alterations in the boundaries in which these interactions are confined, temporarily suppressing the synaptic input of neurons that are excluded from this confinement. Therefore, exclusion should not be confused with elimination. The inclusiveness or exclusiveness of neuron groups is dependent on the timing and complexity of their interaction.

DEVELOPMENT BY GROWTH, ELIMINATION, AND/OR REORGANIZATION?

Net Increase in Cortical Neurons in Early Development

Although conventional wisdom holds that development proceeds through a process of excessive growth and dramatic attrition of neurons and synapses, the available evidence supports a more heterogeneous and differential perspective. Studies have been conducted to calculate the magnitude of neuronal attrition during early development. Harvard neuroanatomist Conel (1939), who provided scientific evidence that supported McGraw's findings regarding neurobehavioral development, first documented changes in the density of cortical neurons in his now classic, longitudinal histological studies involving fetuses and infant brains during the first 15 months. Conel uncovered a reciprocal, rather than linear, pattern of cortical neuron growth and attrition punctuated by overlapping phases of advance and decline. Using more advanced methods of cell counting, Shankle et al. (1998) corroborated and extended Conel's findings by showing that, although there is a considerable reduction of cortical neurons, the amount varies across brain regions, with some areas even showing an increase, such as the multimodal association cortex. Moreover, Shankle calculated that primary visual cortex at birth has double the neurons per column compared with all other gyri combined, indicating that neuron loss is concentrated in this region. Neuron death per month through the 15th month varied from 5% to 20%. Significantly, however, cortical neuron reduction reaches a nadir at 15 months and then increases measurably. Accordingly, neurons per column increase by 6% from 15 to 24 months, by 14% from 24 to 48 months, and by 11% from 48 to 72 months. Thus, there is a moderate depletion of neurons, but most of this loss occurs during the first year and is concentrated in specific areas, such as the visual cortex. After that, however, there is a considerable gain or a 2.2-fold increase of cortical neurons during the next 6 years. Thus, the pattern of neuron growth within 72 months does not conform consistently to the trajectory predicted by the proliferation and elimination theory.

A Plethora of Synaptic Connections

The brain possesses a staggering number of synapses whose possible connections exceed the probable number of particles in the universe. There are an estimated 10 80th particles in the observable universe. In comparison, 60 neurons can create an estimated 10 81st possible connections (Kolb, 1999). By contrast, the 30,000 or so genes that make up the human genome clearly do not possess sufficient information to specify in functional detail more than a tiny fraction of all neurons and synapses. That is why the theory that neurons compete for stimulation to establish stable synaptic connections need not involve the physical elimination of neurons whose synaptic connections are weak or lack synchrony. Estimates regarding the number of synapses that are pruned during early development vary between 20% and 40% (Kolb, 1999). Nevertheless, an estimated ten 14th synapses are believed to survive into adulthood. This superabundance of synapses appears to be the norm. Moreover, establishing an accurate count of synapses over time is beset with many technical problems that may inflate or deflate the actual number (Guillery, 2005). Accordingly, physical growth and elimination through competition alone may play only a limited, time-sensitive role in establishing brain connectivity.

Phases of Synaptic Growth

The synapse is the junction between neurons that enables them to communicate through electrochemical signals. Most synapses occur on dendrites that form on branches on axons, which are the major pathways connecting brain regions. The earliest phases of synaptogenesis begin between 40 and 60 days postconception when subcortical axons penetrate the marginal zone of cortical subplate (see Figure 5.1). By 100 days, synapses then begin to appear on dendrites of axons that reach superficial layers of the

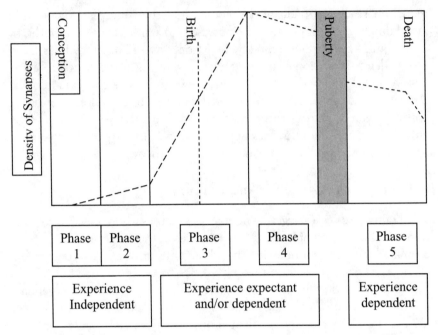

FIGURE 5.1   Change in the relative density of synapses as a function of days
after conception in the primary visual cortex of the macaque. From
"Synaptogenesis, Heterochrony and Epigenesis in the Manmilian Neocortex" by
J. Bourgeois, 1997, Act, 86 (Suppl. 422, pp. 27–33). Copyright 1997 by Taylor &
Francis. Adapted with permission.

cortex. Although independent of external sensory experience, these earliest phases of synaptic growth are governed by electrical and chemical signals generated by spontaneous motor activity.

The third phase that begins 2 months before birth and continues through the 3rd month after birth constitutes a momentous period of rapid synaptic growth. For example, approximately 40,000 new synapses are formed every second in each striate visual cortex in the macaque at birth (Bourgeois, 2002). A plateau is reached in Phase 4 that continues to puberty, in which density reaches a peak that is estimated to be 600 to 900 million synapses per millimeter in the macaque (Bourgeois, 2002). There follows a gradual but continuous decline in density through adulthood. Although it is evident that many synapses are physically eliminated through competitive selective processes, many others remain weak or silent and may be reactivated through stimulation or neuromodulation (Isaac, 2003; Voronin & Cherubini, 2003).

Perhaps the most significant period of synaptogenesis occurs during Phase 3. This is so for at least three reasons. First, sensorimotor association cortexes and other cortical areas develop concurrently during this period, rather than sequentially, facilitating the growth of diverse synapse types needed for simultaneous motor control and sensory processing (Bourgoies, 2001; Shankle et al., 1998). Synaptogenesis proceeds in successive waves across cortical layers, alternating between increased density of synapses on dendritic spines and increased density of synapses on shafts (Bourgeois, 2001). Eventually a stable ratio of 80% excitatory and 20% inhibitory synapses is reached (Goldman-Rakic, Bourgeois & Rakic, 1997). Second, rapid growth is also taking place concurrently in the hippocampus, involving the development of pyramidal cells and other specialized neurons that eventually take over inhibitory functions that are initially performed by GABA-mediated circuits. Even before synaptogenesis is completed, hippocampal neurons are capable of generating synchronous, recurrent, slow electrical waves that contribute to the completion of network circuits (Ben-Ari, 2001). Within 3 to 5 months, infants possess an enormously complex ensemble of neuronal groups fully capable of forming reentrant networks needed to support the development of secondary sensorimotor repertoires.

Synaptogenesis and Brain Electrical Activity

Finally, the cyclical advance of synaptogenesis may depend on successive waves of brain electrical activity and neuromodulation that influence the sequence in which motor and perceptual processes are integrated. It has been customary to extrapolate from adult EEG frequency bands in order to calculate EEG values for infants. But the superficial similarity of adult and infant EEG frequencies may be quite misleading as to the actual underlying neural processes involved. For example, the alpha rhythm has been conventionally associated with the occipital cortex. Yet McGraw's research associate, neurophysiologist J. R. Smith (1939), found evidence that a central alpha rhythm detected in 4-month-olds was more closely associated with motor development and sensorimotor control than vision.

As Marshall, Bar-Haim, and Fox (2002) indicate, Smith's findings have been corroborated by several subsequent studies, which indicate that the 6 to 9 Hz band is comparable to the adult *mu* rhythm emanating from the central sensorimotor region during quiet attentive states. More important, the *mu* rhythm, which is unaffected by changes in visual stimulation, is attenuated by voluntary movement or somatosensory stimulation. Evidence such as this should dispel the notion that early perceptual development is driven by rapid visual development. Vision is dominant in the negative sense that it can overwhelm, capture, and/or distort information retrieved through other modalities, amplifying spatial attributes at the expense of temporal elements (Shimojo & Shams, 2001). But clearly there is a reciprocal relationship between sensory access and motor control that makes perception highly dependent on comparative judgments formed in dynamic situations involving continual adjustments in posture and perspective.

ANOTHER LOOK AT HEBBIAN ORTHODOXY

The proliferation and elimination theory has thrived because it draws support from Hebb's theory at key points. Hebb (1949) contributed to a breakthrough in neuroscientists' understanding of how experience affects the brain and learning occurs. He did so by analyzing how the brain responds to stimulation in early development. Hebb examined how information about stimulus properties is converted into signals that set in motion a succession of synapse-based events that result in learning and memory. Hebb reasoned that initial learning may require a larger portion of cortex, but as this experience is consolidated in memory only a few cells are needed to repeat a learned task. The key to this process of retention resides in the relationship between pre- and postsynaptic firing processes.

Hebb (1949) proposed that the coincident activation of a presynaptic contact with its postsynaptic counterpart strengthens the connection between them. To work effectively, concurrent activation must engage a larger population of neurons organized in what he called *cell assemblies*. Percepts are then formed from information generated by highly distributed neural networks that exhibit considerable redundancy. Accordingly, only a partial or weak stimulus is needed to activate memory that is illustrated by our ability to recognize a partially occluded object. Hebb believed that learning is use-dependent, and thus governed by postsynaptic stimulation and feedback.

Hebb's (1949) theory provoked an ongoing scientific debate about the synaptic and cellular processes that contribute to long-term potentiation (Cooper, 2005). Quartz and Sejnowski (1997) contend that Hebb was right to insist that synapses that fire in close proximity are "closely related semantically" because they believe that "the physical structure of a neural area corresponds to a representational space" (p. 549). However, it is not clear why the spatial structure or geometry of cell assemblies should mirror the spatial features of external stimulis. Binding of features into a coherent unity may involve diverse sensory inputs that are temporally separated and spatially dispersed in the brain.

Hebb's (1949) assumption that the strengthening of synaptic connections requires concurrent synaptic firing also has been challenged. Contiguous neurons do not have to fire at the same time because they each possess a multitude of connections, only a few of which are likely to be involved in concurrent activation. This suggests that stimulation may have differential physical effects depending on the numbers of neurons involved. Some neural effects may be restricted to behavioral processes that are targets of stimulation involving specific skills, as evidenced by increased spine density or dendrite branching. But there are also collateral effects are not confined to local connections, but spread across distantly connected neuron groups through changes in neuromodulation. Synaptic connections are concentrated in short distance local, rather than long distance global networks. For example, one study estimated that 70% of new excitatory synapses in Layer II and III pyramidal cells grow from cells in the near vicinity, limiting the field of influence to a localized area (Nicoll & Blakemore, 1993).

Psychologist Greenough and his colleagues acknowledge that the scope of physical changes in the brain depends on the timing and extent of the sensory stimulation involved. They argue that: "This experience-dependent localized shaping of connectivity suggests that very multimodal and diverse experience (as in environmental complexity) would produce widespread increases in synaptic frequency but that relatively specific experience (as in training tasks) would produce localized increases" (Black & Greenough, 1998, p. 81). Moreover, investigators have found that synaptic enhancement is not limited to those synapses that are stimulated, but spreads to synapses that are not stimulated thus challenging the idea that long-term potentiation requires coincident activation of pre- and postsynaptic terminals.

DOES MEMORY DEPEND ON STORAGE OR RETRIEVAL?

Ever since Bliss and Lomo (1973) corroborated Hebb's theory by showing experimentally that increases in synaptic transmission in neuronal circuits are use-dependent, it has become an article of faith that memory and learning are made possible by long-term potentiation (LTP). This has become the favored explanation because LTP can only be generated through afferent stimulation and can be induced in an associative fashion, whereby a strong and weak input that are simultaneously active will strengthen the weak input. The belief that learning and memory are evidenced by increased LTP has come under increased critical scrutiny, however, as exceptions accumulate and alternative approaches provide new ways to account for the neural dynamics of cognition. Of course, laboratory slice preparations create an artificial environment in which the dentate nucleus of the hippocampus is cut off from several sources of neuomodulation, thus inducing a high level of excitation, but little or no inhibition. Under these conditions, only short-term changes in electrical field potentials have been recorded that are concentrated among a few synapses.

LTP may have broader functional consequences for the brain than learning models suggest. Shors and Matzel (1997) point out that LTP facilitates selective attention by increasing the capacity to recognize contingent relationships among stimuli, such as modality, intensity, or spatial location. For similar reasons, Teyler (2001) argues that LTP is a cellular mechanism that the brain uses to consolidate synaptic gains through increased connectivity, "as opposed to the more limiting view that LTP encodes behavioral experience" (p. 103). Accordingly, LTP and long-term depression (LTD) work hand in hand, switching on and off subsets of neurons to better reflect the changing balance of attention apportioned between more recently acquired experiences and those that reflect more distant memories that are weakening and undergoing reconstruction.

Despite these differences in how to interpret challenges to the LTP model, the belief persists among many infant researchers that the emergence of explicit memory in infants is dependent on storage capacity rather than retrieval. The increase in storage capacity is thought to be directly linked to the processes of synaptic growth and elimination underpinning LTP. Bauer (2004), a primary exponent of this view, contends that memory must be consolidated into a unified trace that is initially processed by the medial temporal lobe and hippocampus. Eventually, these memories are transferred for permanent storage in the association cortexes. Bauer (2004) argues that explicit memory becomes active at the end of the first year, when these neural structures have reached functional maturity. She defines *functional maturity* as that point when "the number of synapses reaches its peak" and defines *full maturity* as that point when "the number of synapses is pruned to adult levels" (Bauer, 2004, p. 360). Although consistent with the proliferation and elimination model of neurodevelopment, this conception of plasticity does not account for the conflicting and uneven dynamics of neurobehavioral integration described before. There may not be any single brain region or site that serves as the sole repository of implicit or explicit memory, but rather there may be a multiplicity of ways that categories can be combined and recombined through highly dispersed and temporally connected and variably modulated neuronal groups.

Bauer (2004) acknowledges that it is difficult to establish whether a memory is lost because of a storage failure or whether the underlying structure for memory remains intact but unavailable for retrieval. Bauer conducted a series of delayed recall tests to infants who were 13, 16, and 20 months olds; the tests involved the recall of visually observed novel, multisequential events. The infants were tested several times to ensure that they had sufficient opportunities to retrieve information from memory that may decay rapidly. However, the younger infants consistently showed more forgetting during retesting than did older infants. Bauer concluded that this demonstrates that storage rather than retrieval processes are more strongly implicated in age-related differential loss of information over time. The problem with this experiment is that if the youngest infants rely more heavily on intersensory cues, they would be handicapped by a test that provides access to memory through only one sensory modality. When Rovee-Collier et al. (2000) administered a delayed recognition task test (discussed in more detail in the next chapter) that involved memory of the act of kicking a mobile attached to the foot, 6- and 9-month-olds sustained recognition after longer delays. Infants apparently acquired an implicit motor memory that was primed when reexposed to the mobile. Accordingly, infants are better able to form and retrieve a categorical memory when motor and sensory processes are simultaneously engaged through reentry than when relying on just one sensory modality.

ORIGINS AND AFTERMATH OF THE EARLY EXPERIENCE DEBATE AND MATURATION CONTROVERSY

The debate over whether behavior is influenced more by heredity or environment, fueled by the rivalry between John Watson and Arnold Gesell, came to a head in the 1930s, arousing an expectation among the public that McGraw's research would decisively resolve the issue (Dennis, 1989). Given this atmosphere, it is not surprising that McGraw's most significant discoveries were overshadowed and that Gesell's ideas were poorly understood because they could not be fit easily into the dichotomy of nature or nurture in development. This debate took place long before neuroscientific research demonstrated how experience shapes neural processes. Neither Gesell nor McGraw possibly could have anticipated that revolution in brain science-one that goes well beyond their limited paradigms. Nevertheless, the highlights of this episode are worth reviewing because they have a bearing on how we understand the relationship between McGraw's research and subsequent neuroscientific studies of experience, brain development, and learning.

George Coghill's Pivotal, but Misunderstood Theory

The confusion surrounding McGraw's findings stemmed primarily from the fact that she and Arnold Gesell, a physician and developmental psychologist, were strongly influenced by neuroembryologist Coghill's research, but they interpreted him differently. Gesell construed the term "maturation" broadly to be a mechanism of growth formative in individual and species development (Hopkins, 2005a) Gesell considered neural maturation to be controlled primarily by subcortical and hence genetically constrained regions of the brain (Dalton, 2002b). Coghill's claim that neural structures anticipate the acquisition of function no doubt strengthened Gesell's conviction that this also was a correct interpretation of Coghill's theory even though Coghill never used the term "maturation" to characterize brain development. Gesell and Thompson's (1934) nativist interpretation of Coghill's ideas is evident in their assertion that,

> Coghill found that the innate maturation of the nervous system determined its primary structure, and that function or exercise did not even hasten the various types of reaction. He infers that the specificity of nervous structures in terms of behavior is "determined by the laws of growth in which the behavior values of the patterns of response have no part." (p. 360)

Nevertheless, Coghill (1929) was clear that neural overgrowth constituted a "structural counterpart to future behavior forms" (p. 109). He contended that these "neural mechanisms of specific behavior . . . must be organized out of elements of experience" (p. 109). Coghill (1926) expressed his point of view about experience most definitively in the following statement:

> It would be difficult to prove that the extension and perfection of particular pattern of response are not facilitated by its performance—for the functioning of growing neurons may facilitate or excite their growth and thus the perfection of the pattern may be hastened through its exercise. (p. 132)

Coghill obviously believed that brain growth is stimulated by experience. He cited evidence that nerve cells differed in the level of sensitivity to excitation, and that dendrites grow in the direction of the sources of stimulation and continue to grow during adult life. He also wrote that "the experience of the individual is a factor in determining the specificity of function of the constituent neurons" (Coghill, 1929, p. 98). It is unlikely that Coghill would have gotten involved in McGraw's research if he really was convinced that behavioral development was a maturational event, and unless he believed that her research was capable of resolving the issue of whether it was possible to accelerate the acquisition of function.

McGraw's successors have not clearly understood her theoretical perspective, nor have they fully appreciated the neuroscientific implications of her work. Thelen (1987), an infant experimentalist, considers Coghill to have advanced a neurogenetic theory, which completely ignores the role of experience in early growth and development. In reflecting on their contribution, in our opinion, Thelen also incorrectly interpreted McGraw's assertion that infant behavior does not become fully integrated until after the onset of cortical control and that this was taken as irrefutable evidence that she was a maturationist. Thelen (1987) claims that McGraw was saying that the "immediate causes of new forms of behavior . . . were reorganizations in the nervous system as it matured and in a systematic and predictable fashion," and that therefore, according to Thelen, McGraw believed that "function emerged from structure and not the reverse" (p. 6). For these reasons, Thelen (1996) claims that McGraw was unable to reconcile the tension between her maturationist and experientialist points of view.

This interpretation is incorrect. McGraw (1943) explicitly acknowledged that, "The problem of developmental or maturational relations between structure and function is more complex than the question of localization of function" (p. 4). McGraw never asserted that the cortex caused or determined motor development, nor did she posit a one-to-one relationship between brain structures and behavior (Dalton, 1996). McGraw was never divided on the relation between structure and function and always considered them to be reciprocally related. She believed that novel behavior is capable of changing how brain networks interact by contributing through repeated practice to a strengthening of some connections and the weakening of others through processes of cortical inhibition. Today, the preponderance of evidence from infant electrophysiological and brain-imaging studies indicates that cortex is involved from birth in motor and perceptual development (Bell, 1998; Bell & Fox, 1994; Johnson, 2000b; Thatcher, 1997). But opinion remains divided as to what role cortex plays in the consolidation of experience.

Thelen (2000) concluded her assessment of these two pioneers in infant development prematurely by saying that, "once major motor milestones were catalogued, there seemed to be little left to do". Moreover, both Gesell and McGraw's theoretical positions appeared to lead to dead-ends in terms of further empirical studies" (p. 388). Gesell and McGraw's research can hardly be singled out as having brought about the death of motor studies, as their ideas never received a proper burial. However, the weight of scientific opinion may be shifting today in favor of a more balanced view of McGraw's theoretical perspective. Developmental scientists are showing signs of discarding the outmoded nature/nurture dichotomy and embracing a new perspective involving the interdependence between brain and behavior in individual development that McGraw first advocated (see e.g., Dalton & Bergenn, 1996; Gottlieb, 1998; Pick, 2003; Touwen, 1995). Hopkins (2005a) underscores that McGraw and Dewey had a recognizably modern perspective closely akin to selectionist theory.

> Both she [McGraw] and Dewey can be read as subscribing to Darwin's theory of natural selection, at least in terms of a metaphor applicable to development. Dewey's selectionist account of development is echoed in McGraw's (1935) conclusion that developing infants are engaged in a process of selecting and refining combinations of movements and postures best suited to gaining ascendancy over a new task or challenge. In this sense, they foreshadowed a key feature of Gerald Edelman's theory of neuronal group selection (p. 40).

McGraw's Studies of Special Stimulation

Coghill strongly influenced McGraw's studies of the relation among brain growth, experience, and learning (Dalton, 1998). Coghill (1930) proposed a fundamental law governing the growth and development of behavior— a conception that anticipated the problematic assumptions about learning and memory that are implicated in the proliferation and elimination theory of brain growth and development. The principle is that development involves the progressive expansion and intermittent contraction of a previously integrated total pattern. Accordingly, the performance of specific skills involves the temporary disengagement of selected movements from a larger, more complex repertoire. The prenatal transition from writhing to fidgety general movements, described in Chapter 3, appears to exemplify this principle in which individual movements become differentiated from larger whole body movements. These separate movements are then reorganized to produce new forms of whole body movements, such as that involved in the transition from crawling to erect locomotion.

Coghill (1933) warned against confusing the difference between the phenomena he called *individuation* and *specialization*. Coghill believed that specialization was closely allied to the objectives of behaviorist conditioning because both processes involve restricting the scope of sensory input and limiting the range of motor response. Instead, Coghill argued that individuation is made possible by internally controlled neural processes of inhibition and not through externally imposed restrictions on sensation or movement. This scheme acknowledges that the organism possesses the ultimate freedom and power to determine how to respond to external stimulation. This is the position that Dewey advanced in his famous critique of the reflex arc theory before the turn of the 20th century (Dalton, 2002a; Dewey, 1972).

Coghill's principle furnished a crucial insight that McGraw exploited in her experimental studies involving special stimulation. He recognized that learning runs contrary to development, when it is based on the segregation of sensory input and specialization of behavior. The assumption that learning new motor skills requires the isolation and control of those movements most immediately and directly involved in their execution seemed contrary to the notion that the value of new skills is determined, in part, by whether they complement and enhance existing skill repertoires. McGraw reasoned that the psychological foundations of learning processes could be better understood if infants are given the freedom in situations involving learning to devise alternative motor strategies that strengthened overall coordination and functional adaptability.

McGraw interpreted this experimentally to mean that, if infants are confronted with uncertain situations involving multiple sources of stimulation and alternative motor options, they are likely to suppress or inhibit an impulsive, reflexive response and mount a coordinated response. Thus, when confronted with uncertainty, she thought that infants are likely to suppress an immediate response until they get a feeling for the situation as a whole. Consequently, McGraw challenged infants, through nonverbal gestures, to extend their proficiency beyond those conditions already under their control, by placing them in situations that required problem solving through inventive motor responses, such as that involved in climbing off a tall stool, roller skating, or riding a tricycle.

McGraw (1935) also observed that each successive phase of development overlaps, enabling infants to retrieve and convert knowledge from past experience to gain an expanded awareness of how previously experienced limits become means to forward progression. Each successive stage of locomotion reintroduces the problem of instability previously mastered. Under these circumstances, the more recently acquired behavior tends to interfere with the earlier one, contributing to a temporary regression or loss of previously attained skills. This phenomenon need not be interpreted as a loss of memory, but the inability to adapt smoothly to a change in perceptual frame of reference brought about by new motor skills. Nevertheless, previously mastered movements and emergent capabilities are actually recombined and reintegrated, during this regressive phase, to form a more complex but sustainable behavior pattern. McGraw believed that this temporary behavioral disorganization was indicative of neural reorganization— a particularly modern view for her era.

Corroborating Evidence From Contemporary Studies

Philip R. Zelazo (1998) took a fresh look at McGraw's evidence highlighting the formative influence of consciousness in early brain development. Zelazo showed that the onset of walking is accelerated when infants acquire experience with assisted stepping and kicking movements because they become aware of how these behaviors are instrumental to forward progression. Zelazo and his colleagues also persuasively demonstrated that newborns exposed to repetitive auditory stimulation turn their heads away from the familiar sound and toward a mildly discrepant sound in predictable ways, suggesting that they are able to remember and recognize the difference between sounds. Zelazo (1998) credited McGraw's methods and insights for enabling him to reveal the mind at work during infancy:

> Clearly the neonate enters the world with a vast repertoire of primary reflexes and more complex reflexive neuromotor pattern. In the absence of stimulation many of these reflexive behaviors seem to become disorganized and disappear. This is not disputed; it is mostly the role of experience in this process that appears to have been undervalued. Moreover, our data more radically assert a higher level of control than anticipated previously by McGraw or others— even higher order control of reflexive neuromotor patterns. . . . It appears that the role of thought in action not only emerges at the end of the first year of life, as McGraw implied, but appears to direct the body ever more consciously from that point on. (p. 468)

In the mid-1970s, Bert Touwen, a Danish developmental neurologist, conducted a series of studies that corroborated McGraw's findings that infant motor development involves extensive variability and behavioral inconsistency. Touwen (1998) contends that these are positive attributes of development, and that it is the capacity to vary, rather than to approximate a norm, that has primary diagnostic significance. Touwen showed that infants adopt alternative styles of locomotion that deviate considerably from stereotypical forms. As noted before, some infants crawl on their stomachs, some rely exclusively on leg propulsion, while others sit up and push or pull themselves around with their hands as if they were paraplegics. Infants also differ in the rate at which they advance to erect locomotion, and a significant number skip crawling and creeping altogether, stand up, and walk with ease. Infants also exhibit considerable inconsistency in their attainment of motor control and revert to more immature (i.e., labor-intensive) methods of movement when they are challenged in the mastery of a particular motor skill. Figuratively speaking, the brain is undecided and not yet fully committed to making stick the alterations in connectivity needed to support a new behavior pattern. Touwen (1995) observes that McGraw was ahead of her time in thinking of motor development in terms of the transition from random to intentional processes of selection by saying:

> McGraw pointed already to the training aspect of the repetition of newly discovered movement patterns. Observation shows that this repetition is not mere copying from the one time to the next; with every performance the infant introduces tiny alterations. In this way he expands his number of strategies for that particular performance and he uses them indiscriminately. During toddler-age the child appears to select which mode of movement fits his present needs best. At the same time functions become operational which had developed already, but which were not yet used routinely. (p. 278)

PLASTICITY, DEPRIVATION, AND NEURAL REORGANIZATION

Unfortunately for McGraw, corroborating studies by Zelazo and Touwen did not appear until after years of misinformation regarding her research had taken a heavy toll. Yet evidence was already mounting from studies of animals in the 1960s indicating that McGraw was correct in her belief that enriched early experience alters brain development. Rosenzweig et al. (1962) and Rosenzweig, Kreech, and Bennett (1963) and his colleagues were the first neuroscientists in the early 1960s to find evidence that experience induces brain growth and alters the level of neurotransmission. Although vital to McGraw's studies, Rosenzweig's findings, discussed later, were not widely disseminated nor did other scientists immediately accept them.

Visual Deprivation and Critical Periods

Only when Hubel and Wiesel (1970) published the results of their studies that kittens deprived of vision in one eye showed a substantial reduction of cortical dendrites in the impaired visual receptive field was experience accorded a crucial role in early development. They determined that visual development is driven by competition to obtain adequate stimulation for normal perception, and that when animals are deprived of vision in one eye the corresponding ocular dominance column will atrophy. The dendrites in the unimpeded eye then grow disproportionately in size and complexity. They also discovered that the extent of functional impairment depends on the timing of the interference and its duration. Early but brief deprivation only slightly favored the open eye. However, the longer the duration of experiential deprivation, the more irreversible the impairment to the closed eye and the more advantage the open eye accrued in growth and functionality. However, their studies emphasized the primacy of critical periods and mired scientists in debates about genetic influences and the negative effects of deprivation, thereby turning attention from the life-long positive brain effects of enriched experience (Bruer & Greenough, 2001).

These studies shifted the terms of the debate among psychologists about critical periods first initiated by Gesell and McGraw. Gesell used the term *readiness* to refer to the period in which learning can begin after brain functions have become well integrated (Dalton, 2002b). McGraw borrowed the term *critical period* from embryologists, but did not retain their intended meaning, which proposed a limited time frame during which neurons either become functional or die. Instead, she used the term to refer to periods during early development when neural connectivity is incomplete and the form that behavior takes is susceptible to stimulation or experiential influences. Unfortunately, as Bruer (2001) observes, the notion that a window of opportunity is genetically closed when a critical period of susceptibility has passed continues to be a widely held view. This is supposedly illustrated by the difficulty of learning a native or foreign language after a certain age, learning how to play a musical instrument, or overcoming the effects of early stress. But today the center of gravity of scientific opinion has shifted in favor of the view that many forms of neural plasticity are retained in adulthood, most dramatically illustrated by compensatory restoration of function resulting from brain damage or dysfunction (Stein, Brailowsky, & Will, 1995). Compensatory change does not entail regrowth, but substitution, whereby neurons supporting different functions switch activity.

Is Vision Paradigmatic of Plasticity and Development?

Unfortunately, ever since Hubel and Weisel's research on visual development, many neuroscientists and developmental psychologists have tended to view the cortical processes by which vision becomes functional as paradigmatic of the developmental processes through which all sensory and motor functions are acquired. The assumptions that brain plasticity is restricted to cortical neurons and that change in the synaptic organization of visual receptive fields does not include subcortical neurons have been challenged by recent neuroscientific evidence. Subcortical contributions to experience-dependent neural reorganization are considerable (Jones, 2000), and small changes in map topography in the brainstem are magnified in the cortex through the thalamus.

Faggin, Nguyen, and Nicolelis (1997) found that somatosensory reorganization takes place nearly simultaneously at cortical and subcortical levels. In their study, they first stimulated rats' whiskers and then injected lidocaine, a local anesthetic. The resulting peripheral sensory deactivation induced an immediate sensory reorganization that included the somotosensory region, thalamus, and brainstem. The loss of peripheral sensation triggered rapid change in the balance of excitation and inhibition of the receptive fields across *all* levels of the somatosensory system. The authors note that neuroscientists who study vision need to conduct similar studies to find out whether cortical reorganization observed in V1 is paralleled by short-term modifications in the subcortical lateral geniculate nucleus (LGN). In a recent fMRI imaging experiment involving binocular rivalry, Wunderlich, Schneider, and Kastner (2005) found that neurons in V1 and LGN showed similar activation and deactivation patterns when subjects were shown high- and low-contrast gratings. This important study indicated that conscious perception is not confined to cortical processing, but extends into subcortical regions of the brain. This buttresses the Faggin et al. (1997) conclusion that, "cortical plasticity is likely to be both guided and constrained by reorganizations in subcortical structures" (p. 9430).

For these reasons, plasticity should no longer be assumed to be an exclusive property of the cortex and visual system, nor should plasticity be equated exclusively with the changing strength and synchrony of synaptic firing. Instead, our contention is that neural plasticity must be construed as a global property of the brain capable of rapidly generating diverse local networks that can be recombined instantaneously to form different networks that vary in size and function. Thus, temporary topographic connections can be formed between large groups of neurons whose dimensions are continually changing (i.e., expanding and contracting) through neuromodulation and in response to sensorimotor demands of experience. Moreover, there is considerable ongoing spontaneous brain electrical activity that strongly influences how experientially generated sensory input affects brain function. As illustrated in chapter 3, an unusually low or elevated pattern of EEG activity in the resting state may distort sensory input, adversely affecting perception.

Receptive fields exhibit flexible and variable response properties whose boundaries are continually modified to reflect the changing multimodal composition of sensory experience. Plasticity is not strictly governed by the onset and offset of basic motor and cognitive functions, but persists as a transformational potentiality that can be revived through multimodal stimulation and by responding to familiar situations with novel behaviors. Neurons are capable of adjusting to the ever-changing balance between excitation and inhibition by scaling their synaptic inputs to maintain an appropriate level of response to new kinds of stimulation (Hensh, 2003). These attributes of plasticity involve the flexible composition of, interaction among, and competition between widely disparate neuronal groups whose functional integration crucially depends on their continuous reciprocal and reentrant communication through behavior.

MODERN CONCEPTIONS OF STIMULATION AND EARLY EXPERIENCE

Dewey's Interactionism

Developmental scientists want to know when and under what circumstances stimulation contributes to recognition of species-specific behaviors. To do so requires that *stimulation* be defined in terms broad enough to encompass the earliest experiences that are likely to affect growth and the sequence of neurobehavioral development. As Dewey perceptively observed nearly a century ago, a stimulus is underdetermined except as it is correlated with a response. Dewey (1981) argued that there is no such thing as an "exclusively peripherally initiated nervous event" because, he observed, every stimulus is accompanied by an "avalanche" of internal excitations (p. 213). Accordingly, stimulation cannot be defined narrowly to consist of those features of objects or events that are perceived within the visual field. This does not specify how individuals learn from experiences involving multiple sources of sensory stimulation and alternative modes of behavioral response. As Milner (2006, p. 42) observes, "most stimuli have hundreds of associations, and all those associations have hundreds of their own, so a single glance, or even a thought, could precipitate an avalanche of simultaneous associations." The probability that one association is selected at a time is very unlikely given the differences in order and timing of associated events. In his famous critique of the reflex arc, Dewey (1972) was not arguing that instruction must take place internally, but that stimulus and response only make sense in terms of their interaction. In attacking the psychological theory that stimulus and response are separable events, Dewey paved the way for modern conceptions of experience and the brain.

Gottlieb's Bidirectionality

Gottlieb (1997), a comparative psychologist, provides a useful definition that is consistent with Dewey's interactive conception of the brain and behavior. He defines *experience* as "the contribution of functional activity at the behavioral and neural levels of analysis, whether the activity arises from external or internal sources" (p. 59). Gottlieb's definition fulfills the conditions of embodiment and recognition by holding that neural processes become functionally active through individual behavior, and that even spontaneously generated brain electrical activity occurring before birth provides a mechanism for the behavioral recognition of species-specific activity. Gottlieb's conception of experience was derived from his remarkable research, which demonstrated that prenatal ducklings not only must be exposed to species-typical calls before birth, but that they must be able to successfully practice making these calls before hatching to recognize their own species after birth. Embryos that were devocalized were unable to recognize their own species even though they were exposed to the species-typical calls before birth.

According to Gottlieb, environment and behavior play complementary roles during early development. Some sensory experiences are clearly fundamental to normal sensory functioning, such as vision or hearing, whereas other forms of stimulation may hasten the acquisition of skills or produce new kinds of behavior. Gottlieb (1999) cites compelling studies which show that experimental animals that receive unexpected or unusually enriched early experiences express more complex RNA sequences, indicating a higher level of brain-based DNA activity. Similarly, rats that receive an unusual level of handling after birth are more resistant to stress and show increased levels of exploratory activity compared with controls. Gottlieb disputes the idea that early development is governed solely by genetic instruction, arguing instead

(A) Unidirectional

Genetic activity (DNA ⟶ RNA ⟶ Protein) ⟶ structural
maturation ⟶ function, activity, or experience

(B) Bidirectional

Genetic activity (DNA ⟷ RNA ⟷ protein) ⟷ structural
maturation ⟷ function, activity, or experience

(C) Bidirectional Influences

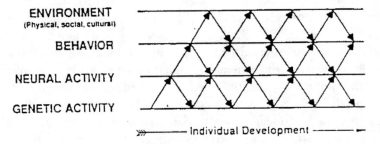

FIGURE 5.2   (A) Unidirectional and (B) bidirectional conceptions of development. (C) A simplified scheme of the multilevel developmental systems view,
showing a hierarchy of four mutually co-acting components, in which there are
top–down as well as bottom–up bidirectional influences.

that it is a product of the co-activation of genetic and experiential factors.
Accordingly, development is not a unidirectional, genetically determined
process, but a bidirectional one involving reciprocal interactions between
biological and experiential factors as illustrated in Figure 5.2.

Is Synaptogenesis a Genetically Controlled Phenomenon?

Greenough and Black (1999) appear to accord a more determinative role
to genetic factors in both experience-expectant and experience-dependent

processes that seems contrary to Gottlieb's notion of bidirectionality. Greenough and Black contend that the synthesis of a protein whose absence is associated with Fragile X mental retardation syndrome (FMRP) may contribute in important ways to synapse production and neural plasticity in animals exposed to enriched experience. "Knockout" mice, whose gene that encodes FMRP has been rendered inactive, are unable to synthesize the protein. Moreover, adults with Fragile X have an excessive number of elongated and thin postsynaptic dendritic spines. Greenough and Black also found that FMRP is strongly expressed during early development and remains active throughout the life span. Finally, they observed that FMRP is elevated in rats that receive enriched experience, and thus suggest that behavior drives the expression of FMRP.

These findings are significant for several reasons that affect how the processes of synaptogenesis are understood. Greenough and Black (1999) contend that rats exposed to enriched experience and those who suffer from Fragile X exhibit strikingly similar patterns of excess synapse production. In fact, there is considerable evidence that the mGLuR5 protein involved in FMRP expression is responsible for a wide array of motor and cognitive impairments, when it is inappropriately released during development (Bear, Huber & Warren, 2004). Greenough and Black (1999) believe this indicates that FMRP expression plays a primary role in the overproduction and subsequent pruning of synapses involved in *all* forms of experience-expectant and experience-dependent development. However, it is not evident how a single gene involved in processes of protein production on individual dendrites is capable of accounting for how global relationships among synapses are altered in response to experience. As Greenspan (2004) cogently observes, selection during development favors the pleiotropic potential of genes to express their phenotype in diverse ways due to the increased opportunity for interaction with one another. Synaptic change is a local phenomenon involving the transient, time-sensitive growth (and retraction) of spines that contribute to temporary enhancements in specific sensorimotor capabilities. Scerif and Karmiloff-Smith (2005) express their reservations about single-gene reasoning by noting that Fragile X involves uneven and paradoxical cognitive effects that cannot be explained by the actions of one gene.

This poses an interesting developmental conundrum: How does the silencing of a protein with ubiquitous functions nonetheless result in an uneven phenotypic profile: Relative regional differences in gene expression can account for some, but not all, neural and cognitive differences across domains. (p. 131)

These heterogeneous uneven developmental outcomes suggest that the mGLuR5 protein may contibute to differences in how genes interact with one another under alternative conditions. Moreover, local mRNA translation allows different synapses to be modified independently within the same dendrite (Pinkstaff et al., 2001). Consequently, Fragile X may result from the selective translation, whereby some proteins are deleted. This same mechanism of selective mRNA production may endow smaller networks of synapses within a larger group with their own unique temporal response properties that enables them to communicate separately. These subgroups may then become segregated or isolated, undermining the integrity of cognitive functions that depend on widely distributed but continuously interactive neuronal groups. Synapses also exhibit differences in strength of firing depending on their responsiveness to neuromodulation. Consequently, the absolute number of synapses and dendritic spines at a given time may be less informative than their differential responsiveness and relationship to other noncontiguous neuronal groups.

EXPERIENCE-DEPENDENT RECOVERY
OF FUNCTION AFTER BRAIN INJURY

Heterogeneous Outcomes

Studies of how normal and brain-lesioned young rats respond to enriched experience demonstrate that the brain makes use of different strategies for the recovery of function depending on the age of injury and scope of the damage. In a series of remarkable experimental investigations, Kolb et al. (1998) found that the results of enriched experience in restoring brain function vary considerably, indicating that recovery of function involves more complex, heterogeneous outcomes than previously surmised. Although experience sometimes leads to more synaptic growth, it can also result in less growth. Kolb et al. (1998) acknowledge that, "although there is a temptation to presume that experiences lead to increased numbers of synapses and probably to increases in glia, it appears that there may be either increases or decreases, the details varying with age and experience" (p. 150). Their studies clearly show that experience can alter different parts of the same neurons differently and independently. An increase in dendritic length increases the number of synapses, whereas a decrease in spine density decreases the total number of synapses. These separate processes may work in tandem to establish the degree of connectivity between short- and long-distance neuronal groups.

Interestingly, the introduction of new neurons in brain-damaged regions in the cerebellum contributes to their integration in networks separated by short distances, but fails to rewire ones separated by long distances (Grimaldi et al., 2005).

Clearly, experiential stimulation produces differential synaptic outcomes. For example, enriched experiences afforded normal rats in the immediate postnatal period did not measurably affect dendrite branching and led to a decrease in spine density. Enriched experience during the juvenile and adolescent periods increases dendritic length, but decreases spine density. In contrast, rats that sustained frontal lesions on the seventh postnatal day showed no change in dendrite branching in response to enriched experience, but did show an increase in spine density associated with a good behavioral outcome. Unlike their younger counterparts, adult rats with frontal lesions showed increased dendritic arborization in parietal cortex, but not in the visual cortex. Apparently, frontal lesions adversely affect the capacity of adjacent parietal neurons to change in response to compensatory experiences. Interestingly, the youngest animals with the largest impairment in behavior benefited the most from enriched experience. The absence of collateral damage enables young rats to mount behavioral strategies that sustain an extensive interaction between brain regions that would otherwise atrophy. These studies suggest that infants with brain-based learning disorders are more likely to benefit from the early exposure to multimodal experiences and behaviors that promote compensatory interactions before these are precluded by abnormal growth. Further analysis of this phenomenon is resumed in chapter 6.

When Is Stimulation Stressful?

The contention that early experiential or social deprivation or stress can cause lasting brain dysfunctions remains controversial. There are those who argue that the conception of experience-expectant brain development based on adequate visual stimulation must be extended to include infant exposure to stimuli that are presented in a safe, nurturing, predictable, repetitive, gradual, and synchronous manner (Perry & Pollard, 1998). The argument is made that infant brain development is strongly influenced by the perceived reliability of caregiving (Glaser, 2000). Social interactions that promote appropriate brain growth are ones that involve visual and tactile contact and talking. Glaser claims that unusual connections are formed in the absence of these interpersonal supports that lead to permanent deficits in cognitive ability. Accordingly, Glaser concludes that stimulation strategies that result in positive learning outcomes are ones that involve consistent and continuous caregiving.

The problem with this argument is that it imposes epistemic and socially mediated constraints on early learning that are contrary to the sponta- neous, random, and self-generated processes through which infants experi- ence their world. Providing a safe and protective environment should not be equated with dispensing certain knowledge. Nor should it be assumed that one style of caregiving is more effective than another in producing effective synaptic connectivity. Typical learning situations vary consider- ably according to the degree of novelty, uncertainty, and stressfulness. Synapse growth may be more responsive to unusual but distinctive patterns of stimulation than ones that are redundant and predictable. Moreover, early enrichment regimes for children at risk may be more effective in pre- venting further declines in intelligence than boosting cognitive abilities beyond an expected developmental range of attainment (Gottlieb & Blair, 2004).

ENRICHED EXPERIENCE AND SYNAPTIC PLASTICITY: ANIMAL STUDIES

Skill Retention Is Practice-Dependent

Studies of enriched experience raise additional questions regarding whether the belief is justified that learning should be evidenced by permanent changes in neural structures supporting memory or cognition. In fact, as Kolb (1995) points out, studies of the stimulation of rats to date have not been able to sustain the neural or behavioral effects beyond a limited period of time. An initial increase in spine density (one indicator of increased synaptic capacity) is often followed by pruning and a dramatic decline in skill enhancement in the absence of continuing practice. The fact that most animal studies restrict stimulation to visual cortical or hippocampal neurons may explain why experientially induced performance is not sustained. Skill retention most likely requires not only procedural and episodic memory, but also the involvement of subcortical structures, such as the cerebellum. Physical changes in the cerebellum are more difficult to document, but which play an essential role in the acquisition as well as the automatization of learned routines. Perhaps permanence is not as important, ultimately, as the capacity to forget extraneous information. Superfluous information may impede decisions involving contextual salience and that demands deci- siveness, as discussed later.

Active Attention Versus Passive Reception

Researchers also discovered that passive repetitive exposure to stimuli alone does not produce neural changes, nor does repetitive motor activity alone produce functional reorganization of receptive field maps (Plautz et al., 2000). Only animals that actively attend to stimuli and/or physically manipulate something exhibit changes in neural substrata (Merzenich & deCharms, 1996). Attention may play a more decisive role in recall, when memory is based on salience and value in problem solving, rather than on the intensity or duration of an experience. In the early 1960s, Rosenzwieg et al. (1963) reported that rats who received training that enabled them to solve more challenging problems to obtain food rewards than their litter mates showed higher AChE levels, a modulatory neurotransmitter strongly associated with selective attention.

Multimodal Versus Unimodal Stimulation

Rosenzweig et al. (1962) and Rosenzweig (1999) also pioneered methods for measuring the effects of enriched experience. These studies are pertinent to a more complete assessment of historical and contemporary studies of special stimulation. Enriched experience (EE) consisted of housing up to 12 rats in large cages filled with many novel and useable objects. Control rats were isolated in individual cages that contained minimal objects. Rosenzweig and his colleagues found small but measurable differences in brain weight of EE rats compared with controls. Significantly, the weight increase was distributed unevenly. The largest gains occurred in the occipital cortex and the smallest in the somesthetic cortex. Interestingly, in other studies described by Kolb and Wilshaw (1998), when monkeys and rats were provided with comparable enriched experiences, only rats, not monkeys, exhibited expansion of the visual cortex. This difference could be explained by the fact that, unlike monkeys, rats have poor visual acuity that is designed primarily for navigation rather than pattern recognition. Visual stimulation enhances rats' capacity to explore objects by combining vision, smell (a primary sense in rats), and touch. This is an important finding that underscores that enriched experience expands the neural basis of perceptual recognition only when it reduces reliance on a single primary sense and engages multisensory processes. This is precisely the stimulation strategy that McGraw employed to enable the experimental twin, Johnny, to master skills considered impossible at his age. Johnny was challenged by novel contexts to recombine previously learned skills in a new sequence of sensorimotor coordinations that enhanced problem solving.

For these reasons, it is important to specify just how much of the brain is actually involved when behavior undergoes change. For instance, Kolb and Wilshaw (1998) observe that voluntary movements, such as reaching in rats, involve complex relationships among balance, weight shifting, and tail use. Change may not be restricted to neurons that control the reaching arm, but may engage other elements of the motor system in varying degrees. Conversely, task-specific skills may enhance neural substrata through excessive or redundant us, which does not contribute to any overall increase in cognitive capacity. Typists possess more elaborate dendrite arborization in somatosensory areas controlling trunk and finger movements. But this form of experience-dependent change does not enhance intersensory processing (Scheibel et al., 1990). Similarly, although useful, increasing the dexterity or speed of pedaling a bicycle may not be as significant as learning how to adjust speed in response to changing racing conditions to conserve physical effort. The latter capability draws on knowledge of the contingencies of order and new ways to attain similar or the same outcomes—a lesson that Lance Armstrong learned to win the *Tour de France* for 7 consecutive years!

Self-Initiative in Challenging Situations

The fact that the activity of EE rats was self-initiated also contributes to striking differences in neural connectivity and learning ability compared with individually caged animals that did not receive special stimulation. As Black and Greenough (1998) report in their review of studies, the superior performance of EE rats did not depend on the volume of neural activity per se, but whether rats were able to initiate and sustain a series of activities. Rats that are exposed to challenging tasks involving balance, agility, and coordination showed increased synaptic growth in the dentate gyrus of the hippocampus, compared with rats that received nonchallenging daily exercise. Interestingly, rats reared in isolation are eventually able to catch up to the performance levels of EE rats. To catch up, isolated rats must receive after intensive training that isolates the specific motor reflexes involved, rather than by facilitating their integration through multimodal stimulation (Rosenzweig, 1998).

Unexpected Experiences

The discovery that younger rats benefit more from early exposure to enriched experience than older rats may be due to the limited capacity of older rats to behaviorally accommodate and integrate new experiences. Young rats were given experiences that are unexpected and not typically available during early rearing. In this instance, the basis of the distinction between experience-expectant and experience-dependent becomes blurred. Experience-expectant neural development is based on the notion that adequate stimulation must reliably occur within a restricted window of opportunity to enable normal exercise of species-specific growth of brain and behavior. Sensory input is considered adequate, when it results in the formation of a normal configuration of receptive fields characteristic of a specific sensory modality. Experience-dependent neural development is driven by experiences that are unique to the individual involving multimodal stimulation. But there is evidence that these two apparently distinct processes can co-occur, expanding neural capacity without undermining the integrity of sensorimotor functions. Adequacy and sufficiency should not be confused. There surely is a minimum level of stimulation necessary for adequate development of single sensory functions, but this may not be sufficient to sustain intersensory integration. Sensory input is rarely confined to the boundaries of a specific receptive field, but often engages several fields simultaneously, enabling the detection and binding of different attributes into a coherent multimodal perception. The conditions that favor change in behavioral phenotypes include variation in early experience and the possession of a brain that is complex and plastic enough to sustain these changes over time (Gottlieb, 1999).

For these reasons, it is not evident that either experience-expectant or experience-dependent motor behavior is necessarily governed solely by whether synaptic response is restricted to sensory-specific stimulus attributes. More important, mastery of a performance involves the concurrent elimination of excess movement and integration of isolated behaviors into seamless, continuous, and fluent motions. However, the elimination of excessive behavior is not necessarily indicative of synaptic elimination. Instead a process of reorganization is occurring, whereby neuronal groups supporting different behaviors selectively interact, changing the scope and composition of neurons and number of synapses involved. In this regard, McGraw's experimental infants typically reverted to more laborious movements each time a task was made more challenging for them at later ages. They were simply reactivating neuronal groups involving synaptic connections governing these behaviors. There may be a point at which synaptic connections become committed and entrenched through repeated firing (see Munakata, Casey, & Diamond, 2004), but this does not prevent the recruitment of weak (i.e., understimulated) synapses in opponent behaviors.

CONCLUSION

The theory that neurobehavioral development depends on the rapid proliferation of neurons, their subsequent dramatic reduction, and the parallel experience-dependent elimination of excess synapses has gained widespread support because it appears to fit the facts of early infancy. Although there is persuasive evidence that these growth-related physical changes in the brain are concentrated in early infancy, it is not evident that the emergence and complex interaction of neuropsychological processes can be explained solely by the marginal rise and fall among a small percentage of the absolutely immense total number of neurons and synapses that survive. Nor do these neural phenomena alone adequately explain how infants learn from experience, acquire new skills, and expand their memories.

The notion that the neurons and synapses that survive do so because they confine their response to a more limited range of sensory inputs sanctions the unwarranted assumption that learning is equivalent to specialization. Learning involves generalization and the ability to expand behavioral repertoires beyond the limits imposed by specific tasks. Training involving redundant stimulation enhances task-specific skills, but it may also recruit a disproportionate number of receptors that could be apportioned among a wider array of sensory functions. Dewey and McGraw, with Coghill's help, anticipated this objection in experimental studies, which demonstrated that learning is precipitated by unexpected events involving the reorganization of response into novel behaviors that contribute to the expansion of a previous repertoire. Experimental studies of rats' brains clearly demonstrate that rats exposed to unfamiliar but enriched experiences showed more dramatic synaptic growth than litter mates who were exposed to familiar exercises and expected experiences. Significantly, only rats and monkeys that initiated and actively attended to experiential challenges exhibited significant synaptic growth. Moreover, lesioned animals respond differently to enriched experiences depending on the timing of the onset and scope of neurobehavioral deficit. These animals show independent changes in dendritic branching and spine density that underscore the complexity and interdependent nature of experience-dependent neural plasticity.

Hebb's theory of neuronal plasticity is alluring because it supports the belief that experiential stimulation provides information that is subsequently encoded and permanently stored in the brain. However, as Kolb reports, enriched stimulation produces only temporary physical changes in rats' brains that disappear in the absence of continued practice. Moreover, as Dewey pointed out over a century ago, stimuli are underdetermined and gain significance only through an active and engaged response. McGraw incorporated this principle in her experimental studies by giving infants the freedom to select an appropriate response. Gottlieb takes Dewey's interactionist conception of experience one step further by underscoring the bidirectional and reciprocal nature of genes and experience. Again, animal studies are instructive in this regard. Rats and monkeys respond differently to neural stimulation because each species engages its primary sensory capacities in different ways. It is evident that perceptual awareness increases and learning improves when experience affords congruent and multimodally integrated, rather than incongruent and nonintegrated, sensorimotor responses. Taken together, these findings from animal studies suggest that neural plasticity and learning involve factors that extend beyond stimulus attributes to encompass the interplay of neuropsychological mechanisms associated with consciousness, such as attention and memory, discussed next.

6

The Neuropsychological Dynamics of Infant Learning

Animal experimentation has been enormously helpful in identifying the physical changes in the brain that occur as a result of manipulating the amount, quality, and duration of stimulation. However, these studies furnish only limited information about how neuropsychological processes contribute to the wide variability in the degree to which children benefit from experience. More fundamentally, we want to know what difference consciousness makes in the effectiveness with which mechanisms of attention and memory are employed to learn from experience and expand our knowledge about the world and ourselves. This chapter assesses the attempts by several prominent developmental and cognitive scientists to understand the neuropsychological mechanisms that impede and facilitate learning among infants who experience and respond to unfamiliar situations differently.

Determining how experience affects brain development and function depends on many factors that have not been clearly distinguished by researchers. Judgments must be made about how sensorimotor processes are engaged, in what sequence, for how long, at what level of effort, and with what degree of attention and memory. It is not simply a question of whether stimulation triggers an appropriate or correct neural response because the brain is not receiving instruction. Nor is it a matter of stimulating the brain to produce a cognitive reproduction of what is observed because representation and reconstruction take place simultaneously. So the relevant question is: Why do some infants and children experience more success in learning and the development of cognitive skills even though their less successful cohorts receive comparable stimulation and undergo similar experiences?

Contemporary research on the perceptual and behavioral effects of brain injury or dysfunction also provides useful knowledge about how one part of the brain affects the functioning of remaining or intact structures. Historically, researchers have subscribed to the view that brain functions conform closely to the boundaries between neuroanatomically distinct structures. This has provided a convenient way to predict the kinds of motor or cognitive impairments likely to occur as a result of injury or dysfunction. However, mounting evidence of the paradoxical effects of many cerebral injuries, such as that involving visual neglect or the sparing of function despite severe damage, has challenged the adequacy of neuroanatomically based models.

Evidence from developmental learning disorders, such as dyslexia, attention deficit, and autism, discussed in this chapter, indicates that these disorders involve multiple negative functional consequences that cannot be traced easily to a single gene or confined to a single brain region. Moreover, the assumption may be unwarranted that the functional necessity of a specific brain region is confirmed by the cognitive consequences of its removal or impairment, as Price and Friston (2002) contend, because functional imaging systems cannot indicate how many regions are jointly activated or even latent, and thus capable of generating the same functional output as the damaged component. Children with brain-based learning disorders appear to engage mechanisms of attention and memory differently from other children, producing divergent neuropsychological outcomes.

Developmental psychologists and cognitive neuroscientists, among others, have examined several factors that appear to significantly affect brain function, including: looking behavior and attention, stimulus attributes, emotional state or temperament, motor experience, conscious control, and contextual memory. Alternative theoretical models have been proposed that differ in terms of the relative weight accorded to each of these factors in experience-dependent learning processes. These differences in theoretical perspective are important to understand. They affect beliefs about the scope and limits of neural plasticity, influence assumptions about the degree of variability in early development, and affect judgments about whether humans possess the capacity to exploit these resources of neurobehavioral modification through explicit strategies.

This chapter concludes by showing how children who vary in brain-based resources for learning deploy mechanisms of attention and memory differently to sustain balance, attain synchrony of motor and perceptual control, and maintain the proportionality of effort needed to attain neuropsychological integration. The compensatory strategies children adopt not only reveal more clearly the crucial role of attention and memory in learning. These remedial strategies are also likely to be effective in enabling children challenged by learning who do not have brain disorders, to increase their level of conscious control of their behavior.

CONSCIOUSNESS AND LEARNING

At this point, a more explicit and empirically testable conceptualization of consciousness is needed to establish its relationship to learning. The argument advanced in the second chapter is that consciousness is an emergent property of neurodevelopmental processes. Consciousness is dependent on the growth and successive interlocking of sensory and motor processes into mechanisms of perception and attention. Several preconditions must be satisfied for neural processes to reach the threshold of consciousness, which are depicted in Table 6.1. As described before, prenatal infants undergo brief episodes of periodic arousal during which time spontaneous movements occur. But without sustained arousal, it is difficult to establish whether fetuses who are temporarily aroused possess any awareness of the nature or source of this stimulation. Only after birth, when infants are capable of sustained arousal, is it possible to establish whether they possess voluntary control of attention. Detecting the difference between internal and external sources of stimulation also is crucial to establishing the boundaries of self. Young infants maintain an egocentric perspective, whereby most events are perceived to be the result of how they feel about or react to them. Not until 7 months are most infants able to distinguish between the proximate source and cause of an event and their own feelings and behaviors during these events.

Another argument made previously is that conscious experience is multimodal, and that any single event is accessible through alternative sensory pathways. Conscious awareness is based on comparative judgments involving the convergence of inputs from different sources. The physical and sensory dimensions of a situation that contribute to its perceptual uniqueness and significance involving light, sound, and tactile feeling are bound together to furnish an overall impression. Yet these separate elements can be recomposed and accessed differently through

Table 6.1
Preconditions of Consciousness

Sustained arousal

Discrimination between internal and externally induced feelings

Concurrent activation and temporal binding of at least two senses

Locomotion

Memory

Synaptic plasticity enabling change in response and memory

Large-scale interaction of neuronal groups through thalamus

memory. Locomotion provides different points of entry to a scene through alternative frames of reference. Attention governs the degree of selectivity with which different inputs reach the threshold of perceptual integration. Even thought involves the imagined or simulated movement and reordering of ideas through the momentum they gain or lose as objects of propositional reasoning. The ability to remember simple sequences of actions or trains of thought would appear then to be necessary to sustain a minimal level of consciousness.

Finally, neural processes capable of supporting consciousness must possess two other attributes essential to local and global processing of sensory inputs and motor outputs. There must be sufficient plasticity to enable flexibility and adaptation. Plasticity must be concentrated during periods of intense growth to facilitate the development and integration of experientially dependent structures and functions. This linkage among early growth, malleability, and integration may be crucial to the development of the mechanisms of consciousness because attention and memory require the simultaneous expansion and contraction of different repertoires of neuronal group interaction. In addition, the brain must possess a rich and diverse number of reciprocal connections through the thalamus between different regions within the cortex and between cortex and subcortex. These reentrant connections, which begin to form late term, facilitate communication between neuronal groups separated by long distances and furnish the global processing that underpins consciousness, learning and memory.

It is also important to establish what role (or roles) consciousness plays in learning. Consciousness functions at the threshold of awareness when a difference or change in state is detected, but there is uncertainty about how to respond. If we accept the principle that individual experience is continuous, but that our conscious awareness is limited by what we selectively attend to while experiencing something, then each successive experience will involve a mixture of implicit and explicit memories, feelings, habits, beliefs, and expectations about future events. Learning seems to require the possession of criteria for distinguishing between novel and familiar things. Accordingly, some common basis of comparison must be employed to establish whether what is observed from one moment to the next differs in some essential respect.

Categorization provides an explicit way of grouping or classifying objects or events with respect to similar or shared features. Categorization helps establish whether salient features change (i.e., added or eliminated, expanded or contracted, in foreground or background, etc.), despite changes in the order in which they are experienced and regardless of individual beliefs and expectations. Learning has to do with deliberately changing how a situation is handled, which makes a difference not only to an immediate outcome, but enables generalization to other situations. Further analysis is needed, however, to establish whether consciousness plays a decisive role in learning and to identify the conditions in which the mechanisms of consciousness involving attention and memory are compromised by brain dysfunction.

Alternative theoretical models have been proposed to explain how learning occurs that differ in terms of the relative weight accorded to experience-independent and experience-dependent learning processes. These factors include looking behavior and attention, stimulus attributes, emotional state or temperament, motor experience, conscious control, and contextual memory. The focus here is to critically examine how these factors affect differently the timing and sequence of neurodevelopmental processes, the capacities they confer, and the limitations they impose on conscious perception and learning. We adopt the position that a more complete understanding of the neuropsychological mechanisms involved in learning will come from a better appreciation for how these and other factors reciprocally interact throughout development.

LOOKING BEHAVIOR AND ATTENTION

The importance of motion and timing in the development of attention is most clearly demonstrated by the uneven processes through which infants acquire peripheral and focal vision. This dramatically affects infant looking behavior. A striking feature of early infancy is that babies undergo a gradual expansion of their temporal and nasal fields of vision from only 32% of adults at 2 months to nearly 70% of adults at 7 months (Maurer & Lewis, 1998). Consequently, infants are challenged to enlarge the breadth and depth of their vision by expanding the range of motor control. Orienting toward peripheral targets develops much sooner than eye movements to the nasal field for reasons that have to do with differences in the development of the brain mechanisms involved. Several interrelated brain regions are involved in the detection of peripheral, visual stimuli that are particularly sensitive to motion. The superior colliculus (SC) controls reflexive eye saccades, while a second, anterior system in the frontal cortex bypasses the SC and facilitates planned saccades to targets. A third system involving the middle temporal and parietal areas of the cortex controls smooth pursuit. A fourth system sets up an inhibitory pathway to the SC from cortical areas through the basal ganglia. As Johnson (1997) points out, these systems do not go online all at once. Consequently, infants exhibit considerable unevenness in sustaining access to focal and peripheral events that depend increasingly on their degree of motor control. This dependency is evident at 2 months, when infants must turn their bodies in the direction of the moving object to sustain visual contact and smooth pursuit. Similarly, maintaining balance in an upright sitting position at 6 to 7 months facilitates the ability to anticipate direction and follow sequence. These attainments depend on the engagement and synergistic coupling of complex motor functions.

The nasal field for focal vision develops more slowly than peripheral vision because it is dependent on several factors related to motor control. Targets within the nasal field or focal vision tend to be more static and require longer fixation. Infants must be capable of resisting distraction and concentrating long enough to detect and discriminate among individual features within a visual array. These efforts to convert random looking into organized forms of attentive behavior succeed only if the preliminary stages of motor control are mastered first, which include the suppression of action and stabilization of posture. The coordination of visually guided behavior requires congruence of visual and proprioceptive signals that, when absent, results in poor perceptual organization (Bahrick & Lickliter, 2000). The tight coupling between motor control and visual perception is no better illustrated than by the overlap between neuronal groups involved in shifts of attention and those governing eye saccades (Rizzolatti, Riggio, & Dascola, 1987). Even covert shifts of attention require the voluntary suppression of eye movement (Corbetta et al.,

1998). These same neuronal groups are also activated during binocular rivalry involving the alternation between foreground and background. For example, Leopold and Logothetis (1999) found that, when exposed to ambiguous scenes, subjects shift their attention from foreground to background. This action helps them find alternative ways to categorize events that have multistable phenomenal properties, enabling them to avoid being locked in to one epistemically privileged perspective.

Infant attention undergoes a series of changes during early development. (see Ruff & Rothbart, 1996, for an overview). Newborns are attracted to peripheral events that involve movement, but are unable to track their trajectory. In the first 2 months, infant attention is drawn to arousing, high-contrast objects such a checkerboards. They frequently fixate on such objects for long periods of time and have difficulty disengaging and looking away partly due to poor control of eye saccades. During the period between 2 and 3 months, infants begin to notice discrepancies, when some part of a larger repetitive pattern differs from the rest. After 3 months, infants more easily disengage from one object and shift to another. The ability to sit up facilitates disengagement by enabling the infant to stabilize posture and rotate the head. From 3 to 14 months, cortex is increasingly involved in locomotion, furnishing the inhibition needed to move head, body, arms, and hands independently. This allows infants to attend and respond selectively to events with different behaviors.

The accumulation of experience and memories from attended events enables infants, in the next several months, to anticipate the outcomes of familiar events and focus longer on novel events whose outcomes are unknown or unexpected. Perhaps the most striking change between 2 1/2 and 3 1/2 years is that the duration of focused attention and concentration more than doubles. This is a mixed blessing. Children attain a high level of self-control, in which movement is minimized and concentration is maximized. This enables children to engage in extended periods of learning involving memorization and subsequent retrieval. But this narrowing of the field of vision makes children vulnerable to attention capture for long uninterrupted periods, and prolonged physical inactivity diminishes cognitive engagement.

Clearly, attention emerges through a developmental process that is not confined to vision. This involves a whole sequence of sensorimotor attainments that overlap and ultimately become integrated. Shifting focus from center to periphery and from foreground to background is not simply a matter of improved vision or eye saccade control. This entails the capacities to inhibit return and attain a stable posture that will sustain this new frame of reference. Similarly, narrowing the field of vision preparatory to focused concentration requires the ability to resist distractions by limiting the range of eye saccades. As becomes clear later, children with brain-based learning disorders experience difficulty in effecting these integrations at different stages in the emergence of attention, compromising the learning process.

STIMULUS ATTRIBUTES

Stabilization of Motion and Form

Many developmental psychologists who study infant perception believe that stimulus properties provide crucial information that ensures that infants respond appropriately to their environment. Kellman and Arterberry (1998) advance the strongest position that stimulus properties play a formative role in the functional development of perception. They contend that an evolutionary "premium is placed on an ontogenetic sequence in which information of highest ecological validity come to function earliest" (p. 137). By *ecological validity* they mean that the most valid information "more accurately indicates physical separation in the environment" (p. 149). This is evidenced by the capacity to detect edges that establish the boundaries of objects. Infants not only must be able to extract form from motion, but also detect the continuity of moving objects that are partially and temporarily occluded. Kellman and Arterberry (1998) conclude incorrectly, in our opinion, that because anticipatory reaching and reaching for stationary objects appear to coincide in the fourth month, this means that, "accurate three dimensional and event perception abilities precede skilled motor behavior" (p. 186). This relegates motor experience to playing a minor role in perceptual discriminations involving motion, distance, and velocity. However, human perception takes place under conditions of physical instability and sensory uncertainty. Counteractions (i.e., saccades or head movements) are required that furnish the most stationary view of objects in three-dimensional space from an allocentric frame of reference (Heron, Whitaker, & McGraw, 2004; Wexler & Boxtel, 2005).

The habits of looking that children acquire strongly influence their patterns of recognition and the capacity to learn by expanding the inclusiveness of their categorizations. In a reassessment of studies of object permanence, Kaufman, Mareschal, and Johnson (2003) suggested that the conflicting evidence regarding whether infants are capable of tracking occluded objects could be explained by the different demands they impose on looking behavior. Some experiments use large, static objects whose appearance and occlusion engage head-centered eye saccades. This form of looking behavior focuses infant attention on surface features that are not easily detectable and recalled. In contrast, smaller, mobile objects appear to engage a body-centered perspective in which infants attend to whether the object is graspable (Mareschal, 2000). Infants tend to track and anticipate better the behavior of smaller objects, according to Kaufman et al. (2003), because motion triggers reaching and increases the probability that hand and eye movement will converge to intercept an object that reappears. In this instance, recognition and recall are enhanced through intersensory redundancy.

Linear Versus Curvilinear Edges and Boundaries

At what point infants are able to identify and categorize the features and anticipate the behavior of specific objects remains controversial. However, it is not evident why visual information about objects that have linear edges and well-defined boundaries or spaces between one another should possess greater ecological validity and be more informative than other stimuli known to capture infant attention, such as curvilinearity, symmetry, and continuity (see Kagan & Herschkowitz, 2005). Rectilinear edge and boundary recognition may not be the most salient signals for infants who possess negligible focal control as described before. In a series of studies in which infants viewed occluded objects under alternative conditions, Johnson, Bremner, and Mason (2000) found that good form rather than proximity supported the perception of object unity. Infants did not perceive unity in displays in which moving rods were placed close together across an occluder until the rod parts' edges lay on a curved shape. Curvature facilitated the recognition of relatable parts across the occlusion gap.

As this example suggests, infants exposed to a Maxwellian environment of unexpected events and uncertain interactions usually get only a fleeting look at most objects, whose edges overlap with the exception of faces, especially mothers' faces. Perhaps that explains why infants look longer at faces that violate vertical symmetry because they become accustomed to seeing faces that maintain an upright rather than a tilted or inverted relationship to the body. Infants may prefer curved lines to straight ones because curved lines form contour patterns whose edges are easier to trace with jerky eye movements than rectilinear forms, which require precisely controlled eye movements. The continuity of trajectory of moving things surely plays a crucial role in enabling infants to effectively anticipate where they will appear next as they move from left to right in the visual field and disappear from view (Haith, 1999).

These kinds of cues are salient because they help reduce the ambiguity inherent in dynamic events by providing an orderly basis for tracking change. Accordingly, early infant perception appears governed primarily by the need to reduce uncertainty associated with movement through strategies of integration that maintain physical balance and proportionality among sensory inputs. Only later on, when toddlers and young children learn how their intentions and goals are affected by contingencies of experience, do their capability to differentiate objects and events in terms of specific attributes and causal relationships become essential to further development and learning.

Is Familiarization a Form of Stimulation?

The belief that infants come preequipped with the capacity to recognize objects that obey the perceptual principles of good continuation and object permanence has been challenged in recent experiments. There is, in fact, persuasive evidence that the familiarization phase of experiments employing the violation of expectation method constitutes an important source of experience that can bias infants' performance. In an interesting test of this phenomenon, Shilling and Clifton (1998) found that infants have the ability to learn and remember physical phenomena after brief training and make accurate predictions based on their newly acquired knowledge of the behavior of objects under alternative conditions. In the first experiment, 8 1/2- to 9-month-old infants were familiarized with a procedure in which a similar looking heavy ball and a light ball were placed at the bottom of a tube on top of a paddle. Infants were given the opportunity to press the paddle and observe that the light ball was lifted while the heavy ball remained on the bottom. They were subsequently tested by exposing them to trials that were inconsistent with the expected behavior of the heavy and light balls. In the inconsistent event, the light ball remained on the bottom and the heavy ball was lifted when the infant pressed the paddle. The infants reliably looked longer at the inconsistent events.

To rule out the possibility that the infants had prior knowledge of the effects of gravity, Shilling and Clifton (1998) reversed the procedure during familiarization by enabling the heavy ball to be lifted by the paddle while the light ball remained on the bottom. When exposed to consistent and inconsistent versions of this trial, infants looked reliably longer at the balls that behaved inconsistently (i.e., when the light balls were lifted and heavy balls remained stationary), although they did not violate the effects of gravity. The infants did not appear to possess special knowledge about gravity, and thus were able to learn and remember arbitrary, contingent relationships during familiarization that enabled them to detect behaviors that violated expectations.

Researchers who propose that infants possess innate computational mechanisms to interpret the behavior of objects, which have been temporarily occluded, may be overlooking the possibility that this knowledge is acquired through experience. As noted before, infant object concepts can be trained during familiarization that temporarily enhances their performance in object-recognition tasks (Scholl, 2004). In an important experiment, Johnson, Amso, and Slemmer (2003) found that 4-month-old infants can be trained to anticipate the movements of occluded objects, significantly enhancing the speed and accuracy of doing so, compared with 6-month-olds who already possess a concept of object permanence. In doing so, they employed a corneal reflection eye tracker, which more accurately measures eye movements than manual visual observations. First they established that infants undergo a transition between 4 and 6 months, as 6-month-olds produced a reliably higher proportion of anticipations than their younger counterparts. In a second experiment, after receiving 2 minutes of familiarization with nonoccluded trials, 4-month-olds' anticipatory eye movements occurred more frequently than 4-month-old controls. Although 6-month-olds continued to have an edge in the speed with which they anticipated the movement of ball from occlusion, there were no significant differences in the timing of the anticipations of the trained 4-month-olds and their older counterparts. A third experiment was conducted to see whether 4-month-olds could generalize from previous experience and show similar increases in occulomotor anticipations when the trajectory of the ball differed in orientation. Four-month-olds showed the same gains in performance, ruling out the possibility that they were simply habituated to the horizontal eye tracking condition.

Quinn and Schyns (2003) demonstrated, in a series of experiments, that 4-month-old infants who are habituated to shapes that violate good

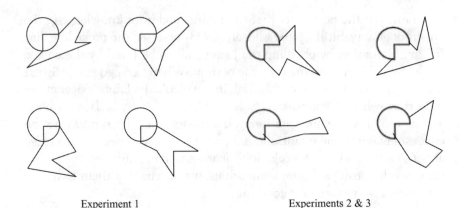

Experiment 1   Experiments 2 & 3

FIGURE 6.1   Results of two different familiarization experiences Experiment 1
    showed that 3- to 4-month-olds could parse a circle in accord with good
continuation from multipart visual patterns consisting of a circle and a complex
polygon. In Experiment's 2 and 3, however, this Gestalt-based parsing process was
interfered with by a category familiarization experience, in which infants were
presented with a set of visual patterns, each one consisting of a 'pacman' shape
and complex polygon. Part 1 of Experiments 2 and 3 showed that the infants
    recognized the pacman shape as familiar, and Part 2 of Experiments 2 and 3
    (a replication of Experiment 1) demonstrated that the representation of the
'pacman' shape blocked the subsequent parsing of the circle in accord with good
    continuation. From "What Goes Up May Corne Down," by P.C. Quinn and
            P. Schyns, 2003, Cognitive Science, 27, p. Copyright 2003.
                            Adapted with permission.

continuation fail to select circles that are partially occluded by other
objects because they are mistakenly perceived to be a noncircular shape.
Infants who were familiarized first with an object shaped like pacman (a
circle with a pie-shaped wedge cut into one side) and then a circle shown
in Figure 6.1 spent less time looking at (i.e., showing surprise) at circles
whose form was partially occluded. The authors concluded that an
infant's perception of feature correlation is biased by its previous history
of categorization experiences.

Autism: A Motion-Dependent Perceptual Disorder?

Children with autism or pervasive developmental delays exhibit severe
deficits in sensorimotor integration, which make it difficult for them to
process and integrate moving stimuli. Autistic children have difficulty

detecting fast-moving objects, they show poor postural reactions to visually detected environmental motion, and they perform poorly in recognizing facial emotions, when this requires the matching of lip movement, tone of voice, and gesture (Gepner & Mestre, 2002a, 2002b). Some cognitive neuroscientists contend that this failure to process global features is indicative of a breakdown of central coherence, whereby contextualized meaning is overwhelmed by an obsessive attention to detail (Happe, 1999). Interestingly, autistic children excel at tasks involving the recognition of static images that engage local rather than global processing capabilities. As noted before, nonautistic children do much better initially at global than local processing—a perceptual ability that depends on the capacity to extract form from motion and, crucially, the ability to detect amodal attributes of intersensory stimulation. Autistic children appear to be locked into a pattern of obligatory looking that normal children transcend by 3 months. This appears to be a compensatory strategy designed to avoid sensory arousal and provide stabilization through gaze that is denied them through lack of motor control. But being locked in deprives them of the fluidity needed to shift attention and put what they are seeing into a larger context.

TEMPERAMENT AND EMOTIONAL STATE

As discussed in the last chapter, infants' capacity to learn from experience may be strongly influenced by temperament or their ability to control their emotions and respond to uncertain or unfamiliar situations positively and effectively. Developmental scientists who study temperament believe that infants vary in terms of how they respond to novel or unfamiliar events. Some babies are distressed by encounters with novel events and seek withdrawal, whereas others approach the unfamiliar with interest, curiosity, and calmness. Kagan and Herschkowitz (2005) speculate that temperament may be strongly influenced by heritable differences in neuromodulation. But the apparent multitude of potential neurochemical interactions involved suggests that the causal factors involved will remain elusive. Moreover, theories that propose that attention is a function of emotional state obscure potential underlying disorders in perception, which may precipitate adverse emotional reactions to unexpected and unfamiliar events.

Kagan (1994) proposed that most infants fall into one of two broad temperamental categories of those who are inhibited, wary, and likely to avoid unfamiliar events and those who are uninhibited and likely to approach novel events with curiosity and interest. Kagan contends that these categories reliably predict behavioral reactions of infants until 11 years of age. One in 4 infants who were either high reactive or low reactive maintained their behavioral profile, whereas only 1 in 20 showed significant change in temperament. According to Kagan and Herschkowitz (2005), these differential reactions to novelty implicate the amygdale, but are driven by surprise rather than fear. Before 7 months, infants are unable to distinguish between events that are menacing or aversive and ones that are unusual but benign. Instead, their attention is captured by discrepant events (i.e., ones that involve unusual contexts or unexpected outcomes). In these instances, infants' expression of irritability or distress may not be temperamental, but indicative of the inability or uncertainty about how to mount an appropriate response to an arousing situation.

Distress, Attention, and Error Correction

There are other cognitive neuroscientists, such as Posner and Rothbart (1998), who identify several networks anchored in the anterior cingulate that modulate the relationship among self-regulation, distress, and attention. They believe that attention requires self-control, and that the cingulate is uniquely suited to revealing conflicts between perceptual accuracy and emotional control. Closely connected to the amygdala and limbic system, the cingulate is purported to contribute to error detection by highlighting their distress over the delay involved in getting caregivers to understand what they want. The feelings they experience often are misperceived as equivalent to physical pain. Perceptual errors such as these are decreased as the resources of self-control are transferred to the control of cognition. For these reasons, Posner and Rothbart (1998) believe that a system for error monitoring, triggered by distress, is already in place long before children attain prefrontal inhibitory control, and that the capacity to control reactions to distress precedes the voluntary control of attention. Accordingly, they conclude that infants posses an emotional awareness that precedes voluntary control.

Nevertheless, it is essentially unclear whether infants possess the ability to accurately discriminate among their own conflicting emotions or to unerringly identify emotions expressed by caregivers. The assumption may not be warranted that the distress associated with the lack of cognitive or motor control can be overcome through mechanisms of error correction in the anterior cingulate gyrus. In an interesting experiment, Caplovitz-Barrett, Campos, and Emde (1996) showed that when parents express conflicting emotions (i.e., a neutral face, but a stern voice) in the presence of a novel toy, infants show greater ambivalence and reluctance to pick up the toy than when voice and expression are congruently neutral or happy. Also infants who are exposed to conflicting expressions of emotion (i.e., happy then angry faces and voices) show more uncertain reactions.

Clearly, the expression of an emotion by itself does not impart sufficient information to resolve conflict and enable decisiveness. Emotions involve specific facial gestures and voice tones whose meaning is dependent on context. Moreover, many emotions are ambiguous and do not possess either positive or negative valence and instead embody mixed feelings, such as the anger and jealously expressed by resentment. Although the anterior cingulate may be uniquely situated to detect conflict, the functional consequences may be closely aligned with signaling the need to eliminate dissonance rather than resolve error (Botvinick, Cohen, & Carter, 2004).

Moreover, the difficulties that dyslexics or children with attention deficit hyperactivity disorder (ADHD) have in dealing with novel or unfamiliar events cannot be explained solely on the basis of defects in cingulate networks. Instead, research indicates that these disorders follow multiple neurodevelopmental pathways that engage mechanisms of inhibition and motivation (Pennington, 2005; Sonuga-Barke, 2005). For example, although almost 80% of children with ADHD have a deficit in at least one measure of executive control, the same is true for nearly half of the control subjects (Nigg et al., 2005). In another study, Sonuga-Barke (2003) found that 29% of ADHD children exhibited both aversion to delay (a motivation problem) and poor inhibitory control or a so-called executive dysfunction. Aversion to delay diminishes the value of future gains even if they exceed those involving immediate gratification.

The difficulty that ADHD patients experience in delaying response appears to be independent of inhibitory deficits. According to Sonuga-Barke et al. (2005), apparently "children with ADHD are able to wait even if waiting involves inhibition, but they often choose not to wait even when waiting does not involve inhibition" (p. 1233). Although the cingulate gyrus might be capable of registering conflicting emotions involved in immediate satisfaction verses postponement, prefrontal regions are more likely to be engaged in the assessment of whether a bigger reward is worth the delay. But this kind of assessment could be

undermined by an underlying sensorimotor disorder in the perception
of time, perhaps involving a breakdown in the detection of intermodal
relationships.

The Temporal and Multimodal
Basis of Attention Deficits

In fact, young dyslexics frequently are also hyperactive, and both dyslexics and children with ADHD appear to experience a similar difficulty in
accurately perceiving, processing, and managing time. The presumption
has been that ADHD children possess intact, normal perceptual functions and memory. However, ADHD children who exhibit weak
inhibitory control also have difficulty perceiving time and correctly estimating the duration of events (Paule et al., 2000; Toplak, Dockstader, &
Tannock, 2006). The cerebellum and cerebellar vermis appear to be
implicated in motor output involving perceptions lasting for milliseconds, while basal ganglia and frontal cortex are involved in perceptions
of longer duration. Many of the symptoms associated with ADHD exhibited in the classroom, such as speaking out of turn, interrupting other
conversations, failing to meet deadlines, or remembering directions indicate a problem of pacing, especially in responding appropriately to situations of short or long duration. Perhaps not surprisingly, ADHD children
also performed with less precision and reliability than controls in reproducing the intervals of tones that were separated by different durations
(Tannock et al., 2000). Performance on these and other tasks indicate
that ADHD children experience uncertainty in accurately gauging the
timing of events involving pacing and recognition of synchrony.

  Only in the last decade have neuroscientists found evidence that
dyslexia also involves deficits in auditory perception that contribute to
difficulties in phonological processing associated with language use and
reading (Merzenich et al., 1998). Computer simulations that slow down
the syllables in words and the cadence of phrases in sentences have contributed to remarkable improvement in word learning and reading in
dyslexics. These exercises sensitize the auditory cortex to a broader band
of sound frequencies involved in the recognition and reproduction of
words. Nevertheless, a recent study was undertaken to determine
whether dyslexic children suffer from a more general auditory perceptual
impairment underlying phonological processing, which involves not just
timing, but the capacity to recognize amodal similarities in sounds and
figures (Kujala, Karma, & Ceponiene, 2001). A training procedure was

administered on a computer screen to dyslexics assigned to an experimental group requiring them to which they match sound patterns with visual patterns. The sound patterns varied in pitch, duration, and intensity and had to be matched to rectangles that differed in terms of length, width, and angle. Performance was measured in terms of number of correctly read words and by changes in electrophysiological response to determine whether changes in reading scores corresponded to increased ERP amplitude. The training group read significantly more words correctly after training than did the control group, and this correlated with an increase in the ERP amplitude.

These study results support the auditory dysfunction theory of dyslexia advanced by Merzenich, but they also extend it. Merzenich and his colleagues argue that dyslexia involves the failure to accurately discriminate rapid acoustic transitions. Although Kujala et al. (2001) did not present stimuli in rapid transition, they did vary the relationship between sound and vision in terms of shared amodal properties closely related to timing. The subjects succeeded in matched the changing visual angle of the rectangles with the appropriate pitch (a sound equivalent of height). They also correctly matching the length of the visual sequence of rectangles with the corresponding duration of sounds (a sound equivalent of timing). The Kujala et al. study suggests that the capacity to identify equivalent functional properties of different sensory inputs is crucial to perceptual discrimination and learning. These discriminations appear to occur early on in perception through reentrant processes involving multisensory inputs and relational knowledge (Edelman, 1987; Lamme, 2004).

POSTURE AND MOTOR EXPERIENCE

Dynamic Systems

Another way of understanding the relationship between experience and the brain is to examine how posture and motor control work in tandem to generate new experiences that remap the brain. Thelen and Smith (1998) have adopted an uncompromisingly experiential theory of infant motor development and learning that draws on Edelman's theory of neuronal group selection. Thelen rejects the Piagetian perspective that through cognitive development we transcend our motor limitations. Instead she argues that our minds are embodied and our perceptual and cognitive skills are derived from the patterns of motor activity. Higher level skills are simply the further elaboration and extension of maps or neural networks constructed through processes of selection and reentry. According to Thelen (2000), "cognition is literally acquired from the outside in and depends on the strength of the perceptual motor pathways that access higher functions" (p. 17). Nevertheless, this assertion is inconsistent with the notion that the selection of repertoires involves internal reentrant neural processes, as well as external, experiential influences, which together contribute to behavioral and cognitive variability.

Thelen drifts further from the nonreductionist orientation of a selectionist framework by attempting to show how the structure of perception and cognition emerge from the physics of the movements involved in learning and skill acquisition. Thelen (2000) observes that infants spontaneously generate patterns of motor activity in the first 3 months through leg kicking. This establishes a preliminary set of movement parameters or maps involving the balance of muscle forces and joint rotations that are gradually reorganized when integrated with advanced forms of locomotion involving reaching, grasping, and other goal-directed movements. The motor-based memories generated through these activities facilitate the recognition and subsequent categorization of acts associated with accomplishing different tasks. Although procedural memory is strongly rooted in the cerebellum and hippocampus, Thelen's dynamical system theory does not seem able to account for episodic and autobiographical memories, which eventually engage parietal and frontal association cortexes.

Interestingly, Thelen's (2000) nearly exclusive focus on reaching rather than grasping perhaps is indicative of her desire to understand the dynamics of motor control. But this leads her to neglect the psychophysical aspects of perception. Thelen contends that rules for learning novel behaviors are task-specific and do not transfer easily from one task to the next. But this sidesteps what many consider to be the hallmark of learning—the capacity to generalize from similar instances. No task or situation is completely unique because there is always some degree of overlap in strategies and movements involved. This behavioral overlap or redundancy is likely to be reflected topographically in neuronal maps, which overlap and match at certain key points.

The apparent inability of infants under 7 months to successfully retrieve objects that have been visibly transferred from under one covered location to another in the A not B test, Thelen (2000) contends, does not signify the lack of prefrontal control, but insufficient opportunities to vary response by devising alternative motor strategies. Thelen's aversion to invoking neural mechanisms of cognitive control to explain cognition stems from an unfounded belief that this involves a tacit form of neural maturationism. As noted before, however, the focal point of brain development is not maturation, but the continuous balance between integration and complexity. These contrasting forces contribute to variability and selectivity involved in brain-based systems that must make choices based on multisensory input and controlled motor output. Thelen does not specify the neuropsychological mechanisms that enable these choices to be made, involving the redirection, suspension, or inhibition of action or change in attitude preparatory to focused or selective attention. As van Geert and Steenbeek (2005) observe, rejecting the idea that mental events represent entities does not require that all attempts to model and explain how brain and body interact be abandoned because of suspect ontological assumptions. We need more neuroscientific knowledge regarding how infants' attempts to solve the neurobehavioral challenges by relying on judgments about capacity and effort in assessing relative weight accorded to sensory inputs in relation to motor outputs. We also need to know how these judgments are related to how the psychophysical challenges of discrimination are solved involving judgments about proportionality, estimating distance and perceiving the relationships among the form, size, shape, movement, and trajectory of things. Together these factors contribute to the comprehension of and controlled response to a situation in its entirety.

Visual Proprioception and Attention

Campos and his colleagues have adopted a different approach in tackling these fundamental issues by demonstrating that the development of locomotor experience changes how attention is deployed. Their framework stresses the importance of self-initiated acts of motor control, a significant factor in animal studies, because they contend that only through the contingencies of movement do infants experience the emotional consequences of their behavior (Campos et al., 2000). Infants' early experiences with crawling, creeping, and, eventually, erect locomotion redirect their attention from nearby to more distant events that have repercussions for other psychophysical and neuropsychological aspects of perception. Locomotion exposes infants to the mechanics of optical flow and the challenge of properly coupling visual and vestibular inputs so that discrepancies in surface features, depth, and peripheral movements can be reconciled. Increased accuracy in these elements of distance perception also improves infants' abilities to hold size and shape constant while moving toward and away from objects in the visual field. Locomotion thus facilitates the ease of transition from an egocentric to an allocentric perspective.

Campos et al. (2000) have shown that the age of onset and the duration of locomotor experience enhance cognitive performance. In a longitudinal study of Chinese infants, Campos attempted to determine whether age of onset of crawling or duration of crawling experience more strongly affected infants' performance on the A-not-B test. They divided the infants into three groups consisting of those who began to crawl sooner than the norm (between 8 and 9 months), those who began walking near the norm of 10 months, and those who were late walkers at 10 1/2 months. Each of the infants was tested over successive months in the A-not-B test. Only the early and late crawlers showed any improvement in the successful retrieval of hidden objects after delays. Significantly, however, only the late crawlers who accumulated the longest duration of crawling experience showed the greatest gains in the A-not-B test. Apparently the longer duration of their experience (perhaps combined with the delay they experienced in their ability to crawl) better equipped them psychologically to tolerate increasingly longer delays before retrieving hidden objects. Just as in the case of children with ADHD described before, the experience of time plays a crucial role in infants' capacity for motor control. The additional crawling experience also may have given them an edge in the A-not-B test because the mastery of crawling frees resources needed to better attend to objects within reach.

Campos' research also challenges the notion, examined previously, that emotional attitudes are acquired in advance of experiences that evoke them. Campos, Bertenthal and Kermoian (1992) found that prelocomotor infants who are exposed to visual cliffs when passively moved in a stroller or carried physically do not respond in a fearful manner. Only infants capable of self-produced locomotion express fear and avoid crawling or walking over a visual cliff. But this isn't because the experience is inherently fearful. Instead, infants experience a discrepancy between information provided by vestibular and somatosensory systems based on motion and visual information based on depth. In the absence of proprioceptive feedback, infants experience postural instability and physiological reactions of imbalance that may produce uncertainty or fear.

CONSCIOUS CONTROL OF ATTITUDES

As noted before, autistic children experience a stress-induced emotional inflexibility that undermines learning and adaptation. However, McGraw (1935) did not believe that the trajectory of normal individual development is prefigured in temperament or that a recurring emotion gets strongly associated with particular experiences. Instead, she believed that attitudes were the result of behavior rather than its cause. She defined *attitudes* to consist broadly of "diffuse or specific feeling tones which accompany a motor action or state of being" (McGraw, 1935, p. 283). Examples of attitudes include receptivity, cooperation, persistence, resistance, and inhibition. More important, she considered attitudes to be the most pervasive and variable or fluctuating aspect of infant behavior. Accordingly, McGraw concluded from her studies of special stimulation that attitudes are subject to greater modification than either somatic or cognitive factors. She also asserted that attitudes are more easily transferable from one situation to another than are motor or cognitive skills, although the consequences for behavior may vary considerably.

Gravity, Balance, and Self-Awareness

McGraw (1935) believed that the attitudes infants acquire in early development contribute to conscious awareness of the consequences of their behavior. McGraw observed that mastery of different forms of locomotion never presents exactly the same problem for each individual. That is because toddlers must resolve the problem of balance encountered during previous stages of neuromuscular development, the neural, psychological, and experiential circumstances of which vary considerably between children. As illustrated in Figures 6.2 and 6.3, each successive phase of locomotor attainment involves a plurality of reciprocally interacting brain regions whose center of gravity depends on the configuration and energetic attributes of the behavior they subserve. For example, infants who crawl on their bellies by pushing with the feet and pulling with the hands are using muscle groups controlled by the brain stem and spinal cord. Unlike infants who crawl on hands and knees, belly crawlers must expend more energy to move forward and, given their limited ability to look ahead, are unlikely to fully engage premotor cortex in anticipatory and planned movements. Hand and knee crawlers have an additional advantage of experiencing what it is like to attain bilateral synchrony in

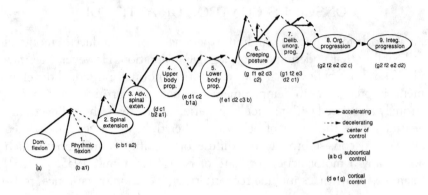

FIGURE 6.2   The development of prone locomotion. McGraw (1941) argued
that the phases through which crawling and creeping emerge reflect the
differential effects of neural growth processes. She hypothesized that the point at
which accelerating and decelerating behaviors intersect constitutes a crucial
transition involving two related events depicted earlier. Each new trait in a
behavior complex (e.g., 1,2,3, etc.) contributing to prone locomotion assumes a
leading position in the sequence until subsequently curtailed or eliminated.
Consequently, excess activity governed by subcortical regions (Traits a–c) is
inhibited with the onset of cortical influences. How long this process takes varies
among children according to rate of physical growth in size and weight (elements
affecting the center of gravity), the timing of synchronization of propulsion and
balance, and the level of awareness exhibited in recognizing and overcoming
limits to forward progression.

the opposing movement of arms and legs—an amodal quality essential to
sensorimotor integration. They also reap perceptual and psychological
advantages by being able to avoid collisions and learn how to reach and
grasp objects that provide satisfaction.

Through these challenges, infants gain an increased awareness of how
their own movements enable them to overcome the limits to forward
progression. Minimal consciousness is attained when an infant is able to
sit up—a behavior that Dewey observed in his own studies in the late 19th
century that led him to conclude that young infants possess consciousness.
Posit consciousness in infants at 3 months. Object consciousness (i.e., the
awareness of the difference between self and other) occurs with the acts of
reaching and pointing. Self-consciousness emerges sometime after the
mastery of erect locomotion, as illustrated in Figure 6.3, when there is an
explicit recognition of a causal relationship between self-initiated
movement and the movement or manipulation of objects.

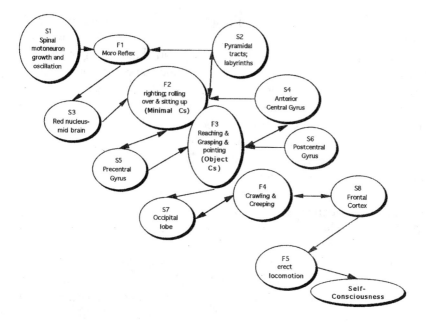

FIGURE 6.3   McGraw's neurobehavioral theory of development and
consciousness. Motorneuron growth and oscillation along the spinal column
commences a sequence of behaviorally mediated neuroanatomical and
neuromuscular reorganizations that sustain successive forms of conscious activity,
culminating in erect locomotion and self-consciousness. Each functional pattern
(F) constitutes the center of gravity of neural structures (S) undergoing
differential growth and reorganization, as illustrated by the neural complex S2
through S5 encircling F2. For example, reciprocal interactions occurring, between
F4 (crawling and creeping) and neuroanatomic structures S4 and S7 contribute
to experiential differences in how each child resolves the problem of balance
encountered in previous stages of locomotion.

The Conservation of Energy in Attitudes

McGraw and her collaborators tried to ascertain whether the physical
strategies and psychological challenges involved in the mastery of functionally specific behaviors, such as learning to walk or scaling inclines, contribute to neurobiological changes resulting in increased awareness and
self-confidence. This also would help decide whether the physical power or
mental effort needed to perform a task, once it is mastered, is reduced and
conserved in recurring attitudes rather than being dissipated. McGraw and
Breeze (1941) believed that the development of erect locomotion furnished

the best evidence obtainable that the attainment of bilateral symmetry in walking involves a redistribution of energy to accommodate new forms, involving reciprocal adjustments between brain and behavior. They demonstrated the possibility of converting the form and timing of gait into equations that measured the difference in amount of kinetic energy expended from the onset to the attainment of erect locomotion. These analyses show that the mastery of balance constitutes the greatest challenge, consumes the most energy, and accounts for the largest variation in form among infants in their efforts to achieve a stable gait. This suggested to McGraw that the challenge of overcoming gravity to attain balance heightens consciousness, redirects and focuses energy, and stimulates interneuronal connections crucial to problem solving and adaptation.

Additional studies by McGraw's associates provided further corroboration for her hypothesis that the gain in neurobehavioral complexity from early stimulation was conserved in the form of psychological attitudes conducive to learning. For example, Weinbach (1938c) found that an infant's proficiency in climbing a slide increases with age, and that power output is adjusted (i.e., decreased) to reflect the child's increased efficiency and competence. McGraw's associate, Vera Dammann (1941), a psychologist, demonstrated that changes in proficiency in mastering a slide were associated with changes in attitude and awareness, indicative of the infant's increased self-confidence. Finally, Weinbach (1937, 1938a, 1938b) devised equations to calculate the effects of physiological growth phenomena involving reciprocal adjustments between the velocity of growth (i.e., rate of energy transformation) of the brain and behavior. His studies suggested that mental energy is concentrated and accumulated rather than dissipated during learning experiences, generating attitudes and beliefs that better reflect judgments based on experience.

Attitude as a Constraint to Learning in Autism

The inability to control adverse reactions to mildly stimulating events has devastating consequences for infants and children with autism because it results in negative attitudes that consume and dissipate energy. It is commonly believed that these noncompliant, resistant, and aversive reactions are the result of poor communication skills. But Zelazo (2001) challenges this view, arguing that these negative attitudes and uncooperative behaviors may be the cause, and not the result, of limitations in self-expression. A self-reinforcing cycle is set in motion by crying, which precludes the development of a tolerance for stress and frustration by permitting escape from stress. Behavioral avoidance of a task eliminates the stress of performing it and reinforces the success of a strategy of escape.

Unfortunately, nearly 75% of autistic children are incorrectly concluded to be mentally retarded because they are unable to express and articulate their needs and communicate with others. To test whether there is a causal relationship between behavior and attitude, a sample of 44 two-year-olds with pervasive developmental disorders or autism received a parent-implemented behavioral therapy for 10 months designed to increase compliance with tasks requiring appropriate forms of self-expression. Zelazo (1997) then administered an information-processing test designed to see whether these toddlers could detect discrepant variations from an original event when it is repeated, a task that is challenging for autisics. He found that 61% of the children had information-processing abilities that equaled or exceeded their chronological ages on conventional tests. This study suggests that an important initial step in enhancing the ability to learn involves exposing young children to experiences that facilitate a change in their attitudes.

NEURODEVELOPMENTAL CONTEXT AND MEMORY

Functional and Effective Networks

Developmental scientists seek McGraw's studies underscore the need to attain a more complete understanding of how the brain and behavior interact and how consciousness contributes to neurobehavioral and neuropsychological complexity and integration. There is mounting evidence that many neural systems are reciprocally engaged in different tasks, but that the specific cognitive functions involved depend on the frequency and duration with which a subset of neuronal groups interact within this larger universe of brain activity. McIntosh (2000), a neurobiologist, proposes a theory that more accurately portrays the highly distributed and interconnected nature of the functioning brain that usually appears in brain-imaging scans. This complexity is often ignored in subsequent analyses designed to pinpoint the most active and presumably determinate region of cognitive function. McIntosh makes an important distinction between functional and effective connectivity that is neglected in most fMRI studies. Two brain regions may exhibit a functional correlation, but may not specify how this correlation comes about. Effective connectivity accounts for the mutual or intervening influences that one region has on another. McIntosh contends that neural context is that pattern of spatiotemporal activity and interactivity that makes a specific brain response unique. This is an emergent property of neuronal processes that is dependent on the temporal order in which they become engaged through behavior. A useful symphonic analogy is the different tone that an instrument establishes as a lead instrument in a concerto versus when it is used in accompaniment. In neural terms, context is evidenced by extensive interaction, as McIntosh (2000) observes that,

> Sensory systems, association systems and motor systems can all impact upon one another through their reciprocal connections. Because of this, the constituents for seemingly related functions can change dramatically, and it is also possible that similar constituents can be engaged across seemingly disparate functions. This reflects the dynamic and adaptive feature of the nervous system. (p. 868)

Neural context is governed by the demands that a specific task imposes on behavior, perception, and memory. For example, Habib et al. (2003) found that, although the hippocampus is involved in discrimination tasks involving familiarity and novelty, the networks that are active in these discrimination processes differ considerably. The significance of these differences in network connections becomes most apparent when the same tasks are performed with either explicit awareness or no awareness. In a study by McIntosh, Rajah, and Lobaugh (2003), subjects who were undergoing fMRI scans were presented with a visual stimulus preceded by one of two tones and asked to tap a computer mouse as soon as they saw the visual stimulus. Although the preceding tone facilitated the response times of all subjects, when the timing of the tone and visual stimulus was varied in a sequence of random and nonrandom presentations, only subjects who detected the nonrandom relationship between tone and visual stimulus were able to improve their response times by correctly anticipating the visual stimulus. Although the medial temporal lobe (MTL), a region involved in episodic memory, was active in both the aware and unaware groups, the scope of network interactions differed significantly. Only in the aware group were long-distance connections activated among the MTL, prefrontal cortex, and parietal areas. The authors concluded that the change in awareness involved in the transition from implicit to explicit knowledge reflects this difference in the scope of MTL regional interactions.

Not every interaction that occurs within a neural context makes a difference by contributing causally to an eventual learning outcome. There are always a multitude of alternative sensorimotor routes that can be taken to attain the same outcome. Most of these pathways involve experientially rich and often implicit interactions that expand variation and enlarge choice, but are not essential in a causally necessary sense. Statistical methods involving backtrace analysis have been employed to filter out incidental relationships to reveal a core of causally and sequentially significant relationships that recur despite changes in context. These methods were employed to show how a brain-based device, with a simulated hippocampus, could learned to find a hidden platform despite variations in the point of departure. The researchers were able to identify a causally efficient pattern of movement embedded within a larger contextually dependent repertoire of movements (Seth, Edelman, & Krichmar, forthcoming).

Infant Memory and Retrieval

Infants appear confronted with precisely this problem of retrieving information from memory that has been acquired through implicit, motor-based learning processes. Psychologists Rovee-Collier, Hayne, and Colombo 2001) have demonstrated, through a series of innovative studies, that infants must rely on multiple pathways of entry to retrieve memories essential to recognition, categorization, learning, and generalization. Access through these pathways involves a variety of different behaviors that include a combination of implicit and explicit strategies. Implicit strategies include noting (identifying relations), shifting (changing the stimulus), refreshing (prolonging or extending activation), and reactivating inactive information. Explicit strategies include imitation, rehearsing, and searching or retrieving. Rovee-Collier and her colleagues have shown that infants are capable of developing explicit strategies by 3 months. Infants were trained to kick mobiles that were suspended over their heads and attached by a ribbon to their feet. Infants retained recognition after short delays, but needed priming after longer periods to attain the same level of performance as before. These attempts to revive infant memories revealed complex interactions between implicit and explicit memory that are time- and context-dependent.

Rovee-Collier, Hayne and Columbo (2001) found more similarities than differences between explicit and implicit memories. They found that the magnitude, duration, and rate of forgetting implicit and explicit memories were about the same during the first year of infancy. The rate of forgetting was particularly sensitive to the number and duration of primes. Brief activations after short periods of delay were more effective in preserving memory than longer activations administered with longer delays after initial training was completed. Contextual information is lost in the course of repeated activations. Implicit memories are more susceptible to this form of forgetting because at the time when young infants are being trained they are unable to behaviorally differentiate a novel mobile from a training one. Once infant memories have become context-free in terms of time and place, a different cue and a different context may reactivate forgotten memories, such as the realization that objects which are kicked can be moved.

A Nonhierarchical Model of Memory

Based on these findings, Rovee-Collier, Hayne and Columbo (2001) question whether it makes sense to conceive of memory in hierarchical terms involving the transfer of information from episodic to semantic systems. They urge instead that memory be conceived as a single system involving different routes of access. This is consistent with the notion that memory is a function of reentry and the capacity of the brain to mix and match inputs against an enormous reservoir of mappings and alternative categorizations. This view is also consistent with a neuroscientific theory that Fuster (2003) has empirically supported. He argues that all cognitive functions consist of "transactions" and that accordingly, the same cortical networks are involved in perception, attention, memory and language.

Neuroscientists who are dissatisfied with these and other limitations of hierarchical conceptions of memory have attempted to build more flexibility into neural modeling by more closely approximating the plastic, self-generating powers of neural networks. Drawing on long-range but differential connectivity of spike-timing-dependent plasticity (discussed before), Izhikevich (2006) demonstrated, in a model, that a network could be generated that consisted of several interacting neuronal groups that exceeded the number of individual neurons or synapses, thus creating an enormous memory capacity (see Figure 6.4). Building in a 4 to 1 ratio of excitatory and inhibitory neurons and connecting them with axons that had finite conduction velocities made this unusual global property possible, whereby neuronal groups were differentiated according to conduction delays.

Through this simulation, Izhikevich (2006) found that the timing of spikes to postsynaptic targets not only affected their strength or weights, but also influenced with whom the neuronal groups will be firing. This allowed the same neuronal groups or subgroups to be apportioned differently depending on the timing of the signal's arrival. This temporal approach differs fundamentally from feed-forward models, Izhikevich contends, because

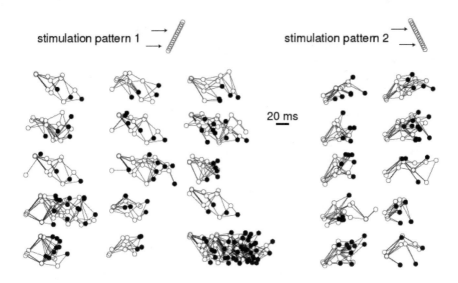

FIGURE 6.4   Expansion of a polychronous network. Persistent stimulation of the network with two spatiotemporal patterns (top) results in the emergence of polychromous groups that represent the patterns; the first few neurons in each group are the ones being stimulated, and the rest of the group activates (polychronizes) whenever the patterns are present. From by Eugene M.Izhikevich, "Polychronization: Computation With Spikes," 18(2), p. 245-282. Copyright 2006, Neural Computation by the Massachusetts Institute of Technology. Reprinted with permission.

the stimulus perturbs ongoing intrinsic activity. Consequently, the same stimulus does not evoke a recurring response pattern each time, but can elicit a different random subset of polychronous groups.

What is peculiar and significant about this dynamic is that each neuron can be a part of many groups, enabling it to fire with one group at one time and another group at a different time. The dimensionality of the memory system as a whole can be enormously expanded by altering the timing of the firing patterns of neuron subgroups. This model allows presynaptic inhibitory neurons to fire first, thus initiating a delay in potentiation—a phenomenon, discussed before, that appears to accompany the onset of cortical influence during the earliest periods of motor development. A different cluster of neuron groups are activated every 20 milliseconds even when the same neurons are stimulated by either Pattern 1 or Pattern 2, as shown in Figure 6.4. After 20 minutes of stimulation, 25 new groups

representation A   representation B

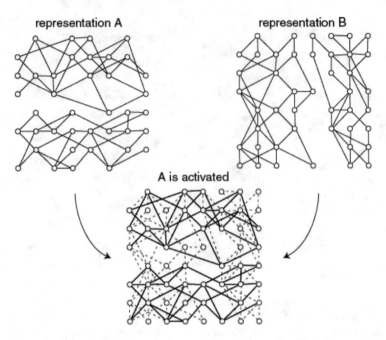

A is activated

FIGURE 6.5   Selective firing of overlapping networks. Stimuli A and B are both
represented by pairs of polychromous groups with overlapping neurons. Selective
attention to Representation A (both groups representing A are active) does not
inhibit neurons involved in Representation B. Because the neurons are shared,
they just fire with the spike-timing pattern corresponding to A. From by Eugene
M. Izhikevich, 2006, Neural Computation 'Polychronization With Spikes,'18(2),
p. 245-282. Copyright by the Massachusetts Institute of Technology. Reprinted
with permission.

emerged: 15 corresponding to the first stimulus and 10 corresponding to
the second stimulus. These groups reflect the memory of input patterns of
the two different stimuli. Each group is in a constant state of competition
to expand the number of neurons that represent the memory of a previously learned pattern of stimulation. This explains why categorizations are
unstable because memories never involve exclusive images or events, but
overlap rendering our conceptualizations incomplete, contextually dependent, and prone to ambiguity.

Izhikevich, Gally, and Edelman (2004) found that activating one neuron group interferes with and distorts the firing patterns of other nearby
groups because they are anatomically interconnected. The independent
activation of two groups may be too weak to interfere with a third group.
Nevertheless, the time-locked coactivation of the two groups may produce

a pattern that is inconsistent with and thus dissolves the third group. Simultaneous co-activation of the two groups alternatively might form a new pattern of neuronal group interaction whose synaptic organization is consistent with the pattern of input from the two groups. As illustrated in Figure 6.5, competition between two groups that share reentrant connections can result in the selective reproduction of one stimulus pattern that temporarily precludes another one from being attended to or remembered. The neurons constituting the pattern of firing related to Stimulus B are capable of firing, but only with a different spike-timing pattern.

Context and the Pattern of Remembering and Forgetting

This timing-dependent model of neuronal group selection and interaction appears better able than a model predicated on storage capacity to account for the patterns of retention, retrieval, and forgetting that Rovee-Collier, Hayne and Columbo (2001) demonstrated in their studies of infant memory discussed before. This is seen most clearly in the author's attempts to determine the effects of a novel prime on the retention of an active memory. They reported that 3-month-old infants typically forget the specific details of a training mobile 3 days after the training. Exposure to a novel mobile 3 minutes after training retroactively temporarily interfered with infants' recognition of the familiar mobile the next day, as did exposure to a novel mobile 3 days after training. However, infants did recognize the original mobile 7 days after exposure.

To analyze the timing of forgetting and remembering in more depth, Rovee-Collier, Hayne and Columbo (2001) studied the responses of 6-month-olds to time-delayed novel primes. Accordingly, when 6-month-olds were primed with a novel Mobile B 1 to 8 days after training, they only recognized Mobile B, but not Mobile A. After delays of 9 to 13 days, they did not recognize either Mobile A or B. However, the infants' training memory of both Mobiles A and B was reactivated 3 weeks after exposure to a novel prime administered 1 day after training, but memory of Mobile B was reactivated only when infants were exposed to a novel prime 13 days after training. What they found is that, after long delays, memory of Mobile A had been replaced by training memory of Mobile B. Whether a training memory is still accessible can facilitate or impede recognition of the original mobile depending on the timing of the prime after the original training event. Interestingly, when two different mobiles are used in alternate training sessions, 3- and 6-month-olds recognize a novel category member C. Under these circumstances, neuronal groups with slightly different configurations are formed, but whose patterns overlap. Infants who receive the same training with two different mobiles in consecutive trials appear to form a single concept of mobile from these overlapping motor maps. Only infants who were exposed to Mobile C after the longest priming delays (6-9 days, but not 1-3 days) responded to Mobile C, indicating that they had recognized Mobile C as falling within the category formed by their motor response to Mobiles A and B, thus expanding the inclusiveness of the concept of mobile.

As these experimental findings suggest, timing plays a crucial role in modulating the competition among overlapping neuronal groups involved in the formation, alteration, and enlargement of infant memory. Neuronal groups must be selectively reactivated by stimulation periodically to reinforce existing connections otherwise synaptic strength quickly degrades and group composition changes. This is illustrated by the need to refresh infant memory with priming sufficient to reactivate waning synaptic strength. But what is important to notice is that the effect of priming on memory depends on how soon priming occurs after initial training and whether follow-up stimulation introduces signals that are congruent or incongruent with a previous pattern of firing triggered by the original stimulus. Brief periods of priming immediately after initial training preserve the experiential context that strengthens recognition. Yet over time, as infants discover subtly different ways to move the mobiles with their bodies, legs, and feet, alternate forms of neuronal group interaction through reentry may have been superimposed on the original, less complex repertoire, changing the neural context.

Under these conditions, the distinctive pattern of temporal firing involved in recognizing Mobile A would be weakened or dissolved in favor of an emergent pattern of temporal interaction favoring the recognition of Mobile B. As the size and strength of intergroup connections grow, reentrant activity enhances or disrupts intragroup firing patterns, and thus either facilitates or impedes memory retrieval. Once the transition to a new level of group interaction has been attained, forgetting what has been previously learned may be more conducive to increased learning and behavioral reorganization than striving to remember a previous skill that is only weakly supported by the neural context. This polychronous model of experience-dependent neuronal group interaction does not entail any permanent increase in the number of synapses and does not require the assumption that memories are permanent. Instead, memory undergoes continuous reorganization in response to the changing context.

CONCLUSION: ATTENTION AND MEMORY MAKE
A DIFFERENCE THAT HAS VALUE

A question was posed at the beginning of this chapter that is crucial to understanding the relationship between experience and the brain: Why do some infants and children experience more success in learning and the development of cognitive skills even though their less successful cohorts receive comparable stimulation and undergo similar experiences? A provisional answer can be formulated by showing how the development of and interaction between attention and memory is governed by neurobiological and neurobehavioral processes that either enlarge or diminish conscious awareness depending on the trajectory and timing of growth processes, the scope of neuronal interactions, the flexibility of attitudes, and the efficacy of judgment. Children who incur neural deficits prenatally or during infancy face challenges in attaining adequate stimulation. They do not possess the means to explicitly recognize which learning strategies are likely to have value in advancing neuropsychological integration. But even newborns with possess healthy brains are still at risk for subsequent learning disorders if their earliest years are experientially impoverished and lack multimodal forms of stimulation.

The kinds of challenges that children with serious learning disorders face in benefiting from experience appear to be directly related to their failure to employ effective strategies to attend to, retrieve, and render explicit the relationship between sensory input and motor output. When these learning mechanisms are compromised, individuals are unable to anchor their experience in a broader phenomenal context and attain the psychological distance required to make explicit adjustments in their learning strategies to access implicit but retrievable knowledge. Children with brain-based learning disorders may simply represent more unusual forms of adaptive perceptual strategies on a continuum, whereby mechanisms of attention and memory are deployed to produce different neuropsychological outcomes. Cognitive deficiencies are more likely to become apparent when motor control is enlisted in the performance of tasks involving attention, underscoring the relationship between motor fluency and cognitive flexibility (Wassenberg, Feron, & Kessels, 2005).

The perceptual challenges that children with autism and dyslexia encounter are clearly rooted in neurobiological dysfunctions beyond their control. There is no simple and straightforward scenario that predicts the onset of autism because behavioral signs only appear after birth

(Zwaigenbaum et al., 2005). The neural defects responsible for the perceptual disorders associated with autism and other brain-based disorders are not easily traced to a single recurring neuroanatomical source, but rather involve the breakdown of interdependent functional networks (Frank & Pavlakis, 2001). Decreased activation in one part of a network may involve increased activation in another, as illustrated by ADHD. Anomalies have been observed in autistic children's visuocerebellar circuits, which disrupt the temporal processing of visual motion. Disruptions in the projections between cerebellum and basal ganglia have been found, which control the sequence and timing of motor output, and the connections between these structures and premotor and parietal cortexes also appear to be adversely affected, thus compromising learning. Damage to cerebellar vermis also may undermine the accuracy of ocular saccades and disrupt vestibular control of balance. Poor visuomotor control also weakens sensory modulation (Courchesne, Yeung-Courchesne, & Pierce, 1999).

These early disruptions in the timing and extent of neural growth can undermine the relationship involved in the construction of primary and secondary repertoires. The adverse consequences of delayed growth before birth are compounded after birth. The brains of autistic newborns are still preoccupied with the construction of primary repertoires just at the time when synaptogenesis undergoes rapid acceleration. This spurt of growth interferes with the completion of the formation of primary repertoires undermining the interactions between key regions involved and delaying the formation of functionally intact secondary repertoires.

For example, in a PET study of autistic adults, Horwitz et al. (1988) found reduced correlations among frontal, parietal, cingulate, and other areas indicating restricted or ineffective connectivity among these distant brain regions. Abnormally excessive synaptic growth within nearby or local groups attenuates these long-distance connections between neuronal groups. Consequently, when the development of local and long-distance connections are out of phase, a series of cascading events contribute to maladaptive selection outcomes. Autistic children also experience a depletion in serotonin synthesis during the first few months after birth that contributes to hemispheric asymmetries in global and local connections, compromising language development (Chandana et al., 2005).

The subsequent train of events would appear to undermine the development of a reliable system of reentry. Courchesne and Pierce (2005) argue that prenatal underdevelopment of cortical minicolumns followed by overdevelopment of others after birth contribute to an imbalance between

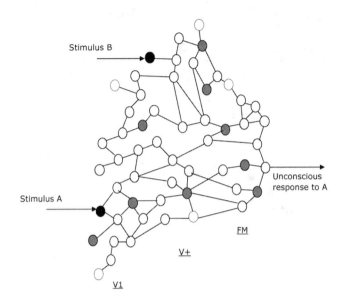

FIGURE 6.6   Visual processing without reentry. Incomplete or incongruent
neural representations of multiple stimuli (visual stimulus A and auditory
stimulus B) may interfere with the feed-forward transfer of visual stimulus A from
VI to frontal or motor regions (FM). Stimuli A and B may still be simultaneously
represented at lower levels of VI, V+, and extrastriate areas. Nevertheless,
feed-forward activation (gray dots), both of selected (i.e., attended) and not
selected inputs, are unconscious, although they may trigger or modify behavior.
From "Separate Neural Definitions of Visual Consciousness and Visual Attention:
A Case for Phenomenal Awareness," by V.A.F. Lamma, 2004, *Neural Networks*,
17, pp. 961–86 Copyright 2004 by Elsevier. Reprinted with permission.

excitation and inhibition. In the absence of clear signaling, functional
boundaries become blurred and responding is underselective and biased to
favor one sensory source of stimulation to the exclusion of alternative
sources, as described before. Local excitation lasts too long and is concentrated within isolated regions of cortex. This may explain why autistics
react negatively to tactile and auditory stimulation because it is perceived
to be much more intense than visual stimulation alone. The poorly modulated firing of minicolumn cells favors short-distance connections over
long-distance ones. Accordingly, the synchrony or spatial and temporal resolution of input from long-distance connections is reduced, impairing reciprocal or reentrant oscillatory signaling between short- and long-distance
neuronal groups—a stage of sensory processing critical for conscious access
to phenomenal experience. Under these circumstances, the interdependence between primary and secondary selection is broken, contributing to

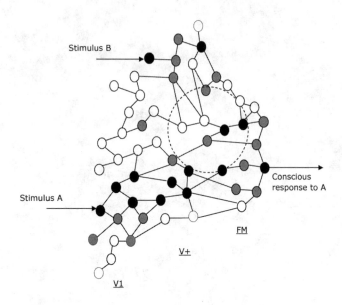

FIGURE 6.7   Visual processing with reentry, phenomenal awareness, and
conscious response. Neurons in activated regions engage in recurrent interactions
between inputs and outputs, which are accompanied by increased synchronous
firing (circles with black and gray shading). The interaction between visual
stimulus A and auditory stimulus B becomes the focus of attention within the
dotted circle. This produces phenomenal awareness of the visual and auditory
inputs. The span of some recurrent interactions increases as a result of selective
attention producing a conscious response to stimulus A. From "Separate Neural
Definitions of Visual Consciousness and Visual Attention: A Case for
Phenomenal Awareness," by V.A.F. Lamme, 2004, *Neural Networks, 17*,
pp. 861–872 Copyright 2004 by Elsevier. Reprinted with permission.

the misalignment of local and global maps, poor recognition, and defective
perceptual categorization. As shown in Figure 6.6, autistic children are
locked into the early stages of sensory processing and fail to reach the
threshold of reentrant interactions needed to sustain phenomenal awareness of the relationship between auditory and visual stimuli, as illustrated
in Figure 6.7. Memory is restricted to the recall of time-locked, repetitively
sequenced, static images that lack a phenomenally grounded context.

Significantly, in their attempts to avoid situations that produce states
of sensory overload and hyperarousal, autistic children develop maladaptive strategies that actually interfere with their need to obtain and effectively utilize multimodal forms of stimulation. This severely limits their
ability to retrieve contextual cues and obtain the psychological distance

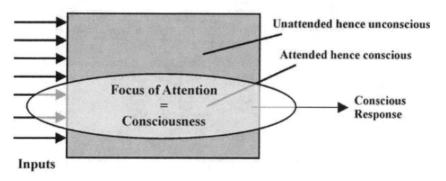

FIGURE 6.8   Effect of narrow focus of attention in autism. Unable to obtain
reliable sensory inputs from peripheral sources, autistics attend to objects or
events that are within the immediate focus of attention. From "Separate Neural
Definitions of Visual Consciousmess and Visual Attention. A Case for
Phenomenal Awareness," by V. A. F. Lamme, 2004, *Neural Networks*, *17*,
pp. 861–872. Copyright by Reprinted with permission.

needed to access different memories that furnish alternative interpretations of what is experienced. Autistic children possess considerable skill
in attending to and remembering visual features of objects and performing tasks that involve redundant and repetitive sequences. However, they
are unable to rapidly disengage, shift attention, and engage in a different
or unfamiliar sequence of activities. They succeed in visually reproducing
exactly what they see, but have great difficulty imaging how these same
objects or events could be organized in a different sequence. Memory
becomes time-locked, contextually static, and categorically changeless.
They essentially develop tunnel vision. Moreover, the strategy of minimizing aversive stimuli by narrowing the realm of attended events results
in the neglect of an unusually large field of unattended but contextually
relevant and retrievable information illustrated in Figure 6.8. Their consciousness is limited to what is in the focus of attention, and their judgments about value are measured negatively in terms of minimizing stress
rather than increasing the span of sensory access and motor control.

Dyslexic children also experience perceptual problems stemming from
incomplete or dysfunctional detection of intersensory relationships that
produce somewhat different consequences for attention and memory
depicted in Figure 6.9. For dyslexics, visual and auditory input is not synchronized, resulting in difficulties in timing and attending to differences
in pace. Unable to engage and focus attention on the meaning of words
whose syntax is elusive, the attention of children with dyslexia is drawn

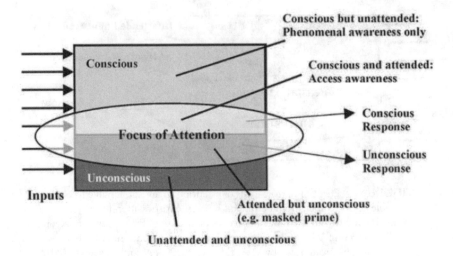

FIGURE 6.9   Effect of wide peripheral awareness in dyslexia. Unlike autistics,
dyslexics posses a much wider conscious and phenomenal access to peripheral
events, but this contributes to divided attention and more complex patterns of
response. From "Separate Neural Definitions of Visual Consciousness and Visual
attention: A Case for Phenomenal Awareness," V. A. F. Lamme, 2004, *Neural
Networks*, 17, pp. 861–872. Copyright by 2004, Reprinted with permission.

to peripheral events that are distracting, but also informative. Hyperactivity
increases the tendency to impulsively attend to looming sources of new
stimulation in advance of adequately comprehending and consolidating
prior experience in memory. This intensifies the crowding among stimuli
vying for attention that is accentuated by inadequate mechanisms for
selection and response according to salience. Nevertheless, in widening
their visual search for contextual information that can be obtained from
the periphery, dyslexics increase their comprehension, although the
meaningfulness and usefulness of this information must be deciphered
from spatially contingent cues, rather than from recurring temporal relationships. Dyslexics, unlike autistics, possess an awareness of a much
wider field of implicit but potentially accessible phenomenal experience.
But this advantage is narrowed by the randomness of search, poor
selectivity, and weakly coupled memories.

    Infants with brain-based learning disorders struggle with and often fail
to recognize how to attain a stable frame of reference, acquire a sense of
proportionality in behavior and attitude, and achieve synchrony between

sensory inputs and motor outputs. These modes of recognition confer value by making judgment effective. Toddlers are able to make judgments based on feeling and noticing the physical and psychological difference between two contrasting states, such as balance and precariousness, proportionate and disproportionate effort, and synchronous and asynchronous states. Synchrony binds movements into patterns or gestures that are more easily remembered and replicated. Autistic and dyslexic children are unable to establish a stable frame of reference that would enable them employ these fundamental modes of judgment. Fixed and inflexible attitudes weaken their capacity to accurately gauge the proportionate amount of energy needed to mount and sustain stable postures. Consequently, autistics and dyslexics consume enormous amounts of energy in fearful avoidance or distraction, rather than conserving energy in attitudes of patient watchfulness and moderation. For these reasons, they experience difficulty attaining motor synchrony and perceptual integration.

Infants enlist these same judgments regarding balance, proportionality, and synchrony involved in physical movement to eventually experience and express meaningfully complex and sometimes conflicting psychological states—capabilities that are severely impaired in children with brain-based learning disorders. Just as infants must experience more than one form of movement to master different postures and forms of locomotion, so too they must be able to undergo and endure different moods and attitudes in order to experience how emotions place different demands on their physical and mental energies. As McGraw noted, attitudes are more variable than emotions and reflect changes in the child's perception of control over a situation and willingness to engage, rather than to withdraw or become psychologically detached.

Judgment performs an accounting function by enabling infants to detect discrepancies, based on force, movement, contrast, and balance, to distinguish between a currently experienced physical or emotional state and a preferred one, and to know what attitude to adopt to attain the desired outcome. Consciousness performs critical roles in determining where the difference lies between precariousness and balance, between asynchrony and synchrony, and between disparity and proportionality. As such, consciousness is not yoked to any one sense, but involves the recognition of amodal qualities that reflect the recurrent but dynamic interactions involved in the transition from one phenomenal state to another. As described in the next chapter, self-consciousness makes possible the juxtaposition of alternative states of existence through language and memory. Learning how to learn ultimately requires the capacity to monitor and modify one's own attitudes and behavior and suspend belief in order to respond to the demands of a situation differently than before.

7

Language, the Self, and Social Cognition

Once sensorimotor control is attained, infants enter a prolonged period of learning how to communicate with language involving the integration of a complex group of competencies and new levels of recognition. The development of a sense of ownership of one's own thoughts involves more than simply distinguishing between self- and non-self-directed activities. Rather, there is a larger need to gain acknowledgment—to be recognized as someone who possesses beliefs and intentions and the capacity to communicate them through symbols that impart meaning and bestow sense. As described before, communication through language is rooted in gestures that combine posture and movement in temporally linked repertoires of action. Sign languages invented by children never previously exposed to spoken language use symbols that integrate manner and path of movement into gestures. A level of combinatorial power comparable to complex linguistic systems is attained with this technique (Senghas, Kita, & Özyürek, 2004). Syntax is essential to secure the precision with which propositions about the world can be stated, but it does not reduce the ambiguity involved in establishing the boundaries of meaning, intentionality, and identity that are often transgressed.

The acquisition and use of language involve the same principles of selection on variation as those entailed in the construction of motor repertoires and gestures. Language development does not closely parallel the neuroanatomical maturation of the brain, but emerges through self-organizing neural networks supporting flexible categories, semantic differentiation, and the gradual and progressive expansion of syntax (Cabeza & Nyberg, 2000; Li et al., 2004). Word and gesture are combined in early childhood, which reflect the intersensory basis of communication and the attempt to link words and behavior in presyntactic but meaningful relationships (Özcahskan & Goldin-Meadow, 2005). Language is acquired and expanded through semantic degeneracy, whereby words that have multiple senses (i.e., polysemy and metonymy) can be arranged syntactically to express unlimited variations in context (Beretta, Fiorentino, & Poeppel 2005). Selection is made on ambiguous words whose core meaning is underspecified by finding a context in which meaning conforms to the intended use or sense. Selection is facilitated through brain-based mechanisms of reentry that enables the rapid sampling of alternative expressions until an appropriate match is found between meaning and form. Language acquires signifying force by matching visual and auditory input, enabling gesture to be coupled with meaningful speech. The translation of sounds into signs and symbols furnishes the delay of action that is needed to redescribe events in propositional form, encompassing the past, present, and future tense.

The experiential and cognitive implications of this conceptualization of language, examined in this chapter, are that the acquisition of knowledge is not a matter of establishing the identity of objects or their correct representation, but of discerning the similarity and divergence among expressions that can be mapped differently. Infant cognition has much to do with understanding how meaning is governed by context and how inference is conditioned by the boundaries between familiar and novel situations and events. Children with brain-based language impairments, such as autism, experience profound difficulty integrating ideas in context to resolve ambiguous meanings, especially ones involving figurative expressions (Norbury, 2005). The underlying neuropsychological sources of these difficulties are discussed in this chapter.

Perhaps the single most important acquisition during infancy is a theory of mind—the recognition that other individuals possess desires, beliefs, and intentions that differ from one's own. An understanding of human intention builds on the processes of boundary recognition involved in other forms of perceptual recognition. Noticing that animate and inanimate objects differ in their capacity for self-movement, and that persons sometimes fail to attain their goals, helps children realize how human intentions can be conceived in terms of beliefs. Accordingly, infants learn that some goals entail long-term objectives requiring that a series of intermediate and transitional steps be taken for their fulfillment. This developmental attainment is significant because it enables children to formulate goals and think about events in conditional terms of if-then. Children also are able to ascribe desires and beliefs to other people and know that they can be mistaken about them and the appropriate conditions of their satisfaction.

There are good reasons to believe that infants show some understanding of intentionality (i.e., what an action is *about*) before they acquire language. This occurs before they fully understand the difference between desires and beliefs and the conditions under which desires are fulfilled and beliefs either are warranted, confirmed, or rejected. Developmental scientists are challenged to understand how infants and children acquire conceptions of objects and events, which form beliefs about how their appearance changes and are transformed under different circumstances. Contemporary research increasingly focuses on whether infants show some implicit understanding of false beliefs before they attain linguistic competence and acquire a theory of mind. This is controversial because some researchers propose that infants possess characteristic expectations about causal relationships and mental efficacy that appear to exceed their own self-knowledge at this age (Onishi & Baillargeon, 2005). This poses an interesting question as to whether children learn more about themselves by observing, simulating, and, perhaps, imitating the actions of others or instead, gain self-knowledge by actively exploring, experiencing, and remembering the consequences of their behavior under different circumstances (Frith & Frith, 2003; Grèzes et al., 2004).

Pinpointing the onset of theory of mind is important because this signals the recognition of subjective states of mind and the possibility of mutual understanding. Observing the emotions expressed by someone else may enable infants to imagine what it would be like to possess the feelings. Infants who observe others in distress tend to react with distress and, eventually, to offer assistance, indicating they recognize that these feelings belong to the other person and not to themselves (Barresi & Moore, 1996). This may signal the capacity to become aware of a subjective state of mind, involving awareness of rather than about some specific and nameable feeling. At an early stage, children begin to conceive of mind as the place where thought takes place, even though misconceptions persist through later childhood about the role of the brain in conscious and voluntary behavior (Corriveau, Pasquini, & Harris, 2005).

Some cognitive neuroscientists and infant experimentalists believe that mirror neurons furnish the basis of intersubjective recognition by enabling the detection of goals and intentions in gesture and movement (Rizzolatti, Fadigo, Fogassi & Gallese, 2002). It is not evident however, that young infants possess sufficient neural connections needed to understand that intentions are about beliefs. Although mirror neurons may subserve the detection of goal-based movements involving reaching toward objects, it appears that the recognition of intentions engages more than just premotor neurons (Frith & Frith, 2003).

GESTURE: CONVERTING MOTION AND SOUND INTO MEANINGFUL SYMBOLS

As noted before, infants at birth produce rhythmically organized sequences of leg and arm movements that eventually are differentiated into stable and separable patterns of behavior. Their earliest vocalizations become easily entrained within these motor rhythms and organized into overlapping cycles involving the alternation between the production of sound and movement (Iverson & Fagan, 2004). These vocalizations are not only influenced by patterns of motor oscillation and the perceived synchrony between visual and auditory cues, but they also reflect the intrinsic phonetic and prosodic bias of the native language (Hollich, Newman, & Jusczyk, 2005). For example, English language users alternate between stressed and unstressed syllables, whereas French speakers give equal emphasis to each syllable of a word. These patterns of accent furnish clues about word boundaries that infants use by 9 months to segment words in speech (Jusczyk, 2002). Before then, at 7 months, infants string pseudosyllables, such as *papapa* and *bababa*, together in babbling phrases whose vowels and consonants reflect the native language phonetic bias. Ten-month-old infants begin to recognize individual words several months in advance of their ability to use them correctly and consistently.

Prelinguistic infants are capable of communicating their desires by gesture, but lack the specificity and precision needed to ensure an appropriate response from caregivers. The efficacy of gesturing appears to depend on whether infants are able to increase the use of cross-modal combinations of physical and vocal elements that reduce the ambiguity of what they are trying to communicate. Clearly, infants undergo a significant transition from 16 to 20 months, whereby one-element utterances of gestures decline while two-word utterances increase dramatically. Nevertheless, cross-modal gestures continue to play an important role after 20 months involving a combination of pointing and referential elements that enable infants to significantly extend the meaning of their intended message (Volterra et al., 2005). When confronted with problem-solving tasks, children frequently make gestures that convey that they are simultaneously considering alternative ways of solving the problem. These competing gestures create mismatches between perception and action, suggesting uncertainty about which course of action to pursue. But they also signal that children are capable of thinking about a problem in more than one dimension (Garber & Goldin-Meadow, 2002).

Infant babbling facilitates the coupling between motor and auditory maps by enabling infants between 5 and 10 months to recognize the relation between self-articulated sounds and the resulting auditory consequences. Babbling is an experience-dependent method of reorganizing sensorimotor maps to better reflect the articulatory parameters and phonetic features of a native language. Even deaf babies babble with their hands, indicating that there is a need to map the perceived structure of language onto the means to produce it (Petitto et al., 2004). Imitation of non-self-produced sound does not explain how this can lead to selection of motor gestures associated with that sound (see Kuhl & Meltzoff, 1996). It would seem more plausible that the frequent experience of self-produced presyntactic syllables makes infants more sensitive to similar patterns of intonation in their native language (Westermann & Miranda, 2004; Friederici, 2005). This is consistent with Gottlieb's (1997) findings, discussed in Chapter 5, that prenatal ducklings learn the auditory characteristics of their own species calls by matching them with their own vocalizations of those calls.

PREVERBAL CONCEPTUALIZATION: EXPERIENTIAL HISTORY AND SCALE

Infant babbling not only furnishes a flexible method for the co-articulation of sounds and gestures, but it breaks down sounds into segments that eventually acquire meaning with syntax. What is so surprising about the relationship between speech and syntax is that auditory percepts do not come labeled, and the acoustic boundaries of speech are flexible rather than static (Liberman & Whalen, 2000). This raises the issue of whether infants possess preverbal concepts that provide the basis for mapping words onto objects and events. As noted in the last chapter, some infant experimentalists contend that infants possess visual biases or perceptual preferences that make movement, cohesion, edges, or other general features stand out. We had reason to qualify this view, however, because it privileges some forms of knowledge over others. Moreover, this perspective ignores the fact that each child experiences a unique history of categorization that enables him or her to organize features in a flexible rather than a fixed fashion (Schyns, 1997). For example, there are many different ways that edges and forms can be perceived and categorized depending on how a child approaches an object and the distance that is maintained. As Kagan's experiments suggest, inhibited children who keep their distance from unfamiliar objects may see them completely differently than children who take a closer look.

A theory is needed that accounts for how preverbal concepts acquire meanings that vary according to context and the contingencies of individual perceptual experience. Moving beyond the assumption that the world is organized into finite sets of fixed features and attributes requires the adoption of pragmatic principles of dimensionality and scale. As Schyns (1997) points out, this does not require dropping the notion of perceptual biases or constraints. Instead, he suggests how the dynamics of categorization and the perceptual choices involved in feature extraction can be reconciled through the adoption of a bidirectonal conception of the relationship between categorization and experience. The world is presented in multiple scales whose features fluctuate in terms of size and shape depending on distance and the focus of attention. At a distance, poison oak looks a lot like any other bush. Only when we draw near and see the distinct leaf form and resin do we recognize it as something familiar (and dangerous). The general category *bush* is replaced by the more specific category *poison oak*, whose meaning is constrained or restricted to a subclass of bushes that have leaves with distinctive edges covered in a whitish resin. Through adjustments in dimensionality and scale, the categorical meaning of *bush* can be expanded and contracted to fit the exact sense intended. In a larger sense, poison oak is a shrub that forms part of the chaparral or community of plants that cover dry, rocky hillsides. As we see, the development of a lexicon engages similar experientially driven processes, whereby the expansion of vocabulary makes possible the acquisition of a wider range of semantically related terms that can be substituted to express differences in sense.

One interesting example of how language structures cognition comes from a cross-national study, which showed that language users differ significantly in the frames of reference they adopt to specify the location of objects relative to other objects (Majid, et al., 2004). Descriptions of the position of objects crucially depend on the perspective adopted. Some cultures, like the Balinese, favor using absolute coordinates like north/south or east/west, whereas English speakers employ relative (i.e., egocentric) or allocentric (i.e., object centered), or some combination of these frames of reference. These cognitive categories of spatial reference differ considerably and seem to align with semantic categories that vary across languages.

In another provocative study, Johnson (2006) conducted a simulation of an exemplar-based, reentrant model of phonological perception intended to pinpoint the mechanisms that account for gender expectations in auditory word recognition. An exemplar model attempts to identify how individuals experience language when it is heard. Johnson believes that Edelman's theory is better able to account for why spoken language enlarges meaning because a neural system based on reentry allows form and meaning to intersect through coordinated patters of activity in both sensory and higher level cortices. His study was based on a reanalysis of Strand's (2000) laboratory study that consisted of three parts. In the first part, 24 listeners (15 female, 9 male) were asked to rate how different pairs of talkers sound (i.e., whether they sounded like men or women). The talkers to be judged included a group of 10 men and 10 women who spoke the same phonetically balanced, monosyllabic, high-frequency words. Another group of listeners (2 male, 8 female) heard the same talkers and were asked to simply identify the gender as male or female. The time it took to identify gender was recorded. In the second part, Strand used multidimensional scaling to identify stereotypical and nonstereotypical male and female talkers. Finally, in the third part, listeners (14 female, 10 male) were asked to repeat out loud the word that the talkers said. The primary finding of the study was that listeners took longer to begin repeating the words produced by nonstereotypical talkers. Listeners clearly have gender expectations, and words produced by nonstereotypical voices contrary to these expectations do not get processed as fast.

In his reanalysis of Strand's (2000) data, Johnson (2006) found an interesting bias at work. Although the percentage of stereotypical female voices whose gender was correctly identified was 75% and their words that were correctly identified was 79%, nonstereotypical females were misidentified as male over 80% of the time. In contrast, the gender of nonstereotypical males was recognized as male 79% of the time, although only 50% of their words were correctly identified. Johnson reasoned that since a spoken language is correlated with multimodal input involving intonation, gesture, pitch and visual imagery, the experience of hearing male and female voices cannot be stored separately apart from the episodic memories in which they are embedded. The longer it takes to process auditory features of spoken words, the more likely it is that sometimes implicitly linked features of an auditory experience get recruited through reentry to reduce the ambiguity involved in recognition.

SPEECH, WORD PRODUCTION, AND EXPERIENCE

Numerous studies conducted in the last two decades present mounting evidence that the development of speech and growth of vocabulary are highly responsive to the nature and quality of caregiver interaction (see Hoff,

2006). The highlights of these studies are worth mentioning because they possess cultural, educational, neurobiological, and intergenerational significance, among other implications.

Word Selection and Direct Conversation

Culture contributes to differences in the way children develop speech and acquire language. North American mothers frequently refer to objects using nouns, whereas Asian mothers use more verbs (Choi, 2000). This may explain the tendency among North Americans to view words as representations, whereas Asians prefer words that connote action. There are other interesting cultural differences in language experience. Western mothers tend to speak directly to children, help them recognize boundaries, and follow their children's attentional focus. This practice stimulates the production of children produce single words and novel combinations of words. In Asian cultures, by contrast, caregivers do not talk directly to children, but they do enable them to watch family activity and jointly focus on shared experiences. In these cultures, children place is a greater reliance on the memorization of overheard speech in chunks that are subsequently analyzed and broken down into component parts (Lieven, 1994). Conse-quently, language is acquired more slowly in cultures where children are not talked to directly.

Syntactic Variation

Conversational style and structure also strongly affect the capacity to learn through syntactic variation. Mothers who employ joint book reading exercises produce more speech per unit of time that is structurally more complex and generate more questions from children about word meaning than from those children who do not participate in joint book reading (Weizman & Snow, 2001). The indeterminacy of word meaning is significantly reduced when child-directed speech is engaged through joint attention (Dominey & Dodane, 2004). There is also evidence that mothers who provide multiple illustrations of the meaning of the same word increase the rate of growth of new vocabulary (Hoff-Ginsberg, 1985). Similarly, children who hear verbs in a greater variety of sentence structures learn how to employ them more appropriately in different syntactic contexts than do children who learn verbs involving fewer applications (Naigles, 1996). Exposing preschool children to metacognitive vocabulary (i.e., think, know, understand, etc.) resulted in increased metacognitive verb production, but did not lead to better comprehension of metacognitive language (Peskin & Astington, 2004). Although adult speech to young children tends to be repetitious, adults who produce utterances that involve small variations in words through substitution or syntax in the order in which they appear in sentences stimulate word learning in children. These forms of elaboration and recasting have been determined to be positive predictors of grammatical development, accounting for between 18% and 40% of the variance between experimental and control groups (Hoff-Ginsberg, 1986). These forms of substitution and changes in word order are the syntactic equivalents of neural degeneracy that make it possible for children to understand that there is more than one way to say the same thing. These early speech practices are also likely to expand the scope in the brain of reentrant connections involved in the matching of meaning and context through multimodal cues.

Birth Order

Finally, there are several interesting studies that document a significant relationship among age, birth order, and the style and rate of language acquisition. The age of caregivers can negatively affect language development. For example, compared with older mothers, adolescent mothers speak less to their children, produce fewer object labels, produce less affective speech, and issue more commands. These children are often delayed in their language development (Culp, Osofsky, & O'Brien, 1996). Birth order also affects language development as well as self-recognition. First-borns benefit from speech because it is directed exclusively at them. They then become intermediaries in the communication link between parents and second-borns, but they do not necessarily impart their syntactic knowledge. Their speech to younger siblings typically involves social-regulatory commands, less complex syntax, and a smaller vocabulary. Although first-borns may have the advantage in vocabulary and syntax, later-borns are more advanced in conversational skill. First-borns possess more object categories, whereas later-borns use more expressive language. First-borns and later-borns also take different routes to syntactic development. First-borns analyze what they are going to say first before speaking, whereas the reverse is the case with later-borns. Evidently, later-borns must work harder to be recognized and become a part of a conversation. Thus, differences in language resources contribute to differential access to communication and recognition (Oshima-Takane & Robbins, 2003).

LANGUAGE AND THE BRAIN

Structural Emergence

It remains uncertain precisely how the brain evolved to sustain the surprising level of symbolic communication and range of comprehension that is involved in the use of language. Clearly two important steps in this process included the development of the larynx and tongue as a tools of articulation and reiteration Liberman & Whalen (2000). Language is pervaded by metaphors that are rooted in characteristically human visual images, feelings, gestures and movement (Lakoff & Johnson, 1980; 1999). According to TNGS (Edelman, 1989), language is a further elaboration of gesture through semantics and syntax. Broca's and Wernicke's areas are likely to have evolved to provide more powerful mechanisms for relating objects and actions by connecting utterances to prelinguistic concepts. But these regions are not solely responsible for language and memory. Reentry provides for the categorization of semantic interpretations of actions by ordering nouns and verbs in syntactic relationships, which reflect the temporal nature of speech. In this sense, reentry is a precondition of language use. The production of speech requires the coordination of a diverse number of cortical and subcortical areas that connect the physical, value categorically based gesture and desire with semantic and syntactic propositions about beliefs, as illustrated in Figure 7.1.

Deacon (1997) proposed an elegant theory to explain how language and the brain co-evolved. Although he speculates about the extent to which the growth of the prefrontal region contributed to the displacement and reapportionment of functions to accommodate language and speech, he resists the temptation to characterize this transition as one that ushered in modularity. Instead he entertains the contrary supposition that language introduced a new mechanism for recruiting overlapping networks to do diverse tasks—ones that require highly distributed parallel processing. More important, Deacon observed that the acquisition and use of language depends on extensive variability in brain organization.

> If brain regions are recruited during language acquisition on the basis of how they map to implicit modally and temporally segregated, parallel computational domains, then we should also expect that the representation of language functions should be diversely and multiply implemented in different individuals' brains, and even within the same brain at different times in the life span or under other special conditions. Also, even within a single brain there may be

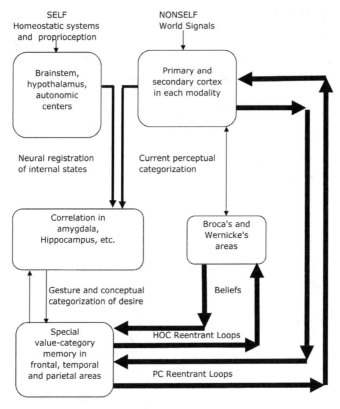

FIGURE 7.1 Emergence of language and higher order consciousness. A new reentrant loop appears with the emergence of language that makes possible the awareness of being conscious. New modes of memory are formed that enable reflection on the relationship between desires rooted in past internal states and beliefs about future states of the world. PC = Primary Consciousness, HOC = Higher Order Consciousness From *Wider Than the Sky: The Phenomenal Gift of Consciousness* by G.M. Edelman, 2004. Copyright 2004 by Yale University Press. Adapted with permission.

some degree of redundancy of functional capacity, so that alternative structures, besides those best optimized for linguistic operations, could be recruited to handle linguistic tasks when these more optimal systems are unavailable (e.g., due to brain damage, to the interference of multilingual communication, or to pressure from simultaneous competing cognitive tasks). Such functional substitutions almost certainly would be associated with a significant decrement in efficiency, precisely because language is not processed by some general learning capacity, but by quite heterogeneous cognitive subsystems, none of which is a language processor by design. (Deacon, 1997, p. 298)

Modeling Word Acquisition

There have been some thoughtful attempts to develop computer-based computational models that explain the neuronal processes in which a lexicon is acquired and arranged in grammatical constructions. For example, Elman (2004) contends that words are stimuli that operate directly on mental states whose meaning is determined by the effects they have on mental states. This is a useful proposal because it treats words as cues to meaning and context, rather than as direct representations of something. Word cues enable predictions about what they mean when put into grammatical context. Elman's approach accommodates the need to show how children learn language incrementally by extracting meaning from word cues.

Neuroscientists face several challenges in modeling and understanding how the infant brain acquires language. First, language acquisition models typically fail to capture the complexity of how words with multiple meanings are processed dynamically by multiple brain regions. Second, models that implement supervised learning regimes involving backpropagation are implausible because children do not receive continuous feedback that corrects errors in their patterns of speech. Children also experience temporary periods of confusion of word use, but they eventually make appropriate semantic distinctions. Third, computational models have not been able to capture the discontinuous spurts and stalls in word acquisition and the periodic confusion about multiple meanings that children exhibit while learning a language (Bowerman, 1978).

A recent model developed by Li et al. (2004) is intended to deal with these and related problems by showing how lexical development occurs through self-organizing neural networks. These researchers constructed a program that simulates the relationship between the increase in vocabulary and growth of topographic maps in the brain. Their model taps into the self-organizing features of neural networks, whereby the configuration of internodal connections is governed entirely by the input. The 500 words fed into the model in 10 growth stages corresponded to the vocabulary of a 30-month-old child. The composition of the words reflected the noun bias typical of English, with 286 nouns, 98 verbs, 51 adjectives, and 65 closed-class words. The more rapid acquisition of nouns resulted in a dense packing of semantically closely related words, such as car and truck, onto the same node. When this happened, it was interpreted as a failure of comprehension because the network cannot differentiate between these two concepts. The higher the word density, the stronger the words must compete during lexical retrieval.

Li et al. (2004) conducted a node-by-node evaluation of semantic relatedness of confused words and found that more than half the category labels among the ambiguous nodes were identical. Confused words that were semantically related increased from 75% at the beginning of the simulation to 90% at the end. It would appear, then, that the difficulty children have in differentiating between the meaning of similar words is a consequence of the way the brain topographically differentiates between meaning and form. The brain appears to favor a strategy of superimposing one form on another that reinforces a literal or dominant meaning until there is some syntactic or contextual cue that enables them to be treated differently. The ability to make these grammatical distinctions, of course, requires several years of formal education for the brain to unpack densely connected maps and redistribute them into syntactically diverse constructions.

Meaning and Multiple Senses

The advent of brain imaging has prompted efforts to better understand the neural processes involved in word recognition. This is a challenging task because most words in English are semantically ambiguous. Many words in the lexicon are homonyms that have more than one meaning, such as bank, which can mean the side of a river or a financial institution. There are many other words that have more than one sense. Ambiguity among related senses is called polysemy. This ambiguity is illustrated by the two different senses of bank appearing in the following two sentences:

1. The bank was robbed.
2. The flood destroyed the bank.

In the first sentence, the bank is an institution, whereas in the second, it is a building. It is also possible for one or more meanings of homonyms to be polysemous. The bank in Sentence 2 could be referring to the side of the river.

The conventional wisdom is that words that have different meanings are easier to recognize than ambiguous ones. Words with different meanings are believed to appear as separate entries in the brain, and thus recognized sooner, as measured by response time, than words that have multiple senses. To test this idea, Beretta et al. (2005) presented subjects with four different groups of homonyms and polysemous words, each of which was presented with nonwords. Their response time signaling positive recognition was measured with MEG recordings. Contrary to expectation, subjects responded more quickly to words that had multiple senses than few senses. Subjects responded more slowly to words with more than one meaning than words with only one meaning. Beretta et al. (2005) concluded that polysemous words do not involve a separate entry, but a core meaning that supports closely related senses. The core meaning possibly consists of a blend of senses that signify contextual variations. There is good evidence that the brain processes meaning bilaterally. The left hemisphere focuses on the dominant or literal meaning while the right hemisphere activates broader semantic fields, which overlap and feature distant or unusual senses (Jung-Beeman, 2005). These studies suggest that word recognition rarely consists of a one-to-one mapping, but, more typically, a one-to-many mapping between the form of a word and its other meanings or senses.

This multivalent aspect of word recognition may help explain the tendency among young children learning their first words to overextend their meaning to include objects that are physically similar in appearance. Infants come prepared to learn words with a stock of general or global concepts (Mandler, 2004). These concepts have less to do with differences in what objects look like that are eventually classified by nouns and more to do with how they move. Nouns constitute the vast majority of words infants learn initially, with verbs and adjectives coming much later. But infants do not possess sufficient knowledge of what really functionally differentiates dogs from cats and cats from foxes. Consequently, when they acquire their first nouns, such as dog, they tend to extend its meaning to include other animals with similar four-legged forms of locomotion. Even among 2-year-olds, 30% of common nouns are understood more broadly than appropriate (Mandler, 2004). The tendency to overextend meaning may actually be advantageous because it increases the stock of semantically closely related words whose differentiation into different forms and meanings awaits the acquisition of verbs and other syntactic tools. Hearing words applied to objects that reflect differences in form and meaning may cause children to attend more closely to those features and functions that had previously not been differentiated.

Unlike children who do not have a language deficiency, children with autism experience difficulty in recognizing similarities and differences in semantic context. They are more likely to underextend meaning because of a failure to recognize words with closely related meanings. When tested against controls, low-functioning autistic children were unable to correctly select the subordinate meaning of words even when they were showed corresponding pictures associated with the dominant and subordinate meanings of the words (Norbury, 2005). Autistics with language impairment also performed more poorly than controls in matching the correct verb with nouns in sentences with ambiguous, closely related constructions, as illustrated by the sentences constructed from the following word choices:

Bill saw/drove/listened to the coach/bus/teacher.
(Sentence construction: Bill drove the teacher and listened to the bus)
Jill hated/felt/treated the cold/weather/flu.
(Sentence construction: Jill hated the flu and treated the weather)

Poor performance on these tasks could be due to the inability to control attention, and thus suppress irrelevant information; it may also stem from deficient working memory for prior linguistic context. Nevertheless, these results strongly suggest that low-functioning autistics exhibit core deficits in semantic knowledge and sentence processing. Imaging studies indicate that adults with autism may be activating a different combination of brain regions than normal adults. Autistic subjects appear to rely less on a region in Broca's area involved in semantic processing in normal adults and instead show increased activation in the middle temporal gyrus and temporal lobe language-related region (Harris et al., 2005). When asked to distinguish the meanings of concrete and abstract words, autistics appeared to expend more effort on abstract words, as if they presented a problem of perception and recognition than one of meaning.

THE NEURODYNAMICS OF LANGUAGE, MEMORY, AND ATTENTION

Within- and Cross-Function Studies

Brain-imaging studies have demonstrated that there is considerable overlap among brain regions involved in a variety of cognitive functions, especially those that involve verbal discriminations. In their meta-analyses of 275 PET and fMRI studies, Cabeza and Nyberg (2000) revealed recurring patterns of large-scale activation associated with higher order cognitive processes. Their analysis is instructive because it reveals the fundamental limitations of so-called within-function studies, which investigate a single cognitive function in isolation, such as attention, working memory or episodic memory. Proponents of within-function studies deny that different functions activate the same region. Instead, they argue that each region actually consists of numerous subregions that are differentially involved in each function.

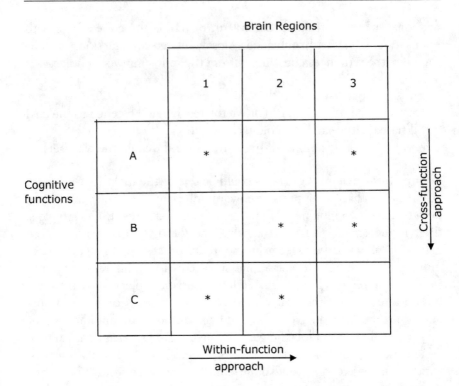

FIGURE 7.2   Within and cross-function approaches to brain imaging. From
Seeing the Forest Through the Trees: The Cross-Function Approach the Imaging
cognition by R. Cabeza and L. Nyberg, in *The Cognitive Electrophysology of Mind
and Brain* by A. Zari and A.M. Proverbio 2002, PP. 41–68. Copyright 2002 by
Elseviono: Reprinted with permission

Cabeza and Nyberg (2002) challenge this position, contending that it is
legitimate empirically to ask whether the same brain region is recruited by
different cognitive functions because the same region may mediate the relationship differently between two different functions, as depicted in Figure 7.2.
The most salient focus for the cross-function approach is the columns rather
than rows because this shows how one region can perform more than one
operation depending on how it interacts with other regions. This point of
view is consistent with the concept of *neural contex*, which was introduced
in Chapter 1 and discussed in Chapter 6 (see McIntosh, 2000).

   Cross-function analyses allow the investigator to determine whether
the frequency of the pattern of regional activation changes depending on

its role in a specific functional process. This issue is particularly pertinent for understanding infant memory because their brains are undergoing differential development that alters the scope and frequency of regional interactions over time. The composition and frequency of brain regions involved during development shift to reflect the transition from implicit procedural memory supported by the cerebellum and basal ganglia to semantic and episodic memories that engage a more diverse combination of cortical and subcortical regions.

Multicomponent Processes of Retrieval and Recall

As noted in Chapter 3, Bauer (2004) contends that improvements in explicit infant memory during the first 2 years depend primarily on increased storage capacity and consolidation, rather than enhanced retrieval (Liston & Kagan, 2002). Bauer defines explicit memory as the ability to recall and recognize names, dates, places, and events. She argues that older children are able to remember more for longer periods of time than infants and younger children. Bauer suggests that this difference in performance is due to the slow development of the dentate gyrus of the hippocampus and the consequent delayed transfer of remembered information for permanent storage in the association cortex.

However, Bauer's emphasis on coding and storage puts undue emphasis on physical location rather than on locus of interaction involving the commingling of different functions. Maguire and Frith (2004) concluded from their brain-imaging studies of semantic encoding of episodic memory that "successful encoding is not invariably associated with activation of one particular brain network" (p. 171). There is simply no single repository for the accumulation of memories because information is multiply encoded that can be flexibly combined and transformed in working memory (Postle, 2005). By adopting this latter perspective, Cabeza and Nyberg (2002) are better able to explain why the transition from simple word recall to semantic and episodic memory, discussed before, involves more than just improvements in coding and storage. These forms of memory involve flexible combination of different functional processes associated with attention, monitoring, and inhibitory control.

A summary of the results of their meta-analysis of adult brain-imaging studies is presented in Figure 7.3. Four cognitive functions were examined (i.e., attention, working memory, episodic encoding and semantic retrieval, and episodic retrieval) to identify their loci and frequency of interaction across different brain regions. Clearly, many of the processes

REGION/BRODMANN AREA

Function	PFC Ant.: 10	PFC DL.: 9, 46	PFC aVL.: 47,45	PFC pVLp.: 44	PFC postDors.: 6	ACC: 32, 24	Precun.: 31
Attention			) 1, 7		⊗1, 2 7	1, 7	
Work Mem.	⊗1,3,4 5	⊗1, 3, 4, 5 6	⊗1, 4, 5, 6	(1, 2, 5, 6	⊗1, 3, 4, 5, 6	1, 4, 5 6	1, 4
Epi.enc/sret.		(1, 4	(1, 4, 5	(1, 4, 5		1, 4	
Epi. ret.	⊗ 1, 4, 5, 6, 7	⊗ 1, 4, 5, 6, 7	⊗1,4, 5, 6,7			1, 4 5. 6. 7	1, 4 5, 6 7
Hypothetical processes	Retrieval and/or monitoring of internally generated information	Monitoring	Semantic processing and inhibitory contol	In left hemisphere: phonological rehearsal	Top-down selection	Initiation of action and/or conflict monitoring	Orienting attention to internally generated information

Function	Pariet: 40,7	Temp.: 21	MTL
Attention	⊗1, 2, 7		⊗ 1, 7
Work Mem.	⊗1, 4, 5, 6		⊗ 5, 6
Epi.enc/sret		1, 4	⊗ 1
Epi.ret.	⊗1, 4, 5, 7	1, 4, 7	⊗ 1, 5, 6
Hypothetical processes	Shifts of attention among external or internal events	Semantic processing	Indexing of descriptions wiithin the focus of consciousness

Abbreviations: epi., episodic; enc., encoding; ret., retreival; sret., semantic retrieval; PFC., prefrontal cortex; ACC, anterior cingulate; precun., precuneus; pariet., parietal cortex; temp., temporal cortex; MTL., medial temporal lobes; ant., anterior; DLl, dorsolateral; aVL., anterior ventrolateral; pVLp., posterior ventrolateral-posterior; postDors., posterior dorsal.

Symbols: (Left lateral ;) right lateral; ⊗ bilateral; ▭ midline. The symbol size corresponds to the relative proportion of activations for each function compared to rest of the functions.

Studies: The numbers adjacent to the symbols refer to the following stuc
1. Cabeza & Nyberg (2002)
2. LaBar et al. (1999)
3. Braver et al. (2001)
4. Nybert et al. (2002a, b)
5. Ranganath & D' Esposito (2001) & Ranagath et al. (2002)
6. Cabeza et al. (2002a)
7. Cabeza et al. (2003)

FIGURE 7.3 Common regions for four cognitive functions and their hypothetical roles in cognition. Data presented in the lower panels are a continuation of data presented in upper panels read from left to right. This matrix demonstrates that cognitive functions involving attention and memory engage a plurality of interacting brain regions whose dimensions and level of activation reflect changes in the complexity of neural processes involved.

presumably performed by the prefrontal cortex do not begin to become available to infants until after 7 months, such as monitoring and inhibition. In their absence, the processes of episodic retrieval and working memory are incomplete. For example, the frequency of activations of stimuli may be lower for infants than the average frequency for adults. Similarly, the relative proportion of activations for each function may be lower for infants compared with adults. Retrieval requires the ability to resist distraction, focus attention, and recognize contextual clues whose mastery is initially limited by the lack of coordination of cognitive skills afforded by a high degree of functional interaction. Infants acquire these abilities through the incremental expansion and eventual integration of several functionally complex brain regions. Episodic memories only become retrievable when semantic processing is sufficiently organized to enable infants to extract meaning from temporally dependent contexts.

Cabeza and Nyberg (2002) and Cabeza et al. (2003) perceptively note that many of the prefrontal cortical (PFC) and parietal occurring during episodic retrieval engage attention rather than memory. The fact that right dorsolateral PFC activations during episodic retrieval are attributed to postretrieval monitoring could be more simply described as sustained attention to retrieval output, with the thalamus orienting attention during retrieval. The involvement of parietal regions in attention, working memory, and episodic retrieval is indicative of their joint role in shifting attention. Attention is shifted not only among external events involving spatial and nonspatial memory, but also among internal events involving the alternation between working memory and episodic retrieval. Finally, the involvement of the medial temporal lobe in all functions may indicate that consciousness is performing an indexing function. The cognitive skill involved in distinguishing the self from other is crucial to self-recognition, the retrieval of episodic memories, and the proper attribution of mental states to oneself and others. Autistics crucially lack the ability to recall memories involving self-attribution, seriously compromising episodic recall (Toichi et al., 2002).

INTENTIONALITY AND THE BOUNDARY BETWEEN PHYSICAL AND MENTAL EVENTS

Recognizing Goals

Infants begin to acquire a rudimentary understanding of intentionality or what something is about through multiple sensory pathways involving reference to goals and intentions. Infants get cues from motion, gesture, speech, and acts of attending that establish a point of reference to distinguish between random occurrences and ones that make sense. The ability to process motion and action into meaningful segments appears fundamental to the recognition of intention. Human action is usually continuous, with few clear boundaries that signal the transition from one action to the next. Infants appear to be sensitive to the structure embedded in intentional action and are able to detect interruptions in the completion of simple actions (Baldwin & Baird, 2001). Infants as young as 6 months are surprised if an inanimate object moves by itself, but they are not surprised if a person moves independently. Similarly, 6-month-olds expect a human hand to reach for the same goal object when the location has been changed, rather than to reach for a different object that is easier to reach (Woodward, 1998). By 14 to 15 months, infants recognize a failed attempt to grasp and retrieve an object and will only repeat a successful version of the same action (Meltzoff & Moore, 1998) and not repeat an accidental action (Carpenter et al., 1998). Despite these capabilities, however, infants at 14 months do not possess a complete understanding of intentional action. Infants need not attribute a mental state or belief to someone performing these actions. All that is needed is an awareness of the most direct and efficient means to obtain a goal; no assumption of mental causation is required (Gergely & Csibra, 2003).

Infants also derive cues from looking, pointing, and naming to detect the relationship between behavior and goals. For example, 12-month-olds use gaze direction and positive emotional expressions to predict adult reaching for an object. Infants expect a person to reach for something they like and not for another object that they are not attending to (Phillips, Wellman, & Spelke, 2002). When hearing a novel word or emotional message, 12- to 18-month-old infants actively rely on cues, such as gaze direction or body posture, to identify the object to which the speaker is referring. Infants older than 18 months resist the impulse to link a novel word with the one they are attending if the speaker fails to indicate that he or she intends to talk about that object (Baldwin, 1993). Infants perceive the difference between goal and non-goal-related movements involved in grasping an object compared with touching it with the back of the hand (Woodward, 1999). These studies illustrate how infants search for and select multimodal signals that best reveal what an utterance is about by furnishing ways to establish the relationship between behavior and goal.

Joint Attention

Converging evidence suggests that a fledgling awareness of mental states is reached at around 18 months. At this time, children are capable of joint attention and pretense. Joint attention is more than simply gaze following. Rather, infants must reliably turn toward a goal that an adult is pointing to that is not already in the line of vision. An important precursor to joint attention is the ability to track sequential changes in body gestures by shifting attention from gaze to hand motions (Amano et al., 2004). According to Carpenter et al. (1998), there is a progression from sharing to following to directing someone else's attention in normal children that is missing in autistic children, who are unable to use another person's gaze or action to plan subsequent actions and properly understand their intention (Pierno et al., 2005). Nevertheless, normal children cannot actually judge very well what someone is looking at from eye direction alone until about 3 years of age (Doherty & Anderson, 1999).

As Frith and Frith (2003) observe, a rigorous definition of *joint attention* would signify an awareness of differences in mental state. This recognition would be evidenced by the child's knowledge that, according to Frith and Frith (2003), "different people can pay attention to different things at the same time, and of the fact that their attention can be 'directed' to coincide with one's own interests" (p. 49). The experience of being aware that one is the object of another person's attention may facilitate the recognition of oneself as capable of attracting attention to fulfill a desire or express an emotion (Reddy, 2003). With pretense, children must be able to detach the meaning of words or objects from conventional usage and substitute other terms or objects that simulate conventional usage. When children use boxes to represent trucks, they learn that they can change what something is about to reflect a different intended meaning.

THE STRUCTURE OF INTENTIONAL STATES

The Conditions of Satisfaction

The philosopher John Searle (1998) developed a useful framework for understanding how we think and reason about the world from an intentional point of view. His conceptualization furnishes insights about how infants develop an understanding of intentional behavior and kinds of mistakes they are prone to make before gaining a more complete understanding of mental states. Searle argues that intentional states are natural phenomena that possess a causal structure that connects neural processes to behavioral outcomes. Conceiving intentionality in this way enables an assessment of the truth of a belief about something according to whether it has practical consequences. Although beliefs may be true or false, the efficacy of desires and intentions depends not on whether they are true or false, but whether they are fulfilled or can be satisfied. That is why Searle believes that "conditions of satisfaction" are crucial to assessing intentionality by providing a warrant as to whether a statement of intention is confirmed by a corresponding state of affairs.

Direction of Fit of Desires and Beliefs

Searle (1998) introduces one other distinction that helps us recognize why beliefs, desires, and intentions must be assessed differently. The truth or consistency of beliefs depends on whether they match some situation or event in the world. In this sense, the direction of fit is between mind and world. In the case of desires and intentions, however, their conditions of fulfillment require a change in the world. Accordingly, the direction of fit is from world to mind. Sometimes the conditions of satisfaction require that the intention functions causally, in the sense that an intention is satisfied only if it causes the intervening behaviors that produce the consequences. Searle stresses that intentions that involve causal self-reference do not imply that the action had to occur or that it is sufficient to determine the outcome. There are numerous contingencies that intervene in the gap between the decision to do something and the eventual outcome that may enhance the possibility of satisfaction and also contribute to unintended consequences.

Infants and young children show progressive changes in their understanding of desires, intentions, and beliefs, as indicated by how they comprehend differently direction of fit and conditions of satisfaction (Moses, Coon & Wusinich, 2000). They begin to realize that not every outcome of their behavior results in a world-to-mind fulfillment of desire, but engages different beliefs, some of which turn out to be incorrect and inconclusive from a mind-to-world perspective. They also learn that language introduces greater ambiguity and uncertainty about meanings. This makes it more difficult for infantts to assess someone else's knowledge and interpret their intentions. As Bartsch and Wellman (1995) observe, 2-year-old children adopt a desire psychology based on their understanding that people are motivated subjectively by what they want. By 3 years, children seem to understand that beliefs differ from desires, but only by 4 years are they able to think of actions as jointly determined by beliefs and desires. Three-year-olds also seem to grasp a causal relationship among desires, outcomes, and emotions that exemplifies the direction of fit between world and mind. They notice that people feel good when they get what they want and express unhappiness when they do not get what they want. Their transition from the use of passive (*me jump*) to active (*I jumped*) pronouns signals a sense of agency or ownership of actions (Clark, 2004).

The fact that reasoning about desires, goals, emotions, and beliefs is governed by different logical conditions and syntactical requirements, as stressed by Searle, does not sanction the view, however, that each of these objects of human cognition are governed by different and separable brain regions. That is why we think it is premature, if not unfounded, for Saxe, Carey, and Kanwisher (2004) to assert that,

> Evidence from developmental psychology unequivocally supports distinct psychological mechanisms for attributing desire/goals, perceptions, and emotions to others (the early-developing theory of mind) from those mechanisms responsible for attributing beliefs. (p. 115)

In fact, there is considerable evidence to the contrary, discussed later, that the same brain regions involved in ascribing desires and goals are also involved in attributions of belief. Intentions are commonly inferred from the observation of outcomes, the assessment of which depends on our beliefs about whether someone believes that his or her goals are attainable by virtue of the actions he or she mounted (Castelli et al., 2002). Moreover, the capacity to modify desires to accommodate new beliefs would seem to require that infants be able to reintegrate these two factors to form a new goal involving a realignment of behavior. This change in how one defines one's own desires in relation to the world would simultaneously engage multiple brain regions as indicated in Figure 7.1.

Perhaps one of the most significant changes in children's understanding of causality and direction of fit is their growing recognition of the different ways that human actions can be explained in terms of psychological states, biological processes, and natural forces. When asked to explain behavior that may or may not be intentional and be subject to more than one influence, 4-year-old children are able to distinguish appropriately between actions more likely (but not exclusively) to be governed by beliefs or desires and ones governed by either reflexes or gravity (Schult & Wellman, 1997). This finding is significant because it reflects children's increased sensitivity to the fact that the same action or outcome can be accomplished and explained in more than just one way—a phenomena in accord with the TNGS principle of degeneracy.

False Beliefs

Children undergo a similar progression in knowing what counts as reliable evidence for fulfilling a desire, carrying out an intention, or confirming a belief. This entails the crucial distinction between thinking that something is the case and knowing it to be true. Young children more easily recognize when a desire or intention is fulfilled because there is usually more than one physical or emotional clue signaling success. What makes assessments of belief more difficult is that beliefs are not direct representations of reality, but action schemas that are conditioned by knowledge of the world. False beliefs are based on inadequate information that does not result in the appropriate action being taken. Preschoolers lack a good conception of how knowledge is acquired and whether available information is also adequate to support a belief. Four- and 5-year-olds show a remarkable indifference to reality and truth by typically reporting that they have always known information that was acquired just recently (Taylor, Esbensen, & Bennett, 1994). Preschoolers also fail to recall both the fact and content of their own recent or present thinking (Flavell, Green, & Flavell, 1995). Similarly, 3-year-olds fail to recall a previously held false belief (i.e., that a candy box unexpectedly contains pencils) and fail to appreciate that someone who was absent when the real contents were revealed will hold a false belief (Perner, Leekam, & Wimmer, 1987).

Research on false belief has become the touchstone for an explanation of how children acquire a theory of mind. The study of theory of mind was initiated by Premack and Woodruff's (1978) seminal study of whether chimpanzees are implicitly aware that different individuals have different thoughts and use this ability to predict their behavior. Although not decisive, the study generated considerable research. Daniel Dennett (1978), a philosopher, proposed a seemingly rigorous test on the basis of a person's false belief. A true belief would not enable an unequivocal test of a theory of mind because it would be impossible to determine whether a person's behavior corresponds to reality or is in accord with his or her own belief about reality. Wimmer and Perner (1983) began a new era in theory of mind research by developing an experimental paradigm that has become a standard version. In this experiment, children listen to a story enacted by two dolls with a piece of candy. The first doll hides the candy in one location and leaves the room. While the first doll is gone, the other doll removes the candy and hides it in another location. When asked where the first doll will look for the candy, 4-year-olds say she will look in the first location. But when 3-year-olds are asked the same question, they say the first doll will look in the second location, thus failing to understand that the first doll has a false belief about the candy's location.

Several different theories have been advanced to explain why 4-year-olds succeed while 3-year-olds fail this test. These theories are controversial because they differ about whether to give the evidence a relatively lean and parsimonious interpretation or provide a richer, more expansive account. Flavell (2000) acknowledges that each approach has its virtues and deficiencies. Lean interpretations argue that we need not impute mental states to infants, as many of the things they do are products of social referencing or conditioning that require no knowledge of subjective experience. They are simply acting on physical cues regarding behavior and not inferring meaning or intention (Haith, 1998). Although acknowledging the need for caution, those favoring a richer interpretation look for signs of the emergence of possible precursors to cognitive achievements. Taking this tact allows investigators to avoid assuming that infants and children are either totally capable or totally incapable of an understanding mental states, but instead look for evidence of a gradual acquisition of knowledge of mental states.

Preverbal Signs of the Recognition of False Belief

There are researchers who are pushing the envelope on the question of when infants show the first signs of recognition of the mental state requirements underlying the false belief test. In a remarkable study, Onishi and Baillargeon (2005) employed a nonverbal violation of expectation method to see if 15-month-old infants expect actor to search for a toy based on her belief about its location, whether that belief was true or false. Accordingly, they predicted that if infants expected the actor to search for the toy based on her belief about its location, rather than on the basis of her knowledge of its actual location, then they will look reliably longer when that expectation is violated. Their predictions were confirmed under both conditions. Infants looked longer when the location the actor searched was inconsistent with her true belief about the toy's location and also when the actor's search was inconsistent with her false belief about the toy's location.

Onishi and Baillargeon (2005) concluded that infants at this age possess an implicit representational theory that others act on the basis of beliefs and that they use this knowledge of mental states to understand their behavior. They reject the notion that children undergo an abrupt change from a nonrepresentational to representational theory of mind. Instead, they claim that it is "more parsimonious that infants attribute to others beliefs that can be shaped and updated by multiple sources of information than to assume that infants form an extensive series of superficial expectations linking different perceptions to different actions" (p. 257).

This controversial study prompted a critical response from Perner and Ruffman (2005). They present two possible explanations for why these infant responses need not involve an understanding of states of mind. First, exposure to stimuli during the familiarization phase may sustain neuron firing patterns sufficient to bias infants to prefer their most recent experience. Second, they suggest that infants may be following a tacit rule that does not require a theory of mind. The rule posits a relationship between seeing and acting, which leads infants to expect that a person will look for something where they last saw it. Moreover, Onishi and Baillargeon (2005) indicated that their study was based on methods used to examine how infants understand another person's goals. In their experiment, object reaches were consistent with the goal of retrieving the object when the object was in the container being reached for. When the object was not there, then infants looked longer at the event. This outcome is consistent with the infant interpreting this as a goal failure that does not require the imputation of a belief.

THE CONDITIONS OF SATISFACTION
OF FALSE BELIEF

There are considerable differences of opinion among developmental scientists about the conditions in which children attain an adequate understanding of false belief. These differences turn on precisely what that attainment signifies. Some argue that children undergo a transition from an object-centered theory of representation to a constructive one that allows for different perspectives and the possibility of misrepresentation (Wellman, 1990). Others contend that children's capacity to succeed in distinguishing between appearance and reality (i.e., that a sponge can represent a rock), a challenge closely related to false belief, contributes to the realization that the same events can be described in different or contradictory ways (Flavell et al., 1995). In contrast, Birch and Bloom (2004) deny that any transition occurs in the structure of thinking. They argue instead that false belief is indicative of the tendency, shared by children and adults alike, to be biased or cursed by their own knowledge, and thereby exaggerate the knowledge possessed by other persons. Finally, Koenig (2002) has a different explanation for over-attributing true beliefs. She contends that children are simply expressing their understanding of the aim of beliefs that they thought to be true. They are confusing the aims of holding beliefs with the need to justify them with evidence.

Counterfactual Conditions

An understanding of false belief obviously involves the ability to represent at least two different mental perspectives and the awareness that two people can respond to a situation differently according to the information they have. Children also face challenges in overcoming an egocentric frame of reference that leads them to impute their own knowledge to others, to confuse the difference between choosing incorrectly and being incapable of choosing because they are uninformed, and to fail to recognize that claims to knowledge must be based on personal experience (Miller, 2000). What makes false belief particularly difficult for children to comprehend is that they must consider how the outcome of events could have been different by reasoning counterfactually. Preschool children's evident inability to understand false belief may be indicative of a more general difficulty in comprehending counterfactual situations (Harris, 1992).

Riggs et al. (1998) examined the possible connection between false belief and counterfactual reasoning experimentally by comparing 3- and 4-year-old children's performance on false belief and physical tasks involving a hypothetical state. They found a significant correlation between errors children make when asked to report a false belief and errors made when asked to report a counterfactual physical state. A recent study reported that the ability to generate different types of counterfactuals accounted for a significant degree of variance in theory of mind performance (Guajardo & Turley-Ames, 2004). Between the ages of 3 and 5 years, children's theory of mind performance and counterfactual reasoning improved and were significantly correlated. Interestingly, children as young as 2 are able to overcome an inclination to bias knowledge of current rather than contrary conditions when they are encouraged to create an alternate reality where outcomes incongruent with everyday experience are possible (Richards & Sanderson, 1999).

Differences in Interpretation

Some researchers contend that the false belief paradigm does not provide any direct evidence regarding whether young children who possess a theory of mind and show knowledge of false belief actually are capable of understanding that beliefs account for differences of interpretation (Carpendale & Chandler, 1996). What seems to elude a 4-year-old's understanding is that people possessing the same information neverthe- less can hold different beliefs about and interpret this same information differently. Even when story characters are given different personal histo- ries and beliefs about the same events and then experience these events at the same time, 5-year-olds who observe them do not show any clear understanding of relevant differences in background and assume instead that everyone whose immediate experiences are the same will also have identical beliefs. Children experience difficulty acknowledging alterna- tive perspectives because it violates their naive belief that objects and events cannot possess more than one name or identity. For example, when directed by a puppet to use the synonym *bunny* for rabbit after the puppet says *rabbit*, 3-year-olds repeated the word the puppet used (Perner et al., 2002). With false belief, children are confronted with two different perspectives toward the same object that they take as evidence of incom- patibility. This conflict is reconciled only when children are able to switch perspectives and learn that two different perspectives are compat- ible with the same underlying truth about something.

UNDERSTANDING THE INFANT MIND AND BRAIN

Imitating Minds

Despite this evidence of the importance of being able to adopt alterna- tive perspectives, even if they appear incompatible, developmental scientists are divided about how children overcome a strong predisposi- tion to give their own beliefs more warrant than they deserve, and to misrepresent the mental states underlying other people's knowledge. Part of the answer may come from a better understanding of how the brain functions to enable the expansion of consciousness to encompass first- and third-person perspectives essential to mental state attribution. Meltzoff (2004), Meltzoff and Moore (1992), and Meltzoff and Decety (2004) advanced perhaps the most ambitious and neuroscientifically sophisticated theory today to explain how infants acquire knowledge of other minds. Meltzoff's work deserves close examination because it high- lights the difficulties developmental scientists face in constructing a neu- roscientifically plausible theory capable of accounting for how children accommodate beliefs that involve perspectives different from their own.

Meltzoff contends, contrary to Piaget, that infant perceptual knowledge does not depend on sensorimotor development. Instead, he argues that infants from birth possess the capacity to recognize equivalences between acts performed by others and those performed by themselves. Meltzoff's contention is based on a series of experimental studies with neonates, which demonstrated that they are capable of deferred imitation. This condition is met when a representation of an event is formed from observation alone without motor involvement. While 3-week-old infants sucked on a pacifier (which blocked them from performing tongue protrusion), an adult demonstrated mouth opening and tongue protrusion, stopped the demonstration, showed a neutral face, and then removed the pacifier. The infants subsequently imitated the gestures even though the target act was no longer visible. However, the fact that the infants imitated tongue protrusion more frequently than mouth opening led other researchers to question whether the infants were actually imitating these gestures or simply showing greater arousal when protruding their tongues than opening their mouths. Anisfeld et al. (2001) found that only tongue protrusion significantly elicited infant response, leading them to conclude that there is no cross-modal transfer that would support the hypothesis that infants imitate oral gestures.

Although a single study reporting contrary evidence alone is not sufficient to overthrow Meltzoff's theory, it does call into question whether infants possess a level of self-awareness needed to truly imitate rather than just mimic something without awareness of whether the actions of two different people are identical. It is not altogether clear how infants establish whether one self-performed action is the same as another and whether a self-performed action is equivalent to one performed by someone else. There are always multiple ways to attain the same goals. Infants possess a limited capacity to detect similarities in movements, as long as they originate from the same place, maintain the same trajectory, and end up in the same place. If any of these elements are altered or undergo variation, infants are unlikely to recognize two actions as identical even though they involve essentially the same goal (Kraebel & Gerhardstein, 2006). Only when 18-month-old infants can detect a goal, despite the failure of an individual to execute the actions to attain it, are they able to complete the actions that would have brought about its realization (Meltzoff, 2004).

Mirror Neurons and Mind Reading

Meltzoff and Decety (2004) believe that mirror neurons furnish a plausible neuroscientific basis to explain how it is possible for infants to imitate intentional behavior. Rizzolatti et al. (1996) discovered that mirror neurons in the monkey premotor cortex discharge during the execution of a goal-directed action and also fire when the monkey observes similar hand action in conspecifics. This instigated subsequent research to find out if humans also possess mirror neurons. Some neuroscientists contended that mirror neurons might bridge the gap between motor cognition and mind reading (Gallese & Goldman, 1998). Brain-imaging studies of human subjects do show the same activation of premotor regions involved in active execution, as well as passive observation as found in monkeys. Nevertheless, other neuroscientists argue that intentions need not be detectable in basic motor acts involving immediate goals (Heyes, 2001; Jacob & Jeannerod, 2005). An intention may involve a temporally distant goal whose attainment involves a complex series of motor acts, no single one of which is sufficient to reveal the ultimate goal. On this view, a motor intention is not equivalent to a social intention.

Meltzoff and Decety (2004) anticipate the objection that the premotor area alone is unlikely to support judgments about intention. Instead, they contend that evidence from brain imaging indicates that imitation engages the inferior parietal cortex—a brain region believed to be involved in distinguishing between action of the self and other. There is some limited evidence that brain functions in the right hemisphere, which include the inferior parietal lobe, develop earlier than the left hemisphere. Decety and Sommerville (2003, p. 632) argue that this would enable infants to view the other "as in some way analogous to the self." But evidence from brain-imaging studies involving adults performing imitation that reversed roles clearly indicates that the distinction between self and other is not lateralized in the right hemisphere. In studies that controlled for whether an individual was imitating or being imitated by another, the left inferior parietal lobe was activated when subjects imitated the other, whereas the right homologous region was associated with being imitated by the other (Morin, 2002). Consequently, even if infants show earlier development of the right hemisphere, they still would not possess the bilateral connections needed to unambiguously distinguish self from other.

Whether individuals view others as similar or dissimilar to themselves significantly depends on the basis of comparison. Comparing the self to the other ("like me") produces more similar self/other ratings. In contrast, comparing others to the self accentuates differences between self and other (Hodges, Bruininks, & Ivy, 2002). The latter perspective requires a world-to-mind direction of fit, a stance that infants governed by "like me" mechanisms are incapable of adopting. If this mechanism is innate, as

Meltzoff (2004) posits, then it is difficult to see how infants could ever replace an egocentric with an allocentric perspective that is required to integrate first- and third-person information (Saxe, 2005).

This relates to a more fundamental problem with simulation theories, the tendency to confuse the difference between instrumental, purposeful behavior and subpersonal, neuronal processes. As Gallagher (2006a: 2006b) cogently observes, individuals do not control the activation of their own brains. Rather, it is the actions of other people that "elicit" a particular level of neuronal activity. Individuals do not possess instrumental control of the activity of mirror neurons, they appear to function automatically. Nor it is it the case, as is typically argued, that neuronal processes are capable of acting "as if" they were carrying out some behavior. Neurons are not capable of pretense. They simply fire in predictable ways that satisfies the need for fidelity. That is why Gallagher (2006a, p 421) is correct to insist that "mirror neurons and shared representations are neutral, that is, they represent neither first-person (my action) nor third-person (your action), but simply action (for which a "who" is not yet determined)."

Self-Awareness and the Sense of Agency

Meltzoff also seems to confuse the difference between experiencing things subjectively and being aware of having distinct mental states associated with these experiences. Although their a newborn's actions are invisible to them, Meltzoff and Decety (2004) argue that the feeling of what it is like to do something is available to them through proprioception. When infants perform actions that provide sensory feedback, they believe that this enables infants to also experience them as mental states. Each mental state is then mapped onto the bodily behavior with which it is associated. Through processes that remain unclear in Meltzoff and Decety's (2004) theory, infants use their self-awareness as a tool to infer by analogy that other people who perform similar behaviors experience the same mental states as they do when they perform them. They acknowledge that this "like me" mechanism works best in predicting mental states that are reliably expressed in explicit physical expressions, such as intentions and desires. But this mechanism does not work very well account very well for how children eventually recognize false beliefs. This is a cognitive achievement that requires knowledge of other minds. It is not evident how infants would map the relationship between behavior and a mental state when they do not coincide. Moreover, there is a difference between experiencing an unfulfilled desire and possessing a mental conception of what it is like to be unfulfilled. As Zelazo (2000) points out, infants are conscious of what they see, but not conscious of seeing what they see as an agent who controls the seeing. *Minimal consciousness*, as Zelazo (2000) defines it, is unreflective, present-oriented, and does not involve an explicit reference to a sense of self. Only later, when children understand that the same world events can be appreciated from decentered, multiple temporal perspectives, are they fully capable of reflective self-consciousness (Zelazo & Sommerville, 2001).

A DEVELOPMENTAL CONCEPTION OF RECURSIVE SELF-CONSCIOUSNESS

A neuropsychologically plausible theory of infant development is more likely to succeed, if it takes into account a broader view of how human consciousness functions at different levels of complexity involving the interaction of language, mind, attention, and memory. We described previously in this chapter how language plays an important role in enabling children to learn that meaning is contextual, that sense depends on intended use, and that mental state words reveal a person's beliefs about the world. Only through mental state words, such as the verbs *think* and *know*, are children able to render a belief independent of the truth value of the sentence regarding a belief, as illustrated in the sentence: "Sally thinks that it is snowing." There is abundant evidence that children's comprehension of this syntactic form precedes and significantly predicts performance on the standard and nonverbal versions of the false belief task (deVilliers & Pyers, 2002).

Attention facilitates a shift in perspective between two different senses involved in, say, treating a goal as an object of action and treating the same goal as an object of a belief. In the former case, it makes sense to characterize the goal as requiring effort to attain, whereas in the latter instance a relevant consideration is whether the goal is attainable. Memory introduces the possibility that the relationship between two events can be described differently depending on temporal context. Recalling an event that occurred yesterday enables children to disengage from states of mind anchored in the present and think of themselves as experiencing a different state of mind. This affords two different self-descriptions of one and the same person. With a little more self-knowledge, children are able to hold a belief about how they will respond to some future contingency and how they might alter past behavior to better handle this hypothetical future event.

As noted before, the acquisition of higher order consciousness, according to Edelman (1989), was made possible by evolutionary changes in the brain that accommodated the tremendous recursive power of language. The changes in the order of magnitude of processing information depended less on neuroanatomical changes than on increased complexity and diversity of neuronal networks. Broca's and Wernike's areas are not special language modules, but epigenetic extensions of systems of categorization, whereby motor maps are converted through gesture and sound to articulate phono- logically distinct words, sentences, and propositions. The developmental implications of this theory are that the infant brain undergoes a transforma- tion in the scope and magnitude of neuronal group connections, which make possible the communication of one's own feelings and beliefs and to understand the beliefs and attitudes of other persons.

Although a first-person perspective is an essential requisite to self- consciousness, it is not sufficient because an individual must be capable of attaining psychological distance and taking the perspective of another individual. Attention, memory, and experience play crucial roles in both distancing the self and switching perspectives. Psychological distance emerges when desires are distinguished from beliefs and world events are distinguished from personal experience. Psychological distance enlarges when there is recursion and the possibility of reflection on the conse- quences for self and other of alternative courses of action (Zelazo and Zelazo, 1998). Distance is also increased with memory. A significant neu- ropsychological consequence of speech and language is that internal models of the remembered self may be constructed that are time- and task-independent. When young children are able to use different verb tenses, they begin to appreciate that the past and future involve events that either happened or will happen at different times, and that these temporally separate events can be distinguished in terms of what one is experiencing now.

Understanding other minds is uniquely dependent on perspective taking and inhibitory control. Children whose knowledge of other minds is impoverished are unable to understand language that involves mental state terms. However, children who are exposed to more metacognitive terms during storytelling do not show greater comprehension of mental state terms than children who received less exposure. Control group children showed greater comprehension of these terms because they had to actively experience and construct their own interpretation of the stories (Peskin & Astington, 2004). Children with poor inhibitory control rarely succeed in restraining prepotent responses long enough to assess whether their own beliefs are well founded. There is clear evidence of a developmental link between theory of mind and self-control, but what is disputed is what makes false belief so challenging for 3-year-olds to understand. Children may not understand that mental thoughts have causal efficacy and/or they may be unable to represent something from an alternative perspective (Muller, Zelazo, & Imrisek, 2005; Perner & Lang, 1999).

The research reviewed in this and previous chapters suggests that infants and children do not possess self-consciousness from birth, but must succeed in handling several levels of motor and cognitive competence before attaining reflective self-consciousness. The mastery of each level of competence provides a gateway to a different level of self-consciousness defined by the degree of recursion, as suggested by Newen and Vogeley (2003). Late-term to 6-month-old infants are capable of nonconceptual categorization. They possess phenomenal or subjective self-acquaintance, but have no awareness of themselves as agents of their own actions. When children between 8 and 12 months are able to classify objects with proper names, they possess a conceptual self-consciousness. This is an important step toward reflective self-consciousness because the child perceives that its body is the center of multimodal experiences, as experienced from an egocentric perspective. Between 1 and 3 years, children gain increasing command over language as a tool for recursion through the use of adjectives, noun, and verb phrases that amplify the scope of meaning and sense of sentences. This supports a sentential consciousness in which one level of description is embedded in and dependent on the meaning of one at another level of description. This closely parallels the processes outlined by Edelman's TNGS by which local maps of single categories are recombined to form global maps embodying concepts that possess greater generality.

Between 3 and 4 years, a crucial moment is reached when children are able to construct mental models of other minds. At this point, children distinguish the difference between a belief about a state of affairs and the actual state of affairs. This state of consciousness can be described as meta-representational. Finally, between 7 and 9 years, children adopt a second-order view of mental events that enables them to reflect on hypothetical events and characterize the relationship among different mental states that occur simultaneously. The first is illustrated by the ability to think counterfactually about a current belief ("How would I think of P if P were not Q but Y?"). The second instance is signified by the ability to express that the correctness of one mental state depends on the validity of another ("John believes that Tom believes that the ball is in the living room").

From a neuroscientfic point of view, an explanation is needed about how the brain represents the self as a conscious entity and how it distinguishes between self-referential states and ones that refer to the mental states of other persons. From a developmental perspective, we need to move beyond the notion that the other is a mirror in which our own identity is reflected and that reading someone else's mind yields veridical perceptions. This has led, in our opinion, to the mistaken conflation of brain areas subserving the recognition of self and other (as proposed by Meltzoff & Decety, 2003) and the dubious idea that imitation involves shared purposes. In this regard, what made the Marx Brothers comedians so amusing is that they exploited the self-perpetuating nature of reciprocal imitation to snare each other in traps with unexpected physical consequences. Certainly this does not mean that we are incapable of intersubjective understanding or agreement about values. But it does require that we view each individual as uniquely constituted by their experiences, beliefs, and values, and that the struggle to understand different perspectives must acknowledge the fundamentally asymmetrical structure of human communication (Ricoeur, 2005).

The privacy of our thoughts and the subjectivity of our first-person experiences are what account for our uniqueness as individuals. However, in a world in which interpersonal understanding necessitates communication through a shared language, beginning in childhood we surrender exclusive control of the meanings of our words, the consequences of our beliefs, and the satisfaction of our desires. Infants and children quickly learn that their desires and intentions are not transparent, and that it takes effort to articulate and enable others to understand what they want and to agree that they should get it. A theory of mind is indispensable not only for mutual recognition, but for the acknowledgment of difference—that two persons can interpret the same event differently, that ambiguity is pervasive, and that persons differ fundamentally about what satisfies their needs and serves their interests. The boundaries of individual identity are not confined to the physical limitations of embodiment, but correspond to life experiences and memories that extend through time. Adults' and children's life histories overlap considerably, reducing the burdens of problem solving and mutual understanding. But these same histories diverge when unexpected contingencies demand novel responses.

To fulfill these competing demands for privacy and accessibility, specificity and semantic diversity, mutual understanding and exclusivity, and familiarity and novelty, we need a brain capable of selectivity and recursion. What determines our behavior is not the state of the world, but our beliefs about the world. Beliefs must be decoupled from the actual state of the world and redescribed from a second-order perspective (i.e., "If P is true, then X will result"). The brain does not detect discrepancies or correct errors; it simply registers the existence of multiple possibilities of response (Edelman, 1987; Frith & Frith, 2003). The brain must also be able to expand and contract the scope of neuronal group connections needed to respond to changes in grammatical complexity and semantic context. Brain electrical activity must be capable of shifting laterally from one hemisphere to the other to meet the changing demands of recognition about whether someone else's intentions are implicated in my beliefs about their behavior.

Some neuroscientists insist that self-recognition and self-awareness result exclusively from right-hemispheric activity (Decety & Sommerville, 2003; Keenan et al., 2001). However, this depends on the context and task. Although recognition of one's own face may be limited to the right hemisphere, more complex tasks involving references to self versus others engage the left hemisphere. When participants were asked to evaluate how well trait adjectives applied to themselves, self-referential tasks produced significantly more activity in the left medial region of the frontal gyrus and left inferior frontal gyrus, compared with control tasks that included non-self-referential assignment of traits. These same areas are involved in the production of inner speech that is also associated with self-awareness (Morin, 2002). In some instances, language tasks will activate the same prefrontal region as theory of mind tasks if the syntax makes sense only by attributing an appropriate intention to the speaker (Ferstl & Cramon, 2002). Similarly, irony requires the listener to recognize that the speaker intends a meaning precisely the opposite of the literal meaning. The process by which we assign and interpret self- and other attributions then appears to be strongly influenced by a bilateral, interactive process of semantic selection, whereby competing activated concepts are sorted and assigned according to behavioral context and sense (Jung-Beeman, 2005).

8

Changing the Phenotype:
Developing the Mind
Through the Brain

This book would not be complete without squarely confronting the most vexing question that developmental scientists face in their attempts to fathom the genetic and experiential forces that shape the relationship among brain, mind, and behavior. This question has to do with how natural, biological, and cultural processes acquire value and how modifications in individual development are proven to be desirable or eventuate in consequences that are considered detrimental to individuals or societies. Of course, we do not possess the power to radically change our phenotype at will, as the human species has evolved as a result of millions of years of adaptations in our mammalian ancestry. Nevertheless, advances in the biological and biomedical sciences are making it possible to accelerate the pace of evolution by producing technologies that alter our individual genetic makeup, physical features, physiology, and even our moods in ways that may change the degree of variability within the species as a whole (Blank, 1999; McKinney, 2000).

Theoretical advances in understanding the relationship between genes, experience and the brain promise to revolutionize the ways that developmental scientists view the potential that humans possess to enlarge their sensory and cognitive capabilities far beyond their natural physical limitations. But the attempt to understand the factors that control neuroplasticity contributes to tension between the preservation of genetically conserved functions that ensure variability and experiential or artificially induced alterations in these functions that either extend or limit the phenotype. The sources and implications of this tension are examined briefly to provide the tools needed to assess the educational and policy implications of neurodevelopmental strategies to enhance learning, as well as to mitigate deficits that prevent learning from occurring.

In this sense, there has always been a tension between evolution and scientific advancement. The integrity of the human species, and life in general, depend crucially on structures, functions, and mechanisms that have been conserved across closely related species. But the preservation of our natural endowments is constantly confronted with the demand for scientific inquiry to understand how the mechanisms of natural endowment function, how they break down, and how they can be repaired or replaced. Through science, engineering, and technology, humans have already extended their capabilities far beyond existing physical and biological limitations. It seems perfectly natural that humans are predisposed to overcome the constraints imposed by the forces of nature, such as gravity and motion, light and darkness, temperature and pressure, among many others, that limit our movement, alter our perceptions, and change the way we think.

Perhaps more important, the absence of gravity in outer space reveals the profound biases in posture, movement, and perception that humans have acquired as a result of evolving in a terrestrial environment. What is important to notice, as indicated by studies of the brain and behavior during the *Neurolab* space shuttle experiments in 1998, is that astronauts are not only required to modify their movements to sustain behavioral functionality or protect against the degeneration of bone and tissue. They also lose their sense of proportionality, balance, synchrony, symmetry, and other amodal attributes of motion and perception that significantly affect their judgment. These modes of perception appear to carry signals that are fundamental to our sense of physical and mental integrity that are not easily dispensed with without altering the behavioral and psychological traits peculiar to terrestrial beings. There is some interesting evidence, examined in this book, that suggests that children and adults who are afflicted by serious neurobehavioral disorders, such as autism, may experience something equivalent to the perceptual distortions induced by weightlessness. This underscores the crucial role of intersensory sources of input in furnishing reliable perceptions of the environment and a stable perspective of oneself in relation to others.

As these examples suggest, every modification we can imagine making to our neurobiological structures and neurobehavioral functions through either genetic alteration, experience or biomedical modification promises unexpected benefits and uncertain risks. The concern that this prospect arouses may not be justified, as clearly we are making incremental and mostly imperceptible changes in our brain and body every moment we breathe and live from one moment to the next. But what we have in mind also concerns changes that occur as a result of institutionalized and organized methods of intervention pursued by schools, hospitals, laboratories, or other human service providers. As publicly accountable entities, they are expected to select, adopt, and pursue policies that enunciate the goals and methods for enabling children to learn or patients to live longer, healthier lives, and so forth. Only when we focus on institutions that possess the prerogatives of selection on a large scale do we begin to glimpse and take seriously the tradeoffs between individual variability and social homogeneity.

Finally, this chapter examines how policies selected to secure measurable educational gains among educable children run the risk of failing to appreciate and respond to the tremendous diversity of children's learning styles and modes of cognition. A balance must be struck between ensuring that every individual meets objective standards or norms of cognitive competence and the need for a diverse workforce capable of contributing in different ways to technological and social advancement. Striking this balance ultimately requires that a concerted effort be mounted to increase knowledge among educators, children, parents, and the business sector about how neural processes affect learning. Success in this endeavor requires increased multisector collaboration among scientists, parents, educators, business, and government to overcome popular misconceptions about the relationship between mind and brain and to embrace scientifically based strategies that enable children with different competences to truly benefit from learning experiences.

STRATEGIES OF INTERVENTION

Genetic Therapy and Early Stimulation

Policymakers and researchers continue to search for techniques that will lead to the early detection and possible prevention of neurodevelopmental disorders. Attaining this goal is not only beset with many technical difficulties and challenges, but is confronted with ethical issues that are politically controversial and publicly divisive. Progress in stem cell research, for example, has been limited by federal policies that have been dominated by special interests that want to curtail efforts to legitimize the transplantation of fetal tissue for therapeutic purposes, forcing some states to adopt less restrictive approaches. We do not review this controversy in any detail. Instead, we believe it is important to examine and compare the feasibility and potential payoff of undertaking genetic or experientially based behavioral strategies designed to prevent or mitigate the adverse consequences of neurodevelopmental disorders. We believe that the knowledge generated by these forms of intervention can be utilized to enhance the acquisition and functional integration of motor and cognitive skills of normal children.

There are numerous neurological disorders that involve genetic dysfunctions whose pathology can only be detected postnatally, such as Tay-Sachs disease, Leigh's disease, and Joubert syndrome. In these cases, postnatal intervention is too late because severe neurodegeneration sets in motion a sequence of physiological and behavioral repercussions that result in early mortality. Not until recently has fetal gene transfer been considered to be a feasible method of gene therapy to change the life course of neurodegenerative disorders (Senut & Gage, 1999). The fetal environment seems well suited to this form of intervention. There is a large population of stem cells that can be easily genetically modified to replace defective genes. In addition, fetuses under 22 weeks may be more immunologically tolerant of products of introduced genes. Moreover, the blood-brain barrier is low enough to enable entry of genetic material into the brain, and genetic material can be introduced either through the placenta or the same way as amniocentesis.

Nevertheless, animal studies indicate that there remain several technical difficulties to overcome for genetic therapy to be a successful prenatal intervention strategy. Perhaps the most challenging problems have to do with timing and targeting. As noted in Chapter 3, a complex sequence of growth-related events unfolds during prenatal development that is time sensitive. To be effective, intervention must occur before irreversible processes are set in motion by the onset of dysfunction. Not only is it difficult to pinpoint precisely when onset of dysfunction occurs, but this may or may not coincide within the window of opportunity when gene transfer can be performed safely. For example, the human fetus may be able to launch an immunological response between 14 and 22 weeks that would lead to the rejection of introduced genes and render ineffective intervention designed to attain a favorable outcome. It is also difficult to confine gene expression to a specific organ for long periods of time. The present routes used for the introduction of genetic material lead to a diffuse targeting involving more than one organ, which may cause unintended multiple genetic interactions involving unanticipated neurobehavioral consequences (Senut & Gage, 1999).

As discussed before, neuronal group interactions that are undergoing changes in composition and complexity can delay or disguise the appearance of a functional deficit and induce a temporary disappearance or permanent reappearance of dysfunctions. This phenomenon is well illustrated by the possibility that a defect in the cerebellum can appear during the first year, when prefrontal cortex and cerebellum have formed only incipient, nonmyelinated connections. The cognitive effects of such disturbances only become evident in the second year, when attention is adversely affected by problems in balance and coordination (Jeyaseelan et al., 2006). The use of stimulation provides more leverage than genetic therapy over experiential factors likely to affect short-term outcomes. Specific brain regions can be more easily targeted by stimulation, and the amount and quality of stimulation can be adjusted to reflect the level of desired impact. Experiential intervention also can be used to increase the level of RNA expression, raising the level of DNA activity and, thus, changing the scope of gene interaction. So one key to more effective intervention is accurate detection of the onset of motor dysfunction. This is when stimulation is timely and likely to succeed in forming compensatory alternative connections and/or triggering complementary forms of genetic expression prior to when faulty connections become permanent. Biotechnology also has a role to play in stimulation strategies. Deep brain stimulation has been increasingly used in last few years to treat the symptoms of Parkinson's disease and essential tremors. This technique involves the insertion of an electrode in the thalamus, which then can be activated by a battery operated neurostimulator implanted in the collarbone. This modulates the electrical signals, which contribute to excessive movement. But neuroscientists discovered recently that when this technique was utilized to stimulate thalamic activity in normal rats their performance on memory tests was enhanced. Shirvalkar et al. (2006) reported that after receiving 30 minutes of stimulation, two genes linked to neural activity and cellular mechanisms of learning became more active in the cortex and hippocampus. The simulated rats explored more than the unstimulated rats and performed much better on object recognition tests. Thalamic stimulation appears to recruit a larger group of neuronal populations than in control rats, contributing to increased alertness and attentiveness. These results are consistent with the idea that the thalamus plays a pivotal role in reentrant processes subserving memory. It is conceivable that brain-based learning disorders involving inadequate or faulty systems of reentry may be partially mitigated in the future by such techniques.

Improving Preterm Outcomes

Increased scientific attention to preterm infants at risk is also providing a much clearer understanding of the kinds of intervention likely to contribute to positive neurobehavioral and neuropsychological outcomes in later childhood. Although the survival rate of preterm infants has improved over the last 10 years, the overall incidence of neurological disorders has not decreased, but remained the same. One recent study reported that 25% of preterm children with extremely low birth weights had neurological abnormalities (Vohr, Wright et al., 2000). Also, up to 50% of school-age infants born before 28 weeks need some kind of educational assistance (Bhutta, Cleves, Casey, Cradock & Anand, 2002). Preterm infants offer a unique opportunity to study the effects of early intervention. Their window of vulnerability to disruption coincides with the period during which they are most responsive to effective intervention. The period between 28 weeks postmenstrual age and 15 months postnatally constitutes the time of greatest risk because neural systems are undergoing accelerated growth, making them particularly vulnerable to disruption (Bhutta & Anand, 2001). Stress in the form of stimulation that continuously pushes physiological processes or behavior out of a state of equilibrium adversely affects motor and cognitive development (de Graaf-Peters & Hadders-Algra, 2006). Prenatal stress can impede the development of sensory maps and disrupt the fine-tuning of thalamocortical projections into cortical and subcortical regions—a process essential to the construction of reentrant processes.

Nevertheless, the fetal brain's extensive plasticity also makes it extraordinarily susceptible to functional enhancement and reorganization. Improvement of neurobehavioral outcomes of preterm infants appears to depend on whether stimulation replicates the environment to which preterms would be exposed if they had not been born prematurely. Preterm infants who receive stimulation that mimics the environment from 22 to 28 weeks are more likely to reap positive gains in neurodevelopment than those who receive stimulation that elicits active responses. The prenatal environment during this early period approximates the conditions of weightlessness, whereby movements are slowed down and the boundaries between separate sensory inputs and motor outputs are blurred and overlap. In an experimentally controlled study, Als et al. (2004) created a treatment was designed to mimic this environment for preterms by physically supporting every movement, slowing the tempo of caregiving, and maximizing the sensory comfort and ease with which their individual needs were attended to. These procedures were designed to minimize abrupt departures from a state of equilibrium. This stimulation regime produced significant gains in brain development both structurally and functionally. In contrast, active strategies involving multimodal and temporally modulated stimulation is an effective strategy for neurobehavioral enhancement from late term through the first 15 months, as documented in previous chapters.

RETRIEVAL-BASED RESOURCES OF EXPERIENTIAL DEVELOPMENT

Increasing the Range of Recognition

As previous chapters indicate, children with brain-based disorders are prevented from exploiting the multiple pathways of retrieval made available by the brain to enable learning to take place smoothly. Their disorders erect barriers to adequate perceptual recognition, which is an essential requisite to the retrieval, processing, and comprehension of information about world events. Consequently, these children are unable to select the appropriate behavioral strategies that contribute to the attainment of an intended learning outcome. Effective remedial interventions are now available to dyslexic children, for example, involving intensive exposure to auditory training that increases the sensitivity of auditory receptive fields to a broader range of frequencies needed to distinguish between phonologically distinct syllables of words (Merzenich et al., 1996). Evidence from brain imaging indicates that this technique not only increases activity in the underactive left-hemisphere Broca's area, but also unexpectedly increases activity in the right hemisphere, revealing a compensatory effect of this remediation strategy (Habib et al., 2003; Temple et al., 2003). Right-hemisphere activations include regions involving attention (anterior cingulate gyrus), memory (left hippocampal gyrus), and word meaning (left temporal gyrus). Consequently, this form of training appears to have released previously untapped mechanisms of reentry, enabling the retrieval of contextual meaning from basic phonetic distinctions. Although autistic children face more formidable difficulties in overcoming their disorders of recognition, they can benefit from interventions that remove the attitudinal and behavioral constraints to learning.

Using Attitudes to Control Effort

There are several strategies that children can employ to increase the range of recognition, retrieval, and learning taking place across different levels of complexity. As noted before, attitudes play a critical role in focusing attention and facilitating the ease with which learning occurs. Attitudes not only affect level of interest and attentiveness, but the willingness to adopt a different approach or method when preferred means fail to attain an intended outcome. Attitude should not be confused with temperament, which is a predisposition to react in a predictable way to unfamiliar or stressful situations through either approach or withdrawal. Attitudes affect openness to new experiences and the amount of effort and time put into exploration, concentration, and reflection. Clearly children differ extensively in the possession of these resources and their ability to modify their attitudes in response to the changing contingencies of experience. Studies reviewed in this book suggest that children who successfully mobilize these attitudinal resources do so because they possess a good sense of time in detecting temporal intervals, pace, and duration. Consequently, they are better able to perceive synchronous movement, notice rhythms in language use, and sustain the tempo of communication involved in interpersonal interaction. They also possess superior self-control—a capability crucial to ensuring that the effort expended is proportionate to the demands of a task.

Exploiting Contingencies of Order

Young children also experience difficulty grasping how outcomes are affected by the contingencies of order. Piaget argued that children only begin to look at a problem sequentially, when they are able to reverse order and trace back through the series of steps that produce an outcome. Although reversibility stresses the importance of a causal understanding of sequence, it does not account for how the attainability of an outcome can be influenced by contingencies of the order in which factors appear in a series. This was the point that McGraw was trying to drive home— one that is characteristic of degenerate systems—that the energetic and cognitive demands of a challenging task can be significantly reduced by reorganizing and remapping the movements involved. By exploiting the close motor relationship between jumping off pedestals and climbing off them, the experimental twin, Johnny, was able to reduce the complexity and lower the energy required to dismount stools by adopting one seamless movement. Thelen and her colleague's subsequent studies confirm that infants' locomotor strategies represent a synthesis of numerous small variations in motor output that disappear in later mappings. This suggests that behavioral and cognitive development depends fundamentally on experiential variation, rather than repetitive order.

If it is the case that memories do not entail veridical duplication or reproduction, but rather are reconstructions whose meaning and significance depend on context, then children who experience more than one way to achieve a goal are more likely to retrieve memories in different sequences. All memories are sequential in that they are based on events that occur in some relevant order. But we are capable of juxtaposing these events in ways that accentuate the meaning and relevance of some events while deemphasizing the importance or pertinence of others. Memory based on past experience increases confidence in our beliefs, but it enables us to respond to future events differently if some of these beliefs are proved to be unwarranted.

Suspending Beliefs

The challenge in childhood is to be able to decouple beliefs from world events and imagine a situation contrary to an existing one. To do so, children must temporarily suspend beliefs about an actual state of affairs and substitute a belief that supports an alternative state of affairs. Children learn how to coordinate descriptions of events that occur at two different times by drawing on memory to compare past events with hypothetical future events. For example, a child can remember going to school yesterday with an umbrella, believing it was going to rain because it was cloudy, although it never rained. That same child could imagine a future state of affairs involving stronger evidence of the likelihood of rain, such as thunder and lightning, that would justify the belief that an umbrella was needed, even though the rain appears only later. Increased experience with thunderstorms may furnish awareness of additional factors in the chain of events that affect the accuracy of weather predictions, such as the shape of cloud formations, a drop in barometric pressure, and an increase in humidity. Accordingly, children draw on past experiences to acquire a more complete understanding of how the outcome of a natural event is affected by experience of additional factors that lead to a change in their beliefs about the causes and order in which the event occurs.

Reconciling Different Perspectives

Finally, not only do children benefit differently from the same experiences, as discussed in Chapter 5, but they also come away from those experiences with contrasting interpretations of their meaning or significance. There seems to be a leap in reflective capacity involved in the transition from knowing that other people sometimes get things wrong involving instances of false belief to the view that the validity of knowledge depends on whether one's interpretation of the facts and beliefs are warranted. As Lalonde and Chandler (2002) observe, there are at least two intermediate stages—one involving the notion that there is more than one way to be wrong, and the other involving the view that there is more than one way to get something right. Exploiting the degenerate structure and recursive nature of behavior, thought, and language traverses these intermediate stages of recognition. Children learn that there is more than one way to be wrong by noticing that an excessive number of movements or gestures do not necessarily result in fulfilling their desires or attaining their goals. Their movements must be coordinated and synchronized to reach a rattle or other desired object. Things get more complicated when infants realize that success cannot be duplicated if the physical surroundings are different or if the context changes. Under these conditions, they must devise alternative solutions to attain the same goal. After the onset of language, they are able to distinguish between their own beliefs and desires and those possessed by other people. Language and syntax enable them to modify the perspective (i.e., first, second, and third person) and temporal standpoint (through memory), by which they characterize their own actions and intentions. Subsequently they are able to assess other individuals' actions, beliefs, and intentions, and to understand how their own behavior is perceived by someone else. Their eventual success in grasping the possibility of multiple and conflicting interpretations appears to depend on how much experience they acquire using language and communicating in situations involving complex social interactions. Enrichment at this level is essential to further gains in reflective self-consciousness.

ARE CHILDREN CARTESIAN DUALISTS?

A considerable amount of space in this book has been consumed with rejecting mind-body dualism, arguing instead that our minds are embodied and that consciousness is the outcome of brain-based functional processes. Nevertheless, developmental psychologist Bloom (2004) insists that babies and adults alike are natural born dualists. The human bias toward dualism is evidenced by children's apparent categorical differentiation between physical objects and intentional minds. To buttress his argument, Bloom cites numerous studies that indicate children tend to view their own identity nearly exclusively in terms of mind and mental states than in terms of brain and neural processes. I think it is worth describing the findings of some of these experimental studies in more detail because they strongly suggest that this proclivity may be more a function of culture, age, and ignorance of brain function rather than an innate predisposition.

Infancy and the Mind-Brain Dichotomy

In their now classic study, Johnson and Wellman (1982) found that young children undergo developmental changes in the way they conceive the distinction between *mind* and *brain*. Four- and 5-year-olds do not differentiate between the two terms and believe that both entities are necessary for mental, but not sensorimotor, actions. Nevertheless, older children begin to make ontological distinctions between mind and the brain that grant equal roles to mind and brain in determining behavior. Unlike their younger counterparts, 7- to 9-year-olds conceive of the brain as functionally interconnected to body parts. They believe that the mind would not exist without a brain, but they do not believe that thinking is involved in involuntary behavior. They also seem infer the existence of imperceptible cognitive processes such as memory and attention underlying mental events.

Children's inclination to equate personal identity with mind rather than with the brain may reflect the fact that adults, when referring to mental states, use the word *brain* infrequently. The word *mind* often appears in expressions that connote disembodiment, such as *losing your mind, out of your mind, mindless, mind-blowing*, and *absent mindedness*. Children receive much more information about the mind in linguistic expressions than about the brain. Consequently, much of the language they use conveys their knowledge and beliefs that the mind, not the brain, is the repository of personal memories (Corriveau, Pasquini, & Harris, 2005). Metaphorical mentalistic expressions can be confusing for young children because they establish causal relationships that are spurious, such as the heart being the seat of emotion (Gottfried & Jow, 2003). The language about mind is misleading because psychological states are characterized as being caused by the mind rather than by the brain. This biased input predisposes children to conceive of the mind as the site of enduring memories even when the mind occupies a different body and brain.

For example, when asked to imagine what a pig would look like and feel like with a human mind, 3- and 4-year-olds believed that the pig would still look and feel like a pig. In contrast, older children believed that, although the pig's appearance would remain unchanged, the pig would act, think, and feel like a child (Johnson, 1990). These judgments are strongly rooted in the belief that the mind is disembodied and not susceptible to physical influences. There is an age-based progression in children's understanding of the role of the brain in establishing identity. Five-year-olds experience difficulty in deciding whether the mind and brain possess material or nonmaterial properties and whether something that is nonphysical can occupy a physical body or organ. Only 7-year-olds view the brain as essential to personal continuity and the capacity to retain memories as constituting personal identity (Corriveau et al., 2005).

Metaphors About Mind and Brain

Linguistic practices and cultural biases strongly influence the development of children's conceptualization of brain function. This predisposes them to adopt the so-called adult notion of the brain as a passive container for the storage of memories, rather than as an active, malleable mechanism involved in the experience-dependent production and integration of thought and behavior (Gibbs & O'Brien, 1990). This notion of containment, a North American construct not shared by Far Eastern cultures, conceives individual consciousness in terms of the contents of thoughts and memories, instead of a process in which sensorimotor functions become integrated. Children are considered to have acquired this adult conception of the mind and brain when they recognize that the memory and identity of an individual whose brain has been transplanted into another individual will retain those memories and identity even though it resides in a different body. However, one cannot assume that memory and identity remain unchanged in imaginary transplants because the brain inhabits a new body, which retrieves experience entirely differently than the previous one. The essential point in these thought experiments that is usually overlooked is that the mind and brain are embodied.

Children appear to undergo a transition in their beliefs about what the brain does that reflects their increased exposure to dominant metaphors about the brain. Although 3- and 4-year-olds do not understand the relationship between the brain and motor control, they do seem to possess the generalized notion that the brain animates thought. Studies of children at this age report that they view the brain as if it were a battery that enables thinking to be turned on and off at will (Gottfried et al., 1999; Gottfried &

Jow, 2003). This suggests that young children have an incipient notion that the brain causes mental states that should not be construed as an error that they eventually outgrow. Nonetheless, it is evident that children are prone to uncritically adopt metaphors that can be misleading.

Mentalistic metaphors, which maintain the artificial separation between mind and brain, may interfere with the child's comprehension of the interdependence of mind and brain. Gottfried et al. (1999) report that, by third grade, children demonstrate a major shift in understanding that the mind and brain are not completely independent of one another, as first graders believe, but are interdependent (i.e., one can't exist without the other). This distinction is ontological in the sense that mental processes are thought to occur *in* the brain, but does not imply any awareness of the functional relationship between perception and action. It is possible that the metaphor of containment enables older children to reconcile their earlier beliefs about the separateness of mind and brain by allowing them to posit abstract entities, such as thoughts and memories, in a physical, material receptacle. They then construe the mind as causally dependent on the brain, in the sense of releasing memories from storage that does not require them to posit any interaction between mind and brain. They also come to see that the brain is necessarily involved in both voluntary and involuntary behavior, although the mind and thinking are not considered to be involved in intentional, motor movements (Johnson & Wellman, 1982).

Contrary to Bloom's assertions, however, young children's understanding of the relationship between mind and brain undergoes a conceptual change that is driven by knowledge and culturally bound linguistic practices. Children initially adopt a naive dualism that reflects their limited knowledge of biological functions. As their knowledge of the biological attributes of brains increases and they are exposed to new words for describing how the brain processes thoughts and stores memories, they acquire the notion that mind and thought are dependent on the brain. There remains, of course, much more to learn about brain-mind and brain-behavior relationships that extend well beyond the preschool years. Nevertheless, a growing body of research, discussed in previous chapters, suggests that 4- to 6-year-olds could become familiarized sooner with a dynamical conception of the brain—one that would coincide with and complement their budding theory of mind. This would have strategic value in enabling children to appreciate that an embodied mind and brain are susceptible to reorganization and reintegration through intentional behavior, and that changing the way we perceive the world alters our beliefs about it (Koizumi, 2004).

Recursion Versus Containment

Perhaps the biggest obstacle to the early acquisition of a dynamic, experience-dependent conception of the brain is the metaphor of containment implicated in the notion that the brain is a storage facility for memories. There is plausible evidence, presented in this book, that there is a continuous trade-off in the brain between certitude and ambiguity, and that the best the brain can do is reconstruct events rather than duplicate them in their entirety. Memory is not veridical, but contextual and time-sensitive. Memory works best when there are multiple forms of access to and retrieval of experientially generated sensory information. That is why the word *recursion* better describes the dynamic nature of neural processes than the term *containment*. Recursion is the brain's solution to overcoming the anatomical limits to circumference and volume by enabling the brain to continuously sample experiential input contextually through alternative sensory pathways involving different levels of neuronal group density and topographical complexity. Recursion multiplies exponentially the power of the brain to do mental work by exploiting the vast interconnectivty that supports alternative interpretations of the same experiences. Plasticity is the brain's method of ensuring flexibility through self-modification and degeneracy, or the possession of more than one way (i.e., through bilateralism) to attain the same outcome. Selection through competition enables the brain to forge temporary connections between brain regions through processes of confinement and correlation, rather than conflict and elimination. Children who possess knowledge of these principles are more likely to benefit from learning strategies, which focus on how to flexibly integrate modes of sensory stimulation and retrieval to increase their conscious control of their behavior.

EDUCATIONAL STRATEGIES

Head Start and the IQ Debate

In the early 1960s, national policymakers moved in the direction of embracing an experiential and dynamic view of early brain development and learning. However, the evolution of Head Start preschool programs illustrates how easy it is for policymakers to become trapped into thinking that learning can be measured exclusively in terms of cognition. Head Start was originally created to mitigate the adverse affects of poverty on learning by providing compensatory programs designed to overcome social, economic, health, and family-related barriers to learning. The broad goal was enrichment to enhance individual motor, cognitive, and emotional development. Unfortunately, during the first decade of Head Start, when there were strong pressures to produce immediate results, social scientists increasingly relied on standard measures of intelligence to document program performance. When initial evaluations reported as much as 10-point gains in intelligence quotients (IQs), it became increasingly difficult politically to oppose the continued reliance on IQ as a measure of program success. Only later, when it became clear that increases in IQ were only temporary and disappeared, as Head Start children advanced through elementary school, did this method of program evaluation become a liability for program administrators (Zigler & Meunchow, 1999).

Early Head Start: Development, Learning, and Social Competence

Perhaps the most creditable evidence that Head Start and related programs have succeeded in demonstrating a strong relationship between development and learning comes from a recent control group evaluation of Early Head Start. Begun in 1995 to serve low-income families with infants and toddlers, Early Head Start is a comprehensive dual-generation program designed to enhance children's development and increase parental involvement in their children's learning while strengthening families. The experimental intervention consisted of three different models: a center-based approach, in which all interaction took place away from home; a mixed approach involving a combination of center-based activities and home visits; and an exclusively home-based model. At the time of the evaluation, there were 700 funded programs nationwide. The evaluation consisted of a randomized trial of 3,001 families in 17 programs.

The results are consistent with data discussed in previous chapters underscoring the significant roles that joint attention and communicative interaction play in a child's early development of language, narrative skills, and theory of mind. In their study, Love et al. (20005) found that 3-year-old children performed better in both cognitive and language development, displayed more emotional engagement with parents, sustained attention longer during play, and showed less aggressive behavior than did control children. When compared with their counterpart controls, Early Head Start parents provided more emotional support, provided more stimulation in language use and learning, read more to their children, and spanked them less. More important, the strongest and most impressive gains based on these measures occurred in programs that offered a mix of center-based and home-visiting models.

The Conundrum of Performance

Head Start persists as one of this nation's longest running social experiments because it reflects the widespread belief that early experience can make a difference in children's ability to learn. Nevertheless, as children enter K-12, the utilization of scientifically based knowledge of child development is sidelined by the nearly exclusive emphasis on cognition. The most striking and ironical consequence of this is the growing number of school children who, nearing graduation, fail to demonstrate even a minimum level of competence in language, reading comprehension, and mathematics. The failure of the American educational system to produce a workforce that meets basic standards of literacy, and one that attains proficiency in math and science, threatens the economic competitiveness and future security of the nation. Unfortunately, anxious policymakers have chosen to respond to this threat by pursuing dubious methods of securing accountability among educators for student learning outcomes.

The current reliance on so-called high-stakes tests results in a measurement-driven instructional strategy that is showing signs of homogenizing an otherwise heterogeneous curriculum. But it also risks imposing a much more insidious outcome—a unitary conception of learning. A test-based pedagogy conceives of children as passive recipients of knowledge whose success in learning is determined solely by how much information they can absorb and how quickly they can retrieve it to find the correct answer (Kornhaber & Orfield, 2001). Not only is this conception of learning based on whether information is retained or stored for eventual recall (the containment model of memory and the brain), but it forces students to confine their attention to a more restricted realm of information than that afforded by active exploration and social interaction. Children snared in these learning regimes are unlikely to develop problem-solving skills in situations involving uncertainty and novelty that confront individuals and organizations, which together must anticipate and creatively respond to future economic and social contingencies.

FORGING A SCIENCE AND EDUCATION NETWORK

The challenge to bring science to bear on educational practice is not unprecedented. Educators, parents, and policymakers confronted a similar situation in the 1920s and 1930s, when the heredity verses environment debate came to a head and the public looked to science for answers (Dennis, 1995). Significantly, an extraordinary partnership was forged among philanthropic foundations, educational advocates, parent groups, and researchers intended to ground educational practice in the principles of developmental science. Describing this historically significant initiative in more detail is worthwhile because it is pertinent to assessing recent attempts to secure public support for educational reform.

The Rockefeller and Macy Foundation Interdisciplinary Initiatives

While an officer of the Rockefeller Foundation in the 1920s, Lawrence K. Frank, a student and protégé of John Dewey, spearheaded a remarkable effort to create a child study network. Frank's (1962) successful organization of an international and interdisciplinary network of academically based researchers demonstrated a foresight unparalleled today. Frank sought to create through this network of academic institutes at Columbia, Iowa, Berkeley, Minnesota, Yale, and other universities an alliance between parent groups and researchers that would widely disseminate knowledge about child development, arousing public support for more innovative approaches to learning and childrearing. Frank also succeeded in persuading social scientists to form a professional society dedicated to interdisciplinary developmental research. The *Society for Research in Child Development*, established in 1933, continues to flourish today under leaders and members who occupy strategic positions in government agencies and commissions. Dewey, a founding board member of the Josiah Macy, Jr., Foundation (1930-1944), and Frank, Vice President from 1936 to 1941, continued their efforts to promote interdisciplinary research and sponsor conferences designed to synthesize the latest knowledge about the relationship among mind, brain, and behavior (Dalton & Baars, 2003).

Dewey and Frank construed interdisciplinary research broadly to involve collaboration among scientists from different fields who are committed to integrated methods of inquiry. Hopkins (2005) perceptively observes that interdisciplinary research should be carefully distinguished from multi- and cross-disciplinary variants. *Interdisciplinarity* involves disciplines working together on a common problem with the explicit goal of adapting theory and methods to establish a broader perspective. A common language is adopted, and an effort is made to develop generalizations based on convergent findings. *Multidisciplinarity* involves different disciplines working on a common problem, but does not involve adjustments in theory or methods. More weight is given to divergent findings that limit the susceptibility of a problem to an integrated solution. *Cross-disciplinarity* represents an even more limited from of collaboration than the other two. Researchers may choose to work temporarily in a discipline outside their chosen field or obtain training in another field to supplement knowledge acquired elsewhere. The pioneers in the field of developmental science came from many disciplinary backgrounds, including embryology, ethology, comparative psychology, and the biological sciences. Through their combined efforts, they adopted new perspectives and forged innovative theories grounded in the experimental study of infants and young children (Oppenheim, 1992).

In constructing this interdisciplinary network, Frank pursued a holistic Deweyan goal of reconstructing the relationship between science and society (Dalton, 2002). Frank recommended the creation of a prototype of a laboratory nursery school that essentially fulfilled the aims first envisioned by Dewey at his laboratory school at the University of Chicago in 1896. It would provide an observational laboratory for researchers, a training school for teachers and child-care workers, and a demonstration center for parents. Frank (1924) advised that the program of child and parent education be based on the Deweyan philosophy of "learn by doing, where the working out of a project empirically is emphasized rather than the study of principles and where observation of actual procedure looms more important than study from books" (p. 3). Teacher's College was the first recipient of a grant from the Laura Spelman Rockefeller Memorial to establish a laboratory nursery school, and many others followed that conducted longitudinal studies of growth and learning.

Frank's holistic model was based on Dewey's interactionist conception of mind and experience. The university-based child study institutes were allowed to pursue different research strategies and given flexibility to decide which specific programs should be implemented, as long as they focused on common developmental problems and issues. Flexible relationships or partnerships could be forged between institutes and parent-run community programs that facilitated the reciprocal flow of information. In practical terms, this reciprocal interactionist model enabled initiative and innovation to emerge from almost any part of the system without altering the overall focus and direction. For example, parent groups might provide special experiential insights that lead researchers to refine their studies, or teachers might provide valuable feedback regarding successes or failures in adapting childrearing methods to accommodate new knowledge. Clearly, no one element was intended to dominate the others, but all were to engage in a collaborative and constructive interaction, blending knowledge and experience into effective educational strategies. Head start programs, among other public and private child care services, may still provide the best community-based laboratories to bring different constituencies together to sponsor interdisciplinary studies of how early experience influences the brain. Head Start enrolls children during a crucial period of neurobehavioral and psychological development that needs to be better understood.

Private and Public Sector Partnerships

An ambitious initiative of this kind clearly requires that partnerships be formed and sustained that cut across constituencies with different goals and interests. Forming communities that pursue common interests must overcome many hurdles involving differences in professional perspective, experience, specialization, and political accountability, to name just a few factors. Collaborative ventures involving bisectoral partnerships with shared but limited goals have predominated. In this regard, philanthropic foundations have sponsored the development of research networks with limited cross-disciplinary collaboration dedicated to basic research on the relationship between brain function and learning. For example, since 1998, the John D. and Catherine T. MacArthur Foundation and the James S. McDonnell Foundation have sponsored a network of developmental scientists representing different fields to study how experience affects brain development. Since 1994, the Swartz and Sloan Foundations have co-sponsored five centers for theoretical computational neurobiology that seek to develop an integrated approach to understanding brain function. But neuroscientists remain divided, as noted in Chapter 1, about which theoretical perspectives regarding brain function show the most promise in generating successful strategies of learning. There are also numerous private, nonprofit organizations that focus more on applied research dedicated to treating and preventing brain-based learning disorders, such as dyslexia and autism. These organizations tend to adopt a strategy of advocacy and mobilization that engages special interests, such as parent groups, in public policies intended to remedy a specific disorder.

Only rarely do educators obtain the knowledge and tools to apply the latest neuroscientific advances to classroom teaching (Bruer, 1997). After years of scientific research on sound-recognition disorders, Michael

Merzenich, Paula Tallal, and their collaborators formed Scientific Learning, a corporation that markets Fast Forward, a computerized program that helps dyslexic children learn how to read. They have also created a Web site, *BrainConnection.com*, which provides educators with an analysis of the educational implications of the latest neuroscientific research and regularly schedules training sessions for interested educators, clinicians, and parents.

Despite these occasional breakthroughs, the goal of translating basic research into applied knowledge remains largely unfulfilled. Mindful of this gap between theory and practice, the National Academy of Sciences sponsored two important volumes that attempt to synthesize scientific knowledge about experience and the brain and demonstrate how it can be incorporated into child-care and educational practices. *From Neurons to Neighborhoods: The Science of Early Childhood Development* (Shonkoff & Phillips, 2000) presented a synthesis of early intervention program evaluations based on the input of a panel of experts in the developmental sciences. This volume presents a masterful analysis of the implications that this research poses for how best to organize and implement child-care programs. In another volume, *How People Learn: Brain, Mind, Experience and School*, Bransford, Brown, and Cocking (2000) demonstrate how knowledge about the brain can be used to teach early classes in science and math. Blakemore and Frith (2005), who are neuroscientists, undertook a more persuasive and accessible effort to provide a highly accessible description of showing how neural processes contribute to success and failure to learn resulting from dysfunctional brains.

Initiatives involving multiple sector partners have been mounted recently by the National Science Foundation, which formed an alliance with several major foundations, corporations and universities. That support special K-12 projects. These projects are designed to reverse the dramatic decline in students in the United States who pursue degrees in science, engineering and technology (Dalton, 2002) In 2004, the NSF launched a multimillion dollar initiative to create four Science of Learning Centers at Dartmouth, Boston University, Carnegie Mellon University the University of Washington. These centers seek to convert new discoveries about the brain into usable classroom techniques that will enable teachers to increase the educational attainments of their students. On the whole, these special programs need to make more use of scientific knowledge about the brain to improve learning outcomes among students. Teachers need to be persuaded by scientists that brain-based techniques can be employed that will affect how children attend to, access, retrieve, and remember experiences that enhance learning. The problem is that there is little consensus among scientists about what constitutes learning and how to define knowledge.

To be successful, strategies such as these must embrace the notion that learning involves the body, brain and mind simultaneously. Infants and young children acquire skills that are not apparent in the initial stages of learning but emerge from an interrelated series of neurobehavioral and neuropsychological reconstructions involving different degrees of complexity and integration. The capacities to vary behavioral and emotional response play critical roles in children's cognitive achievements. Children must be able to discover more than one solution to each problem. They must also be capable of emotional engagement and detachment and be willing to scrutinize their beliefs. The flexible adoption of different attitudes frees energy for reconnoitering a problem from a new perspective that may result in its resolution.

Neuroscience has become a powerful tool in revealing how the developmental pathways involving the brain, mind and behavior are integrated. Further advances in understanding how infants and children learn will depend increasingly on knowledge about how the brain develops, how it is organized and how it adapts to unforeseen situations. Theory and evidence go hand in hand. In our opinion, theoretical perspectives that yield new discoveries will be ones that squarely confront and critically examine epistemological assumptions about the relationship between perception, knowledge and learning discussed in this book. These philosophical commitments must be given the same level of scrutiny as is now accorded the evidence regarding the developmental basis of infant learning. We believe that increased philosophical and scientific self-consciousness will lead to a new level of rigor in our understanding of the neuropsychological foundations of human experience and learning.

References

Als, H., Duffy, F. H., McAnulty, G. B., Rivkin, M. J., Vajapeyam S., Mulkern, R.V., Warielf, S. K., Huppi, P., Butler, S. C., Conneman, N., Fischer, C., & Eichenwald, E. C. (2004). Early experience alters brain function and structure. *Pediatrics, 113,* 846–857.

Amano, S., Kezuka, E., & Yamamoto, A. (2004). Infant shifting attention from an adult's face to an adult's hand: A precursor of joint attention. *Infant Behavior and Development, 27,* 64–80.

Anderson, D. L., Campos, J. J., & Barbu-Roth, M. A. (2004). A developmental perspective on visual proprioception. In P. Bremner & C. Slater (Eds.), *Theories of infant development* (pp. 30–69). New York: Blackwell.

Anisfeld, M., Turkewitz, G., Rose, S. A., Rosenberg, F. R., Sheiber, F. J., Couturier-Fagan, D. A., Ger, J. S., & Sommer, I. (2001). No compelling evidence that newborns imitate oral gestures. *Infancy, 2,* 111–122.

Avillac, M., Deneve, S., Olivier, E., Pouget, A., & Duhamel, J.-R. (2005). Reference frames for representing visual and tactile locations in the parietal cortex. *Nature Neuroscience, 8,* 941–949.

Ayers, A. J. (1972). *Sensory integration and learning disorders.* Los Angeles: Western Psychological Services.

Bahrick, L. (1992). Infants' perceptual differentiation of amodal and modality-specific audiovisual relations. *Journal of Experimental Child Psychology, 53,* 180–199.

Bahrick, L. (1994). The development of infants' sensitivity to arbitrary intermodal relations. *Ecological Psychology, 6,* 111–123.

Bahrick, L., Flom, R., & Lickliter, R. (2002). Intersensory redundancy facilitates discrimination of tempo in 3–month-old infants. *Developmental Psychobiology, 41,* 352–363.

Bahrick, L., & Pickens, J. (1994). Amodal relations: The basis for intermodal perception and learning in infancy. In D. Lewkowicz & R. Lickliter (Eds.), *The development of intersensory perception* (pp. 205–233). Hillsdale, NJ: Lawrence Erlbaum Associates.

Bahrick, L. E., & Lickliter, R. (2000). Intersensory redundancy guides attentional selectivity and perceptual learning in infancy. *Developmental Psychology, 36,* 190–201.

Baldwin, D. A. (1993). Early referential understanding: Infants' ability to recognize referential acts for what they are. *Developmental Psychology, 29,* 832–843.

Baldwin, D. A., & Baird, J. A. (2001). Discerning intentions in dynamic human action. *Trends in Cognitive Sciences, 5,* 171–178.

Baron-Cohen, S. (1999). Does the study of autism justify minimalist innate modularity? *Learning and Individual Differences, 10,* 179–191.

Barresi, J., & Moore, C. (1996). Intentional relations and social understanding. *Behavioral and Brain Sciences, 19,* 107–154.

Bartsch, K., & Wellman, H. M. (1995). *Children talk about mind.* New York: Oxford University Press.

Bauer, P. (2004). Getting explicit memory off the ground: Steps toward construction of a neuro-developmental account of changes in the first two years of life. *Developmental Review, 24,* 347–373.

Bear, M., Huber, K. M. & Warren, S. T. (2004). The mGluR theory of fragile X mental retardation. *Trends in Neurosciences, 27,* 370–377.

Beilin, H. (1994). Jean Piaget's enduring contribution to developmental psychology. In R. D. Parke, P. A. Ornstein, J. Rieser, & C. Zahn-Waxler (Eds.), *A century of developmental psychology* (pp. 257–290). Washington, DC: American Psychological Association.

Bell, M. A. (1998). Frontal lobe function during infancy: Implications for the development of cognition and attention. In J. E. Richards (Ed.), *Cognitive neuroscience of attention: A developmental perspective* (pp. 287–315). Mahwah, NJ: Lawrence Erlbaum Associates.

Bell, M. A., & Fox, N. A. (1994). Brain development over the first year of life: Relations between electroencephalographic frequency and coherence and cognitive and affective behaviors. In G. Dawson & K. W. Fischer (Eds.), *Human behavior and the developing brain* (pp. 314–345). New York: Guilford.

Ben-Ari, Y. (2001). Developing networks play a similar melody. *Trends in Neurosciences, 24,* 353–360.

Benes, F. M. (1997). Cortiolimbic circuitry and the development of psychopathology during childhood and adolescence. In N. Krasnegor, G. Lyon, & P. Goldman-Rakic (Eds.), *Development of the prefrontal cortex: Evolution, neurobiology and behavior* (pp. 85–116). Baltimore: Paul H. Brookes.

Beretta, A., Fiorentino, R., & Poeppel, D. (2005). The effects of homonymy and polysemy on lexical access: An MEG study. *Cognitive Brain Research, 24,* 57–65.

Berthoz, A. (2000). *The brain's sense of movement.* Cambridge, MA: Harvard University Press.

Bhutta, A. T. & Anand, K. J. S. (2001). Abnormal cognition and behavior in preterm neonates linked to smaller brain volumes. *Trends in Neurosciences, 24,* 129–130.

Bhutta, A T., Cleves, M. A., Casey, P. H., Cradock, M. M., & Anand, K. J. (2002). Cognitive and behavioral outcomes of school-aged children who were born preterm: A meta-analysis. *Journal of American Medical Association, 288,* 728–737.

Birch, S. A. J., & Bloom, P. (2004). Understanding children's and adult's limitations in mental state reasoning. *Trends in Cognitive Sciences, 8,* 255–260.

Black, J. E., & Greenough, W. T. (1998). Developmental approaches to the memory process. In J. Martinez & R. Kesner (Eds.), *Neurobiology of learning and memory* (pp. 55–88). New York: Academic Press.

Blakemore, S. J., & Frith, U. (2005). *The learning brain: Lessons for education.* Oxford: Blackwell.

Blank, R. H. (1999). *Brain policy: How the new neuroscience will change our lives and our politics.* Washington, DC: Georgetown University Press.

Bliss, T. V. P., & Lomo, T. (1973). Long-lasting potentiation of synaptic transmission in the dentate area of the anesthetized rabbit following stimulation of the preforant path. *Journal of Physiology, 232,* 331–356.

Bloom, P. (2004). Descartes' Baby: How the science of child development explains what makes us human. New York: Basic Books.

Borbely, A. A. (1982). A two-process model of sleep regulation. *Human Neurobiology, 1,* 195–201.

Botvinick, M. M., Cohen, J. D., & Carter, C. S. (2004). Conflict monitoring and anterior cingulate cortex: An update. *Trends in Cognitive Sciences, 8,* 639–646.

Bourgeois, J.-P. (1997). Synaptogenesis, heterochrony and epigenesis in the mammalian neocortex. *Acta Paediactrica, 86*(Suppl. 422), 27–33.

Bourgeois, J.-P. (2002). Synaptogenesis in the neocortex of the newborn: The ultimate frontier for individuation? In H. Lagercrantz, M. Hanson, P. Evrard, & C. Rodeck (Eds.), *The newborn brain: Neuroscience and clinical applications* (pp. 91–113). Cambridge, England: Cambridge University Press.

Bowerman, M. (1978). Systematizing semantic knowledge: Change over time in the child's organization of word meaning. *Child Development, 49,* 977–987.

Bransford, J. D., Brown, A. L., & Cocking, R. R. (Eds.). (2000). *How people learn: Brain, mind, experience and school* (exp. ed.). Washington, DC: National Academy Press.

Braver, T. S., Barch, D. M., Kelley, W. M., Buckner, R. L., Cohen, N. J., Miezin, F. M, Snyder, A. Z., Oliner, J. M., Akbudak, E., Conturo, T. E., & Petersen, S. E. (2001). Direct comparison of prefrontal cortex regions engaged by working and long-term memory tasks. *Neuroimage, 14,* 48–59.

Bruer, J. T. (1997). Education and the brain: A bridge too far. *Educational Researcher, 26,* 4–16.

Bruer, J. T., & Greenough, W. T. (2001). The subtle science of how experience affects the brain. In D. B. Bailey, Jr., J. T. Bruer, F. J. Symons, & J. W. Lichtman (Eds.), *Critical thinking about critical periods* (pp. 209–232). Baltimore: Paul H. Brookes.

Cabeza, R., Dolcos, F., Graham, R., & Nyberg, L. (2002). Similarities and differences in the neural correlates of episodic memory retrieval and working memory. *Neuroimage, 16,* 317–330.

Cabeza, R., Dolcos, F., Prince, S. E., Rice, H. J., Weissman, D. H., & Nyberg, L. (2003). Attention-related activity during episodic memory retrieval: A cross-function fMRI study. *Neuropsychologia, 41,* 390–399.

Cabeza, R., & Nyberg, L. (2000). Imaging cognition: II. An empirical review of 275 PET and fMRI studies. *Journal of Cognitive Neuroscience, 12,* 1–47.

Cabeza, R., & Nyberg, L. (2002). Seeing the forest through the trees: The cross-functional approach to imaging cognition. In A. Zani & A. M. Proverbio (Eds.), *The cognitive electrophysiology of mind and brain* (pp. 41–68). Amsterdam: Elsevier.

Calvert, G. A., & Thesen, T. (2004). Multisensory integration: Methodological approaches and emerging principles in the human brain. *Journal of Physiology, 98,* 191–205.

Campos, J. J., Anderson, D. I., Barbu-Roth, M. A., Hubbard, E. M., Jertenstein, J. J., & Witherington, D. (2000). Travel broadens the mind. *Infancy, 1,* 149–219.

Campos, J., Bertenthal, B. J. & Kermoian, R. (1992). Early experience and emotional development: The emergence of wariness of heights. *Psychological Science, 3,* 61–64.

Caplovitz-Barrett, K., Campos, J. J., & Emde, R. N. (1996). Infants' use of conflicting emotion signals. *Cognition and Emotion, 10,* 113–135.

Cariani, P. (1997). Emergence of new signal-primitives in neural systems. *Intellectica, 2,* 95–143.

Carpendale, J. I. M. & Chandler, M. J. (1996). On the distinction between false belief understanding and subscribing to an interpretive theory of mind. *Child Development, 67,* 1686–706.

Carpenter, M., Nagel, K., & Tomasello, M. (1998). Social cognition, joint attention and communicative competence from 9-15 months of age. *Monographs in the Society for Research in Child Development, 63*(4, Serial No. 255).

Casey, B. J., Durston, S. & Fossella, J. A. (2001). Evidence for a mechanistic model of cognitive control. *Clinical Neuroscience Research, 1,* 267–282.

Castelli, F., Happe, F., Frith, U., & Frith, C. (2002). Movement and mind: A functional imaging study of perception and interpretation of complex intentional movement patterns. *Neuroimage, 12,* 314–325.

Chaminade, T., Meltzoff, A. N., & Decety, J. (2005). An fMRI study of imitation: Action representation and body schema. *Neuropsychologia, 43,* 115–127.

Chandana, S. R., Behen, M. E., Juhász, C., Muzik, O., Rothermel, R. D., Mangner, T. J., Chakraborty, P. K., Harry, T., & Chugani. D. C. (2005). Significance of abnormalities in developmental trajectory and asymmetry of cortical serotonin synthesis in autism. *International Journal of Developmental Neuroscience, 23,* 171–182.

Choi, S. (2000). Caregiver input in English and Korean: Use of nouns and verbs in book-reading and toy-play contexts. *Journal of Child Language, 27,* 69–96.

Chugani, H. T. (1996). Neuroimaging of developmental nonlinearity and developmental pathologies. In R. W. Thatcher, G. Reid Lyon, J. Rumsey, & N. Kransnegor (Eds.), *Developmental neuroimaging: Mapping the development of the brain and behavior* (pp. 187–196). San Diego: Academic Press.

Clark, E. V. (2004). How language acquisition builds on cognitive development. *Trends in Cognitive Sciences, 8,* 472–478.

Coghill, G. E. (1926). The mechanism of integration in *Amblystoma punctatum. Journal of Comparative Neurology, 41,* 95–152.

Coghill, G. E. (1929). *Anatomy and the problem of behavior.* New York: Hafner.

Coghill, G. E. (1930). The structural basis of the integration of behavior. *Proceedings of the National Academy of Sciences, 16,* 637–643.

Coghill, G. E. (1933). The neuroembryonic study of behavior: Principles, perspectives and aims. *Science, 78,* 131–138.

Conel, L. (1939). *The post-natal development of the human cerebral cortex: Vol. 1. Cortex of the newborn.* Cambridge, MA: Harvard University Press.

Cooper, S. J. (2005). Donald O. Hebb's synapse and learning rule: A history and commentary. *Neuroscience and Biobehavioral Reviews, 28,* 851–874.

Corbetta, M., Akbudak, E., Conturo, T. E., Snyder, A. Z., Ollinger, J. M., Drury, H. A., Linenweber, M. R., Petersen, S. E., Raichle, M. E., Van Essen, D. C., & Schulman, G. A. (1998). Frontoparietal cortical networks for directing attention and eye movements. *Neuron, 21,* 761–773.

Correia, M. J. (1998). Neuronal plasticity: Adaptation and re-adaptation to the environment of space. *Brain Research Reviews, 28,* 61–65.

Corriveau, K. H., Pasquini, E. S., & Harris, P. L. (2005). "If it's in your mind, it's in your knowledge": Children's developing anatomy of identity. *Cognitive Development, 20*, 321–340.

Courchesne, E., & Karen Pierce, K. (2005). Why the frontal cortex in autism might be talking only to itself: Local over-connectivity but long-distance disconnection. *Current Opinion in Neurobiology, 15*, 225–230.

Courchesne, E., Yeung-Courchesne, R., & Pierce, K. (1999). Biological and behavioral heterogeneity in autism: Role of pleiotropy and epigenesis. In S. Broman & J. Fletcher (Eds.), *The changing nervous system: Neurobehavioral consequences of early brain disorders* (pp. 292–338). New York: Oxford University Press.

Culp, A. M., Osofsky, J. D., & O'Brien, M. (1996). Language patterns of adolescent and older mothers and their one-year-old children: A comparison study. *First Language, 16*, 61–76.

Dalton, T. C. (1996). Was McGraw a maturationist? *American Psychologist, 51*, 551–552.

Dalton, T. C. (1998). Myrtle McGraw's neurobehavioral theory of development. *Developmental Review, 18*, 472–503.

Dalton, T. C. (2000). The developmental roots of consciousness and emotional experience. *Consciousness and Emotion, 1*, 57–91.

Dalton, T. C. (2002a). *Becoming John Dewey: Dilemmas of a philosopher and naturalist.* Bloomington: Indiana University Press.

Dalton, T. C. (2002b). Arnold Gesell and the maturation controversy. *From Past to Future. Clark Papers on the History of Psychology, 3*, 7–31.

Dalton, T. C. (2005). Challenging philosophical assumptions about mind. *Trends in Cognitive Sciences, 9*, 356–365.

Dalton, T. C., & Baars, B. (2003). Consciousness regained: The scientific restoration of mind and brain. In T. C. Dalton & R. B. Evans (Eds.), *The life cycle of psychological ideas: Understanding prominence and the dynamics of intellectual change* (pp. 203–250). New York: Kluwer/Academic Plenum.

Dalton, T. C., & Bergenn, V. W. (Eds.). (1995). *Beyond heredity and environment: Myrtle McGraw and the maturation controversy.* Boulder, CO: Westview.

Dalton, T. C., & Bergenn, V. W. (1996). John Dewey, Myrtle McGraw and logic: An unusual collaboration in the 1930s. *Studies in History and Philosophy of Science, 27*, 69–107.

Dammann, V. T. (1941). Developmental changes in attitudes as one factor determining energy output in a motor performance. *Child Development, 12*, 241–246.

Davis, B. E. & Moon, R. Y. (1998). Effects of sleep position on infant motor development. *Pediatrics, 102*, 1135–1141.

Deacon, T.W. (1997). *The symbolic species: The co-evolution of language and the brain.* New York: Norton.

DeCasper, A. J., Lecanuet, J.-P, Busnel, M.-C., Granier-Deferre, C., & Maugeais, R. (1994). Fetal reactions to recurrent maternal speech. *Infant Behavior and Development, 17*, 159–164.

Decety, J., & Sommerville, J. A. (2003). Share representations between self and other: A social cognitive neuroscience view. *Trends in Cognitive Sciences, 7*, 527–533.

de Graff-Peters, V. B., & Hadders-Algra, M. (2006). Ontogeny of the human central nervous system: What is happening when? *Early Human Development, 82*, 257–266.

D'Elia, A., Pighetti, M., Moccia, G., & Santangelo, N. (2001). Spontaneous motor activity in normal fetuses. *Early Human Development, 65*, 139–147.

Dennett, D. C. (1978). Beliefs about beliefs. *Behavioral and Brain Sciences, 1*, 568–570.

Dennis, P. (1989). "Johnny's a Gentleman but Jimmy's a Mug": Press coverage during the 1930's of Myrtle McGraw's study of Johnny and Jimmy Woods. *Journal of the History of the Behavioral Sciences, 25*, 356–370.

Dennis, P. (1995). Johnny and Jimmy and the maturation controversy: Popularization, misunderstanding and setting the record straight. In T. C. Dalton & V. W. Bergenn (Eds.), *Beyond heredity and environment: Myrtle McGraw and the maturation controversy* (pp. 67–76). Boulder: Westview.

Descartes, R. (1985). Treatise on man. In *The Philosophical Writings of Descartes* (J. Cottingham, Trans.,Vol. 1, pp. 99–108). Cambridge: Cambridge University Press. (Original publication 1664)

de villiers, J., & Pyers, J. E. (2002). Complements to cognition: A longitudinal study of the relationship between complex syntax and false-belief-understanding. *Cognitive Development, 17*, 1037–1060.

Dewey, J. (1972). The reflex arc concept in psychology. In J. A. Boydston (Ed.), *John Dewey: The early works* (Vol. 5, pp. 96–110). Carbondale, IL: Southern Illinois University Press. (Original publication 1896)

Dewey, J. (1981). Experience and nature. In J. A. Boydston (Ed.), *John Dewey: The later works* (Vol. 1, pp. 3–328). Carbondale, IL: Southern Illinois University. (Original publication 1925)

Dewey, J. (1989). Art as experience. In J. A. Boydston (Ed.), *John Dewey: The later works, 1925–1953* (Vol. 10, pp. 7–397). Carbondale, IL: Southern Illinois University Press. (Original publication 1934)

DiPietro, J. A., Costigan, K. A., & Pressman, E. K. (2002). Fetal state concordance predicts infant state regulation. *Early Human Development, 68*, 1–13.

Doherty, M. J., & Anderson, J. R. (1999). A new look at gaze: Preschool children's understanding of eye-direction. *Cognitive Development, 14*, 549–571.

Dominey, P. F., & Dodane, C. (2004). Indeterminacy in language acquisition: The role of child directed speech and joint attention. *Journal of Neurolinguistics, 17*, 121–145.

Edelman, G. M. (1974). The problem of molecular recognition by a selective system. In F. J. Ayala & T. Dobzhansky (Eds.), *Studies in the philosophy of biology*. London: Macmillan.

Edelman, G. M. (1987). *Neural Darwinism: The theory of neuronal group selection*. New York: Basic Books.

Edelman, G. M. (1989). *The remembered present: A biological theory of consciousness*. New York: Basic Books.

Edelman, G. M. (2003). Naturalizing consciousness: A theoretical framework. *Proceedings of the National Academy of Sciences, 100*, 5520–5524.

Edelman, G. M. (2004). *Wider than the sky: The phenomenal gift of consciousness*. New Haven, CT: Yale University Press.

Edelman, G. M. (2006). *Second nature: Brain science and human nature*. New Haven, CT: Yale University Press.

Edelman, G. M., & Gally, J. (2001). Degeneracy and complexity in biological systems. *Proceedings of the National Academy of Sciences, 98*, 13763–13768.

Elman, J. L. (2004). An alternative view of the mental lexicon. *Trends in Cognitive Sciences, 8,* 301–306.

Elman, J. L., Bates, E. A., Karmiloff-Smith, A., Parisi, D. & Plunkett, K. (1996). *Rethinking innateness: A connectionist perspective on development.* Cambridge, MA: MIT Press.

Faggin, B. M., Nguyen, K. T., & Nicolelis, A. L. (1997). Immediate and simultaneous sensory reorganization at cortical and subcortical levels of the somatosensory system. *Proceedings of the National Academy of Sciences, 94,* 9428–9433.

Ferstl, E. C., & von Cramon, D. Y. (2002). What does the frontomedian cortex contribute to language processing: Coherence or theory of mind? *Neuorimage, 17,* 1599–1612.

Finger, S. (2000). *Minds behind the brain: A history of the pioneers and their discoveries.* New York: Oxford University Press.

Finlay, B. L. (2005). Rethinking developmental neurobiology. In M. Tomasello & D. Slobin (Eds.), *Beyond nature/nurture: Essays in honor of Elizabeth Bates* (pp. 195–218). Mahwah, NJ: Lawrence Erlbaum Associates.

Finlay, B. L., & Darlington, R. B. (1995). Linked regularities in the development and evolution of mammalian brains. *Science, 268,* 1578–1584.

Fischer, K. W., & Bidell, T. R. (1998). Dynamic development of psychological structures of action and thought. In R. Lerner (Ed.), *Handbook of child psychology* (Vol. 1, pp. 457–561). New York: Wiley.

Fischer, K. W. & Rose, S. P. (1994). Dynamic development of coordination of components of brain and behavior: A framework for theory and research. In G. Dawson & K. W. Fischer (Eds.), *Human behavior and the developing brain* (pp. 3–66). New York: Guilford Press.

Flavell, J. H. (2000). Development of children's knowledge about the mental world. *International Journal of Behavioral Development, 24,* 15–23.

Flavell, J. H., Green, F. L., & Flavell, E. R. (1995). Young children's knowledge about thinking. *Monographs of the Society for Research in Child Development, 60* (1, Serial No. 243).

Fodor, J. (1983). *The modularity of mind.* Cambridge, MA: MIT Press/ Bradford Books.

Frank, L. K. (1924, May 23). *Memorandum: Child study and parent training* (Box 315, Subseries 5, Series 3, pp. 1–3). Laura Spelman Rockefeller Memorial, Rockefeller Archive Center, Tarrytown, New York.

Frank, L. K. (1962). The beginnings of child development and family life education in the twentieth century. *The Merrill-Palmer Quarterly of Behavior and Development, 8,* 207–227.

Frank, Y., & Pavlakis, S. G. (2001). Brain imaging in neurobehavioral disorders. *Pediatric Neurology, 25,* 278–287.

Freud, S. (1953a). The unconscious. In J. Strachey (Ed.), *The standard edition of the complete psychological works of Sigmund Freud* (Vol. 14., pp. 161–204). London: Hogarth.

Freud, S. (1953b). Project for a scientific psychology. In J. Strachey (Ed.), *The standard edition of the complete psychological works of Sigmund Freud* (Vol. 1., pp. 1–385). London: Hogarth.

Friederici, A. D. (2005). Neurophysiological markers of early language acquisition: From syllables to sentences. *Trends in Cognitive Sciences, 9,* 481–488.

Frith, C., & Frith, U. (1999). Interacting minds: A biological basis. *Science, 286,* 1692–1695.

Frith, C. D., & Friston, K. J. (1997). Studying brain function with neuroimaging. In M. D. Rugg (Ed.), *Cognitive neuroscience* (pp. 169–196). Cambridge, MA: MIT Press.

Frith, U., & Frith, C. D. (2003). Development and neurophysiology of mentalizing. In C. D. Frith & D. M. Wolpert (Eds.), *The neuroscience of social interaction: Decoding, imitating and influencing the actions of others* (pp. 44–74). Oxford: Oxford University Press.

Fuster, J. M. (2002). *Cortex and mind: Unifying cognition.* New York: Oxford University Press.

Gallese, V., & Goldman, A. (1998). Mirror neurons and the simulation theory of mind reading. *Trends in Cognitive Sciences, 12,* 493–501.

Garber, P., & Goldin-Meadow, S. (2002). Gesture offers insight into problem solving in adults and children. *Cognitive Science, 26,* 817–831.

Georgopoulos, A. P., Schwartz, A. R., & Kettner, R. E. (1986). Neuronal population coding of movement direction. *Science, 233,* 1416–1419.

Gepner, B., & Mestre, D. (2002a). Rapid visual-motion integration deficit in autism. *Trends in Cognitive Sciences, 6,* 455.

Gepner, B., & Mestre, D. (2002b). Postural reactivity to fast visual motion differentiates autistic children from children with Asperger syndrome. *Journal of Autistic Developmental Disorders, 32,* 231–238.

Gergely, G., & Csibra, G. (2003). Teleological reasoning in infancy: The naive theory of rational action. *Trends in Cognitive Sciences, 7,* 287–292.

Gesell, A., & Thompson, H. (1934). *Infant behavior: Its genesis and growth.* New York: McGraw-Hill.

Gibbs, R. W., & O'Brien, J. E. (1990). Idioms and mental imagery: The metaphorical motivation for idiomatic meaning. *Cognition, 36,* 35–68.

Gibson, J. (1950). *The perception of the visual world.* Boston: Houghton-Mifflin.

Glaser, D. (2000). Child abuse and neglect and the brain—A review. *Journal of Child Psychology, 41,* 97–116.

Gottfried, G. M., Gelman, S. A., & Schultz, J. (1999). Children's understanding of the brain: From early essentialism to biological theory. *Cognitive Development, 14,* 147–174.

Gottfried, G. M., & Jow, E. E. (2003). "I just talk with my heart": The mind-body problem, linguistic input and the acquisition of folk psychological beliefs. *Cognitive Development, 18,* 79–90.

Gottlieb, G. (1997). *Synthesizing nature/nurture: The prenatal roots of experience.* Mahwah, NJ: Lawrence Erlbaum Associates.

Gottlieb, G. (1998). Myrtle McGraw's unrecognized conceptual contribution to developmental psychology. *Developmental Review, 18,* 337–448.

Gottlieb, G. (1999). *Probabilistic epigenesis and evolution.* Worcester, MA: Clark University Press.

Gottlieb, G., & Blair, C. (2004). How early experience matters in intellectual development in the case of poverty. *Prevention Science, 5,* 245–252.

Greenough, W. T., & Black, J. E. (1999). Experience, neuroplasticity and psychological development. In N. A. Fox, L. A. Levitt, & J. G. Warhol (Eds.), *The role of early experience in infant development* (pp. 29–40). New York: Johnson and Johnson Pediatric Institute.

Greenspan, R. (2004). *E Pluribus Unum, Ex Uno Plura*: Quantitative- and single-gene perspectives on the study of behavior. *Annual Review of Neuroscience, 27,* 79–105.

Grèzes, J., Frith, C. D., & Passingham, R. E. (2004). Inferring false beliefs from the actions of oneself and others: An fMRI study. *Neuroimage, 21,* 744–750.

Grimaldi, P., Carletti, B., & Rossi, F. (2005). Neuronal replacement and integration in the rewiring of cerebellar circuits. *Brain Research Reviews, 49,* 330–342.

Groome, L. J., Mooney, D. M., Holland, S. B., Smith, L. A., Atterbury, J. L., & Dykman, R. A. (1999). Behavioral state affects heart rate response to low-intensity sound in human fetuses. *Early Human Development, 54,* 39–54.

Groome, L. J., Singh, K. P., Bentz, L. S., Holland, S. B., Atterbury, J. L., Swiber, M. J., & Trimm III, R. F. (1997). Temporal stability in the distribution of behavioral states for individual human fetuses. *Early Human Development, 48,* 187–197.

Gross, C. G. (1998). *Brain, vision, memory: Tales in the history of neuroscience.* Cambridge, MA: MIT Press.

Guajardo, N. R., & Turley-Ames, K. J. (2004). Preschoolers' generation of different types of counterfactual statements and theory of mind understanding. *Cognitive Development, 19,* 53–80.

Guillery, R. W. (2005). Is postnatal neocortical maturation hierarchical? *Trends in Neurosciences, 28,* 512–517.

Habib, R., McIntosh, A. R., Wheeler, M. A., & Tulving, E. (2003). Memory encoding and hippocampally-based novelty and familiarity discrimination networks. *Neuropsychologia, 41,* 271–279.

Hadders-Algra, M. (2000a). The neuronal group selection theory: A framework to explain variation in normal development. *Developmental Medicine and Child Neurology, 42,* 566–572.

Hadders-Algra, M. (2000b). The neuronal group selection theory: Promising principles for understanding and treating developmental motor disorders. *Developmental Medicine and Child Neurology, 42,* 707–715.

Hadders-Algra, M. (2001). Development of gross motor functions. In A. F. Klaerboer & A. Gramsbergen (Eds.), *Handbook of brain and behavior in human development* (pp. 539–568). London: Kluwer/Academic.

Hadders-Algra, M., Brogan, E., & Forssberg, H. (1996). Training affects the development of postural adjustments in sitting infants. *Journal of Physiology, 493,* 289–298.

Hadders-Algra, M., & Forssberg, H. (2001). Development of motor functions in health and disease. In H. Lagercrantz, M. Hanson, P. Evrard, & C. Rodeck (Eds.), *The newborn brain* (pp. 479–507). Cambridge, England: Cambridge University Press.

Haith, M. (1998). Who put the COG in infant cognition? Is rich interpretation too costly? *Infant Behavior and Development, 21,* 167–179.

Haith, M. (1999). The emergence of future-oriented thinking in the early years. In N. Fox, L. A. Leavitt, & J. G. Warhol (Eds.), *The role of early experience in infant development* (pp. 225–248). New York: Johnson and Johnson Pediatric Institute.

Haith, M., Hazan, C., & Goodman, G. S. (1988). Expectation and anticipation of dynamic visual events by 3.5 month-old babies. *Child Development, 59,* 467–479.

Hamburger, V., & Levi-Montalcini, R. (1949). Proliferation, differentiation and degeneration in the spinal ganglia of the chick embryo under normal and experimental conditions. *Journal of Experimental Zoology, 111,* 457–502.

Happé, F. (1999). Autism: Cognitive deficit or cognitive style? *Trends in Cognitive Sciences, 3*, 216–222.

Harman, P. M. (1982). *Energy, force and matter. The conceptual development of nineteenth century physics.* Cambridge, England: Cambridge University Press.

Harris, G. J., Chabris, C. F., Clark, J., Urban, T., Aharon, I., Steele, S., McGrath, L., Condouris, K., & Tager-Flusberg, H. (2005). Brain activation during semantic processing in autism spectrum disorders via functional magnetic resonance imaging. *Brain and Cognition, 61*, 54–68.

Harris, P. L. (1992). From simulation to folk psychology: The case for development. *Mind and Language, 7*, 120–144.

Hebb, D. O. (1949). *The organization of behavior.* New York: Wiley.

Hensh, T. K. (2003). Controlling the critical period. *Neuroscience Research, 47*, 17–22.

Heron, J., Whitaker, D., & McGraw, P. V. (2004). Sensory uncertainty governs the extent of audio-visual interaction. *Vision Research, 44*, 2875–2884.

Heyes, C. (2001). Causes and consequences of imitation. *Trends in Cognitive Sciences, 5*, 253–280.

Hodges, S. D., Bruininks, P., & Ivy, L. (2002). It's different when I do it: Feature matching in self-other comparisons. *Personality and Social Psychology Bulletin, 28*, 40–53.

Hoff, E. (2006). How social contexts support and shape language development. *Developmental Review, 26*, 55–88.

Hoff-Ginsberg, E. (1985). Some contributions of mother's speech to their children's syntactic growth. *Journal of Child Language, 12*, 367–386.

Hoff-Ginsberg, E. (1986). Function and structure in maternal speech: Their relation to the child's development of syntax. *Developmental Psychology, 22*, 155–163.

Hollich, G., Newman, R. S., & Jusczyk, P. W. (2005). Infants' use of synchronized visual information to separate streams of speech. *Child Development, 76*, 598–613.

Hopkins, B. J. (2005a). Neuromaturational theories. In B. J. Hopkins, R. G. Baar, G. F. Michel, & P. Rochat (Eds.), *The Cambridge encyclopedia of child development* (pp. 37–48). London: Cambridge University Press.

Hopkins, B. J. (2005b). The challenge of interdisciplinarity: Metaphors, reductionism, and the practice of interdisciplinary research. In B. J. Hopkins, R. G. Baar, G. F. Michel, & P. Rochat (Eds.), *The Cambridge encyclopedia of child development* (pp. 25–34). Cambridge, England: Cambridge University Press.

Horwitz, B., Rumsey, J. M., Grady, C. L., & Rapoport, S. I. (1988). The cerebral metabolic landscape in autism. Intercorrelations of regional glucose utilization. *Archives of Neurology, 45*, 749–755.

Hubel, D. H., & Wiesel, T. N. (1970). The period of susceptibility to the physiological effects of unilateral eye closure in kittens. *Journal of Physiology, 206*, 419–436.

Isaac, J. T. R. (2003). Postsynaptic silent synapses: Evidence and mechanisms. *Neuropharmacology, 45*, 450–460.

Iverson, J. M., & Fagan, M. K. (2004). Infant vocal-motor coordination: Precursor to the gesture-speech system? *Child Development, 75*, 1053–1066.

Izhikevich, E. (2006). Polychronization: Compuation with spikes. *Neural Computation, 18*, 254–282.

Izhikevich, E., Gally, J. A., & Edelman, G. M. (2004). Spike-timing dynamics of neuronal groups. *Cerebral Cortex, 14*, 933–944.

Izhikevich, E. M. (2003). Simple model of spiking neurons. *IEEE Transactions on Neural Networks, 14*, 933–944.

Jacob, P., & Jeannerod, M. (2005). The motor theory of social cognition: A critique. *Trends in Cognitive Sciences, 9*, 21–25.

James, D., Pillai, M., & Smoleniec, D. (1995). Neurobehavioral development in the human fetus. In J. P. Lecanuet, W. P. Fifer, N. Krasnegor, & W. P. Smotherman (Eds.), *Fetal development: A psychobiological perspective* (pp. 101–127). Hillsdale, NJ: Lawrence Erlbaum Associates.

James, W. (1981). *The principles of psychology: Vol. 1*. Cambridge, MA: Harvard University Press.

Jeyaseelan, D., O'Callaghan, M., Neulinger, K., Shum, D., & Burns, Y. (2006). The association between early minor motor difficulties in extreme birth weight infants and school age attention difficulties. *Early Human Development, 82*, 249–255.

Johnson, C. N. (1990). If you had my brain, where would I be? Children's understanding of the brain and identity. *Child Development, 61*, 962–972.

Johnson, C. N., & Wellman, H. M. (1982). Children's developing conceptions of the mind and brain. *Child Development, 53*, 222–234.

Johnson, K. (2006). Resonance in an exemplar-based lexicon: The emergence of social identity and phonology. *Journal of Phonetics 34*, 485–499.

Johnson, M. H. (1997). *Developmental cognitive neuroscience*. Malden, MA: Blackwell.

Johnson, M. H. (2000a). Functional brain development in infants: Elements of an interactive specialization framework. *Child Development, 71*, 75–81.

Johnson, M. H. (2000b). Cortical specialization for higher cognitive functions: Beyond the maturational model. *Brain and Cognition, 42*, 124–127.

Johnson, S. P., Bremner, J. G., & Mason, U. C. (2000). The role of good form in young infants' perception of partly occluded objects. *Journal of Experimental Child Psychology, 76*, 1–25.

Johnson, S. P., Amso, D., & Slemmer, J. A. (2003). Development of object concepts in infancy: Evidence for early learning in an eye-tracking paradigm. *Proceedings of the National Academy of Sciences, 100*, 10568–10573.

Jones, E. G. (2000). Cortical and subcortical contributions to activity-dependent plasticity in primate somatosensory cortex. *Annual Review of Neuroscience, 23*, 1–37.

Joseph, R. (2000). Fetal brain behavior and cognitive development. *Developmental Review, 20*, 81–98.

Jung-Beeman, M. (2005). Bilateral brain processes for comprehending natural language. *Trends in Cognitive Sciences, 9*, 512–518.

Jusczyk, P. W. (2002). Language development: From speech perception to first words. In A. Slater & M. Lewis (Eds.), *Introduction to infant development* (pp. 147–166). Oxford: Oxford University Press.

Kagan, J. (1994). *Galen's prophecy: Temperament and human nature*. New York: Basic Books.

Kagan, J., & Herschkowitz, N. (2005). *A young mind in a growing brain*. Mahwah, NJ:Lawrence Erlbaum Associates.

Karmiloff-Smith, A. (1998). Development itself is the key to understanding developmental disorders. *Trends in Cognitive Sciences, 2*, 389–398.

Kaufman, J., Mareschal, D., & Johnson, M. H. (2003). Graspability and object processing in infants. *Infant Behavior and Development, 26*, 515–528.

Kellman, P., & Arterberry, M. E. (1998). *The cradle of knowledge: Development of perception in infancy*. Cambridge, MA: MIT Press.

Kennan, J. P., Nelson, A., O'Connor, M., & Pascual-Leone A. (2001). Self-recognition and the right hemisphere. *Nature, 409*, 305.

Kisilevsky, B. S., Fearon, I., & Muir, D. W. (1998). Fetuses differentiate vibroacoustic stimuli. *Infant Behavior and Development, 21*, 25–46.

Kiuchi, M., Nagata, N., Ikeno, S., & Terakawa, N. (2000). The relationship between the response to external light stimulation and behavioral states in the human fetus: How it differs from vibroacoustic stimulation. *Early Human Development, 58*, 153–165.

Koch, C. (2004). *The quest for consciousness: A neurobiological approach*. Englewood, CO: Roberts & Company.

Koenig, M. A. (2002). Children's understanding of belief as a normative concept. *New Ideas in Psychology, 20*, 107–130.

Koizumi, H. (2004). The concept of "developing the brain": A new natural science for learning and education. *Brain and Development, 26*, 434–441.

Kolb, B. J. (1995). *Brain plasticity and behavior*. Mahwah, NJ: Lawrence Erlbaum Associates.

Kolb, B. (1999). Neuroanatomy and development overview. In N. A. Fox, L. A. Leavitt, & J. G. Warhol (Eds.), *The role of early experience in infant development* (pp. 5–14). New York: Johnson and Johnson Pediatric Institute.

Kolb, B., Forgie, M., Gibb, R., Gorny, G., & Rowntree, S. (1998). Age, experience and the changing brain. *Neuroscience and Biobehavioral Reviews, 22*, 143–159.

Kolb, B., & Wilshaw, B. (1998). Brain plasticity and behavior. *Annual Review of Psychology, 49*, 127–141.

Kornhaber, M. L., & Orfield, G. (2001). High-stakes testing policies: Examining their assumptions and consequences. In G. Orfield & M. L. Kornhaber (Eds.), *Raising standards or raising barriers: Inequality and high-stakes testing in public education* (pp. 1–18). New York: The Century Foundation Press.

Kraebel, K. S., & Gerhardstein, P. C. (2006). Three-month-old infants' object recognition across changes in viewpoint using an operant learning procedure. *Infant Behavior and Development, 29*, 11–23.

Krekelberg, B., Kubischik, M., Hoffman, K.-P., & Bremmer, F. (2003). Neural correlates of visual localization and mislocalization. *Neuron, 37*, 537–545.

Krichmar, J., & Edelman, G. M. (2003). Brain-based devices: Intelligent systems based on principles of the nervous system. *Proceedings of the IEEE/RSJ International Conference on Intelligent Robots and Systems* (pp. 940–945) Lausanne, Switzerland: IROS.

Kuhl, P. & Meltzoff, A. N. (1996). Infant vocalization in response to speech: Vocal imitation and developmental change. *Journal of the Acoustic Society of American, 100*, 2425–2438.

Kujala, T., Karma, K., Ceponiene, R., et al. (2001). Plastic neural changes and reading improvement caused by audiovisual training in reading impaired children. *Proceedings of the National Academy of Sciences, 98*, 10509–10514.

LaBar, K. S., Gitelman, D. R., Parrish, T. B., & Mesulam, M. (1999). Neuroanatomic overlap of working memory and spatial attention networks: A functional MRI comparison within subjects. *Neuroimage, 10*, 695–704.

Lagercrantz, H., & Herlenius, E. (2001). Neurotransmitters and neuromodulators. In H. Lagercrantz, M. Hanson, P. Evrard, & C. Rodeck (Eds.), *The newborn brain* (pp. 139–165). Cambridge, England: Cambridge University Press.

Lakoff, G. & Johnson, M. (1980). *Metaphors we live by.* Chicago: University of Chicago Press.

Lakoff, G. & Johnson, M. (1999). *Philosophy in the flesh: The embodied mind and its challenge to western thought.* New York: Perseus.

Lalonde, C. E., & Chandler, M. J. (2002). Children's understanding of interpretation. *New Ideas in Psychology, 20,* 163–198.

Lamme, V. A. F. (2004). Separate neural definitions of visual consciousness and visual attention: A case for phenomenal awareness. *Neural Networks, 17,* 861–872.

Lecanuet, J.-P., Granier-Degerre, C., Jacquet, A.-Y., Capponi, I., & Ledru, L. (1993). Prenatal discrimination of a male and a female voice uttering the same sentence. *Early Development of Parenting, 2,* 217–228.

Lecanuet, J.-P., & Schaal, B. (1996). Fetal sensory competencies. *European Journal of Obstetrics & Gynecology and Reproductive Biology, 68,* 1–23.

Leopold, D. A., & Logothetis, N. K. (1999). Multistable phenomena: Changing views of perception. *Trends in Cognitive Sciences, 3,* 254–263.

Lewis, M. D. (2005). Self-organizing individual differences in brain development. *Developmental Review, 25,* 252–277.

Lewkowitz, D. (1994). Development of intersensory perception in infants. In D. Lewkowicz & R. Lickliter (Eds.), *The development of intersensory perception* (pp. 165–203). Hillsdale, NJ: Lawrence Erlbaum Associates.

Li, P., Farkas, I., & MacWhinney, B. (2004). Early lexical development in a self-organizing neural network. *Neural Networks, 17,* 1345–1362.

Liberman, A. M., & Whalen, D. H. (2000). On the relation of speech to language. *Trends in Cognitive Sciences, 4,* 187–196.

Lichtman, J. W. (2001). Developmental neurobiology overview: Synapses, circuits and plasticity. In D. B. Bailey, J. T. Bruer, F. J. Symons, & J. W. Lichtman (Eds.), *Critical thinking about critical periods* (pp. 27–44). Baltimore: Paul H. Brookes.

Lickliter, R., & Bahrick, L. E. (2000). The development of infant intersensory perception: Advantages of a comparative convergent-operations approach. *Psychological Bulletin, 126,* 260–280.

Lieven, E. V. M. (1994). Crosslinguistic and cross cultural aspects of language addressed to children. In C. Gallaway & B. J. Richards (Eds.), *Input and interaction in language acquisition* (pp. 74–106). Cambridge, England: Cambridge University Press.

Liston, C., & Kagan, J. (2002). Memory enhancement in early childhood. *Nature, 419,* 896.

Love, J. M., Eliason, E. E., et al. (2005). The effectiveness of Early Head Start for 3-year-old children and their parents: Lessons for policy and programs. *Developmental Psychology, 41,* 885–901.

Macaluso, E., Frith, C. D., & Driver, J. (2000). Modulation of human visual cortex by cross-modal spatial attention. *Science, 289,* 1206–1208.

Maguire, E. A., & Frith, C. D. (2004). The brain network associated with acquiring semantic knowledge. *Neuroimage, 22,* 171–178.

Majid, A., Bowerman, M., Kita, S., Haun, D. B. M., & Levinson, S. C. (2004). Can language restructure cognition? The case for space. *Trends in Cognitive Sciences, 8*, 108–114.

Mandler, J. M. (2004). Thought before language. *Trends in Cognitive Sciences, 8*, 508–518.

Mareschal, D. (2000). Object knowledge in infancy: Current controversies and approaches. *Trends in Cognitive Sciences, 4*, 408–416.

Marshall, P. J., Bar-Haim, Y., & Fox, N. A. (2002). Development of the EEG from 5 months to 4 years of age. *Clinical Neurophysiology, 113*, 1199–1208.

Martensen, R. L. (2004). *The brain takes shape: An early history.* New York: Oxford University Press.

Maurer, D., & Lewis, T. L. (1998). Overt orienting toward peripheral stimuli: Normal development and underlying mechanisms. In J. E. Richards (Ed.), *Cognitive neuroscience of attention: A developmental perspective* (pp. 51–102). Mahwah, NJ: Lawrence Erlbaum Associates.

Maxwell, J. C. (1892). *Matter in motion.* New York: Van Nostrand.

McGraw, M. B. (1935). *Growth: A study of Johnny and Jimmy.* New York: Appleton-Century-Crofts.

McGraw, M. B. (1941). Development of neuromuscular mechanisms as reflected in crawling and creeping behavior of the human infant. *Journal of Genetic Psychology, 58*, 83–111.

McGraw, M. B. (1943). *The neuromuscular maturation of the human infant.* New York: Columbia University Press.

McGraw, M. B. (1946). Maturation and behavior. In L. Carmichael (Ed.), *Manual of child psychology* (pp. 332–369). New York: Wiley.

McGraw, M. B., & Breeze, K. (1941). Quantitative studies in the development of erect locomotion. *Child Development, 12*, 295.

McIntosh, A. R. (2000). Towards a network theory of cognition. *Neural Networks, 13*, 861–870.

McIntosh, A. R., Rajah, M. N., & Lobaugh, N. J. (2003). Functional connectivity of the medial temporal lobe relates to learning and awareness. *The Journal of Neuroscience, 23*, 6520–6528.

McKinney, M. (2000). Evolving behavioral complexity by extending development. In S. T. Parker, J. Langer, & M. McKinney (Eds.), *Biology, brains and behavior: The evolution of human development* (25–40). Santa Fe, NM: School of American Research.

McKinney, M. J., & McNamara, K. J. (1991). *Heterochrony: The evolution of ontogeny.* New York: Plenum.

Meltzoff, A. N. (2004). The case for a developmental cognitive science: Theories of people and things. In G. Bremner & A. Slater (Eds.), *Theories of infant development* (pp. 145–173). Oxford, England: Blackwell.

Meltzoff, A. N. & Decety, J. (2004). What imitation tells us about social cognition: A approchement between developmental psychology and cognitive neuroscience. In C.D. Frith & D. M. Wolpert (Eds.), *The neuroscience of social interaction: Decoding, imitating and influencing the actions of others* (pp. 44–74). Oxford: OxfordUniversity Press.

Meltzoff, A. N., & Moore, M. K. (1992). Early imitation within a functional framework: The importance of person identity, movement and development. *Infant Behavior and Development, 15*, 479–505.

Meltzoff, A. N., & Moore, M. K. (1998). Object representation, identity, and the paradox of early permanence: Steps toward a new framework. *Infant Behavior and Development, 21*, 201–235.

Mergner, T., & Rosemeier, T. (1998). Interaction of vestibular, somatosensory and visual signals for postural control and motion perception under terrestrial and microgravity conditions—a conceptual model. *Brain Research Reviews, 28*, 118–135.

Merzenich, M. M., & deCharms, R. C. (1996). Neural representations, experience and change. In R. Ilinais & P. Churchland (Eds.), *The mind-brain continuum* (pp. 61–81). Cambridge, MA: MIT Press.

Merzenich, M., Miller, S., Jenkins, W. M., Saunders, G., Protopapas, A., Peterson, B., & Tallal, P. (1998). Amelioration of the acoustic reception and speech reception deficits underlying language-based learning impairments. In C. V. Euler (Ed.), *Basic neural mechanisms in cognition and language* (pp. 143–172). Amsterdam: Elsevier.

Merzenich, M. M., Nelson, R. J., Stryker, M. P., Cyander, A., Schoppman, A., & Zook, J. M. (1984). Somatosensory cortical map changes following digit amputation in adult monkeys. *Journal of Comparative Neurology, 224*, 591–605.

Metzinger, T., & Gallese, V. (2003). The emergence of a shared action ontology: Building blocks for a theory. *Consciousness and Cognition, 12*, 549–571.

Miller, S. A. (2000). Childrens's understanding of preexisting differences in knowledge and belief. *Developmental Review, 20*, 227–282.

Milner, P. M. (2006). Trains of neural thought. *Canadian Psychology, 47*, 36–43.

Mirmiran, M., & Kok, J. H. (1991). Circadian rhythms in early human development. *Early Human Development, 26*, 121–128.

Morin, A. (2002). Right hemispheric self-awareness: A critical assessment. *Consciousness and Cognition, 11*, 396–401.

Morokuma, S., Fukushima, K., Kawai, N., Tomonaga, M., Satoh, S., & Nakano, H. (2004). Fetal habituation correlates with functional brain development. *Behavioral Brain Research, 153*, 459–463.

Moses, L. J., Coon, J. A., & Wusinich, N. (2000). Young children's understanding of desire formation. *Developmental Psychology, 36*, 77–90.

Müller, U., Zelazo, P. D., & Imrisek, S. (2005). Executive function and children's understanding of false belief: How specific is the relation? *Cognitive Development, 20*, 173–189.

Munakata, Y., Casey, B. J., & Diamond, A. (2004). Developmental cognitive neuroscience. *Progress and Potential, 8*, 122–128.

Nagarajan, S., Mahncke, H., Salz, T., Tallal, P., Roberts, T., & Merzenich, M. M. (1999). Cortical auditory signal processing in poor readers. *Proceedings of the National Academy of Sciences, 93*, 2664–2669.

Naigles, L. (1996). The use of multiple frames in verb learning via syntactic bootstrapping. *Cognition, 58*, 2212–2251.

Newen, A., & Vogeley, K. (2003). Self-representation: Searching for a neural signature of self-consciousness. *Consciousness and Cognition, 12*, 529–543.

Nicoll, A., & Blakemore, C. (1993). Patterns of local connectivity in the neocortex. *Neural Computation, 5*, 665–680.

Nigg, J. T., Willcut, E. G., Doyle, A. E., & Sonuga-Barke, J. S. (2005). Causal heterogeneity in attention-deficit/hyperactivity disorder: Do we need neuropsychologically impaired subtypes? *Biological Psychiatry, 57,* 1224–1230.

Nijhuis, J. G. (1995). Physiological and clinical consequences in relation to the development of fetal behavior and fetal behavioral states. In J. P. Lecanuet, W. P. Fifer, N. Krasnegor, & W. P. Smotherman (Eds.), *Fetal development: A psychobiological perspective* (pp. 67–83). Hillsdale, NJ: Lawrence Erlbaum Associates.

Nijhuis, J. G. (2003). Fetal behavior. *Neurobiology of Aging, 24,* S41–S46.

Norbury, C. F. (2005). Barking up the wrong tree: Lexical ambiguity resolution in children with language impairments and autistic spectrum disorders. *Journal of Experimental Child Psychology, 90,* 142–171.

Nyberg, L., Forkstam, C., Petersson, K. M., Cabeza, R., & Ingvar, M. (2002a). Brain imaging of human memory systems: Between-systems similarities and within-system differences. *Cognitive Brain Research, 134,* 281–292.

Nyberg, L., Marklund, P., Persson, J., Cabeza, R., Forkstam, C., Petersson, K. M., & Ingvaer, M. (2002b). Common prefrontal activations during working memory, episodic memory and semantic memory. *Neuropsychologia, 41,* 371–377.

O'Donovan, M. J. (1999). The origin of spontaneous activity in developing networks of the vertebrate nervous system. *Current Opinion in Neurobiology, 9,* 94–104.

Okado, N., & Kojima, T. (1994). Ontogeny of the central nervous system: Neurogenesis, fibre connection, synaptogenesis and myelination in the spinal cord. *Clinics in Developmental Medicine, 94,* 31–46.

Onishi, K. H., & Baillargeon, R. (2005). Do 15-month old infants understand false beliefs? *Science, 308,* 255–258.

Oppenheim, R. W. (1988). Ontogenetic adaptations in neural and behavioral development: Toward a more "ecological" developmental biology. In A. Hill & J. J. Volpe (Eds.), *Fetal neurology* (pp. 16–30). New York: Raven.

Oppenheim, R. W. (1992). Pathways in the emergence of developmental neuroethology: Antecedents to current views of neurobehavioral ontogeny [Special Issue]. *Journal of Neurobiology, 23,* 1370–1403.

Oshima,-Takane, Y., & Robbins, M. (2003). Linguistic environment of second-born children. *First Language, 23,* 21–40.

Özcahskan, S., & Goldin-Meadow, S. (2005). Gesture is the cutting edge of early language development. *Cognition, 96,* B101–B113.

Paule, M. G., Rowland, A. S., Ferguson, S. A., Chelonis, J. J., Tannock, R., Swansn, J. M., & Castellanos, F. X. (2000). Attention hyperactivity/deficit disorder: Characteristics, interventions and models. *Neurotoxicology and Teratology, 22,* 631–651.

Peinado, A. (2000). Traveling slow waves of neural activity: A novel form of network activity in developing neocortex. *The Journal of Neuroscience, 20,* 1–6.

Peinado, A. (2001). Immature neocortical neurons exist as extensive syncitial networks linked by dendrodendritic electrical connections. *Journal of Physiology, 55,* 620–629.

Peirano, P., Algarin, C., & Uauy, R. (2003, October). Sleep-wake states and their regulatory mechanisms throughout early human development. *Journal of Pediatrics,* pp. 570–579.

Pennington, B. (2005). Commentary: Toward a new neuropsychological model of attention-deficit/hyperactivity disorder: Subtypes and multiple deficits. *Biological Psychiatry, 57,* 1221–1223.

Penrose, R. (1994). *Shadows of the mind: A search for the missing science of consciousness*. Oxford, England: Oxford University Press.

Perner, J., & Lang, B. (1999). Development of theory of mind and executive control. *Trends in Cognitive Sciences, 3*, 337–344.

Perner, J., Leekam, S. R., & Wimmer, H. (1987). Three year-olds' difficulty with false belief: The case for a conceptual deficit. *British Journal of Developmental Psychology, 5*, 125–137.

Perner, J., & Ruffman, T. (2005). Infants' insight into the mind: How deep? *Science, 308*, 214–216.

Perner, J., Stummer, S., Sprung, M., & Doherty, M. (2002). Theory of mind finds its Piagetian perspective: Why alternative naming comes with understanding belief. *Cognitive Development, 17*, 1451–1472.

Perry, B., & Pollard, R. (1998). Homeostasis, stress, trauma and adaptation. A neurodevelopmental view of childhood trauma. *Child and Adolescent Clinics in North America, 7*, 33–51.

Peskin, J., & Astington, J. W. (2004). The effects of adding metacognitive language to story texts. *Cognitive Development, 19*, 253–273.

Petitto, L. A., Holowka, S., Sergio, L. E., Levy, B., & Ostry, D. J. (2004). Baby hands that move to the rhythm of language: Hearing babies acquiring sign languages babble silently on the hands. *Cognition, 93*, 43–73.

Phillips, A. T., Wellman, H. M., & Spelke, E. S. (2002). Infants' ability to connect gaze and emotional expression to intentional action. *Cognition, 85*, 53–78.

Piaget, J. (1928). *Judgment and reasoning in the child*. London: Kegan Paul, Trench and Trubner. (Original publication in French, 1923)

Pick, H. (2003). Development and learning: An historical perspective on acquisition of motor control. *Infant Behavior and Development, 26*, 441–448.

Pierno, A. C., Mari, M., Glover, S., Georgiou, I., & Castiello, U. (2005). Failure to read motor intentions from gaze in children with autism. *Neuropsychologia, 44*, 1483–1488.

Pinkstaff, J. K., Chappell, S. A., Mauro, V. P., Edelman, G. M., & Krushel, L. A. (2001). Internal initiation of translation of five dendritically localized neuronal mRNAs. *Proceedings of the National Academy of Sciences, 98*, 2770–2775.

Pittman, R., & Oppenheim, R. W. (1979). Neuromuscular blockade increases motoneuron survival during normal cell death in the chick embryo. *Nature, 271*, 364–366.

Plautz, E. J., Millikan, G. W., & Nudo, R. J. (2000). Effects of repetitive motor training on movement representations in adult squirrel monkeys: Role of use versus learning. *Neurobiology of Learning and Memory, 74*, 27–55.

Posner, M. I., & Rothbart, M. K. (1998). Attention, self-regulation and consciousness. *Philosophical Transactions of the Royal Society of London, 353*, 1915–1927.

Postle, B. R. (2005). Working memory as an emergent property of mind and brain. *Neuroscience, 139*, 23–38.

Pozzo, T., Papaxanthis, C., Stapley, P., & Berthoz, A. (1998). The sensorimotor and cognitive integration of gravity. *Brain Research Reviews, 28*, 92–101.

Prechtl, H. F. R. (1997). State of the art of a new functional assessment of the young nervous system: An early predictor of cerebral palsy. *Early Human Development, 50*, 1–11.

Preissl, H., Lowery, C. L., & Eswaran, H. (2004). Fetal magnetoencephalography: Current progress and trends. *Experimental Neurology, 190*, S28–S36.

Premack, D., & Woodruff, G. (1978). Does the chimpanzee have a theory of mind? *Behavioral and Brain Sciences, 1*, 515–526.

Price, C. J. & Friston, K. J. (2002). Degeneracy and cognitive anatomy. *Trends in Cognitive Sciences, 6*, 416–421.

Purves, D. (1988). *Body and brain: A trophic theory of neural connections.* Cambridge, MA: Harvard University Press.

Purves, D. (1994). *Neural activity and the growth of the brain.* Cambridge: Cambridge University Press.

Purves, D., & Lotto, B. (2003). *Why we see what we do: An empirical theory of vision.* New York: Sinauer Associates.

Quartz, S., & Sejnowski, T. J. (1997). The neural basis of cognitive development: A constructivist manifesto. *Behavioral and Brain Sciences, 20*, 537–596.

Quinn, P. C. (2002). Categorization. In M. Lewis & A. Slater (Eds.), *Introduction to infant development* (pp. 115–131). New York: Oxford University Press.

Quinn, P. C., & Schyns, P. (2003). What goes up may come down: Perceptual process and knowledge access in the organization of complex visual patterns by young infants. *Cognitive Science, 27*, 923–935.

Ranganath, C., & D'Esposito, M. (2001). Medial temporal lobe activity associated with active maintenance of novel information. *Neuron, 31*, 865–873.

Ranganath, C., Johnson, M. K., & D'Esposito, M. (2002). Prefrontal activity associated with working memory and episodic long-term memory. *Neuropsychologia, 41*, 378–389.

Reddy, V. (2003). On being the object of attention: Implications for self-other consciousness. *Trends in Cognitive Sciences, 7*, 397–402.

Reeke, G. N., Jr., Sporns, O., Gall, W. E., Tononi, G., & Edelman, G. M. (1993). A biologically based synthetic nervous system for a real world device. In R. J. Mammore (Ed.), *Artificial neural networks for speech and vision* (pp. 457–473). London: Chapman and Hall.

Revonsuo, A. (2000). Prospects for a scientific research program on consciousness. In T. Metzinger (Ed.), *Neural correlates of consciousness: Empirical and conceptual questions* (pp. 57–76). Cambridge, MA: MIT Press.

Revonsuo, A. (2001). Can functional brain imaging discover consciousness in the brain? *Journal of Consciousness Studies, 8*, 3–23.

Richards, C. A., & Sanderson, J. A. (1999). The role of imagination in facilitating deductive reasoning in 2-, 3- and 4 year olds. *Cognition, 72*, 1–9.

Ricoeur, P. (2005). *The course of recognition* (D. Pellauer, Trans.). Cambridge, MA: Harvard University Press.

Riggs, K. J., Peterson, D. M., Robinson, E. J., & Mitchell, P. (1998). Are errors in false belief tasks symptomatic of a broader difficulty with counterfactuality? *Cognitive Development, 13*, 73–90.

Rizzolatti, G., Fadiga, L., Fogassi, L., & Gallesse, V. (2002). From mirror neurons to imitation: Facts and speculation. In A. N. Meltzoff & W. Prinz (Eds.), *The imitative mind: Development, evolution and brain bases* (pp. 247–266). Cambridge, England: Cambridge University Press.

Rizzolatti, G., Riggio, L., & Dascola, I. (1987). Reorienting attention across the horizontal and vertical meridians: Evidence in favor of a premotor theory of attention. *Neuropsychologia, 25*, 31–40.

Roberts, T. D. M. (1995). *Understanding balance: The mechanics of posture and loco-motion*. London: Chapman and Hall.

Rose, D. F., & Eswaran, H. (2004). Spontaneous neuronal activity in fetuses and newborns. *Experimental Neurology, 190*, S37–S43.

Rosenzweig, M. R. (1998). Historical perspectives on the development of the biology of learning and memory. In J. L. Martinez, Jr., & R. P. Kesner (Eds.), *Neurobiology of learning and memory* (pp. 1–53). San Diego: Academic Press.

Rosenzweig, M. R. (1999). Effects of differential experience on brain and cognition throughout the life span. In S. H. Broman & J. M. Fletcher (Eds.), *The changing nervous system: Neurobehavioral consequences of early brain disorders* (pp. 25–50). New York: Oxford University Press.

Rosenzweig, M. R., Kreech, D., & Bennett, E. L. (1963). Effects of differential experience on brain AchE and ChE and brain anatomy in the rat, as a function of stain and age. *American Psychologist, 18*, 430.

Rosenzweig, M. R., Kreech, D., Bennett, E. L., & Diamond, M. C. (1962). Effects of environmental complexity and training on brain chemistry and anatomy: A replication and extension. *Journal of Comparative Physiological Psychology, 55*, 429–437.

Rovee-Collier, C., Hayne, H., & Colombo, M. (2001). *The development of implicit and explicit memory*. Amsterdam: John Benjamins.

Ruff, H. A., & Rothbart, M. K. (1996). *Attention in early development: Themes and variations*. New York: Oxford University Press.

Salenius, S., & Hari, R. (2003). Synchronous cortical oscillatory activity during motor action. *Current Opinion in Neurobiology, 13*, 678–784.

Saxe, R. (2005). Against simulation: The argument from error. *Trends in Cognitive Sciences, 9*, 174–179.

Saxe, R., Carey, S., & Kanwisher, N. (2004). Understanding other minds: Linking developmental psychology and functional neuroimaging. *Annual Review of Psychology, 55*, 87–124.

Scerif, G., & Karmiloff-Smith, A. (2005). The dawn of cognitive genetics? Crucial developmental caveat. *Trends in Cognitive Sciences, 9*, 126–135.

Scheibel, A. B., Conrad, T., Perdue, S., Tomiyasu, U., & Weschler, A. (1990). A quantitative study of dendrite complexity in selected areas of the human cerebral cortex. *Brain and Cognition, 12*, 85–101.

Schilling, T. H., & Clifton, R. (1998). Nine-month-old infants learn about a physical event in a single session: Implications for infants' understanding of physical phenomena. *Cognitive Development, 13*, 165–184.

Schneck, C. M. (2001). The efficacy of a sensorimotor treatment approach by occupational therapists. In R. Huebner (Ed.), *Autism: A sensorimotor approach to management* (pp. 139–177). Gaithersburg, MD: Aspen.

Scholl, B. J. (2004). Can infants' object concepts be trained? *Trends in Cognitive Sciences, 8*, 49–51.

Schore, A. (1994). *Affect regulation and the origin of the self: The neurobiology of emotional development*. Hillsdale, NJ: Lawrence Erlbaum Associates.

Schult, C. A., & Wellman, H. M. (1997). Explaining human movements and actions: Children's understanding of the limits of psychological explanation. *Cognition, 62*, 291–324.

Schyns, P. G. (1997). Categories and percepts: A bi-directional framework for categorization. *Trends in Cognitive Sciences, 1*, 183–189.

Searle, J. (1998). *Mind, language and society.* New York: Basic Books.

Searle, J. (2004). *Mind: A brief introduction.* New York: Oxford University Press.

Senghas, A., Kita, S., & Özyürek, A. (2004). Children creating core properties of language: Evidence from an emerging sign language in Nicaragua. *Science, 305,* 779–1782.

Senut, M.-C., & Gage, F. H. (1999). Prenatal gene therapy: Can the technical hurdles be overcome? *Molecular Medicine Today, 5,* 152–156.

Seth, A. K., Baars, B. J., & Edelman, D. B. (2005). Criteria for consciousness in humans and other mammals. *Consciousness and Cognition, 14,* 119–139.

Seth, A. K., Edelman, G. M., & Krichmar, J. L. (forthcoming). Distinguishing cause from context in neural dynamics during spatial navigation.

Seth, A. K., McKinstry, J. L., Edelman, G. M., & Krichmar, J. (2004). Visual binding through reentrant connectivity and dynamic synchronization in a brain-based device. *Cerebral Cortex, 14,* 1185–1199.

Shankle, W. R., Romney, R., Kimball, A., Landing, B. H., & Junko, H. (1998). Developmental patterns in the cytoarchitecture of the human cerebral cortex from birth to 6 years examined by correspondence analysis. *Proceedings of the National Academy of Sciences, 95,* 4023–4028.

Shaw, C. A., & McEachern, J. C. (2001). Traversing levels of organization: A theory of neuronal plasticity and stability. In C. A. Shaw & J. C. McEachern (Eds.), *Toward a theory of neural plasticity* (pp. 427–438). New York: Psychology Press.

Shilling, T. H. & Clifton, R. K. (1998). Nine-month-old infants learn about a physical event in a single session: Implications for infants' understanding of physcial phenomena. *Cognitive Development, 13,* 165–184.

Shimojo, S., & Shams, L. (2001). Sensory modalities are not separate modalities: Plasticity and interactions. *Current Opinion in Neurobiology, 11,* 505–509.

Shonkoff, J. P., & Phillips, D. A. (2000). *From neurons to neighborhoods: The science of early childhood development.* Washington, DC: National Academy Press.

Shors, T. J., & Matzel, L. D. (1997). Long-term potentiation: What's learning got to do with it? *Behavioral and Brain Sciences, 20,* 597–655.

Shultz, T. R., & Mareschal, D. (1997). Rethinking innateness. Learning and constructivism: Connectionist perspectives on development. *Cognitive Development, 12,* 563–586.

Siegler, R. S. (2002). Variability and infant development. *Infant Behavior and Development, 25,* 550–557.

Smith, J. R. (1938). The electroencephalogram during normal infancy and childhood: Rhythmic activities present in the neonate and their subsequent development. *Journal of Genetic Psychology, 53,* 431–453.

Smith, J. R. (1939). The occipital and pre-central alpha rhythms during the first two years. *Journal of Psychology, 7,* 223–227.

Smith, J. R. (1941). The frequency growth of the human alpha rhythms during normal infancy and childhood. *Journal of Psychology, 7,* 177–198.

Sonuga-Barke, E. J. S. (2003). The dual pathway model of AD/HD: An elaboration of neuro-developmental characteristics. *Neuroscience and Biobehavioral Reviews, 27,* 593–604.

Sonuga-Barke, E. J. S. (2005). Causal models of attention-deficit/hyperactivity disorder: From common simple deficits to multiple developmental pathways. *Biological Psychiatry, 57,* 1231–1238.

Spelke, E. S., Breinlinger, K., Macomber, J., & Jacobson, K. (2002). Origins of knowledge. *Psychological Review, 99*, 605–632.

Spence, C., Shore, D. I., & Klein, R. M. (2001). Multisensory prior entry. *Journal of Experimental Psychology, 130*, 799–832.

Sperry, R. W. (1943). Visuomotor coordination in the newt after regeneration of the optic nerve. *Journal of Comparative Neurology, 79*, 33–55.

Srinivassen, R., Russell, Edelman, D. P., Tononi, G. (1999). Increased synchronization of neuromagnetic responses during conscious perception. *The Journal of Neuroscience, 19*, 5435–5448.

Stein, B. E., & Meredith, M. A. (1993). *The merging of the senses.* Cambridge, MA: MIT Press.

Stein, B. M., Meredith, M. A., & Wallace, M. (1994). Development and the neural basis of multisensory integation. In D. Lewkowicz & R. Lickliter (Eds.), *The development of intersensory perception* (pp. 81–106). Hillsdale, NJ: Lawrence Erlbaum Associates.

Stein, D. G., Brailowsky, S., & Will, B. (1995). *Brain repair.* New York: Oxford University Press.

Strand, E. (2000). *Gender stereotype effects in speech processing.* Unpublished doctoral dissertation, Ohio State University.

Taga, G., Ikejiri, T., Tachibana, T., Shimojo, S., Soeda, A., Takeuci, K., & Konishi, Y. (2002). Visual feature binding in early infancy. *Perception, 32*, 273–286.

Tannock, R., Hetherington, R., Ickowicz, A., Schachar, R., & Hockenberry, M. (2000). Time perception in attention-deficit/hyperactivity disorder: Effects of co-morbid reading disorder and methylphenidate. *American Journal of Psychiatry, 157*, 851–880.

Tassi, P., & Muzet, A. (2001). Defining the states of consciousness. *Neuroscience and Biobehavioral Reviews, 25*, 175–191.

Taylor, C. M., Kennett, S., & Haggard, P. (2002). Vision modulates somatosensory cortical processing. *Current Biology, 12*, 233–236.

Taylor, J. G. (2001). Functional brain imaging to search for consciousness needs attention. *Journal of Consciousness Studies, 8*, 39–43.

Taylor, M., Esbensen, B. M., & Bennett, T. T. (1994). Children's understanding of knowledge acquisition: The tendency for children to report they have always known what they have just learned. *Child Development, 65*, 1581–1604.

Temple, E., Deutsch, G. K., Poldrack, R. A., Miller, S. L., Tallal, P., Merzenich, M. M., & Gabrieli, J. D. E. (2003). Neural deficits in children with dyslexia ameliorated by behavioral remediation: Evidence from functional MRI. *Proceedings of the National Academy of Sciences, 100*, 2860–2865.

Teyler, T. J. (2001). LTP and the superfamily of synaptic plasticities. In C. A. Shaw & J. C. McEachern (Eds.), *Toward a theory of neuroplasticity* (pp. 101–117). Philadelphia: Psychology Press.

Thatcher, R. (1997). Human frontal lobe development: A theory of cyclical cortical reorganization. In N. Krasnegor, G. Lyon, & P. Goldman-Rakic (Eds.), *Development of the prefrontal cortex: Evolution, neurobiology and behavior* (pp. 85–116). Baltimore: Paul H. Brookes.

Thelen, E. (1987). The role of motor development in developmental psychology: A view of the past and an agenda for the future. In N. Eisenberg (Ed.), *Contemporary topics in developmental psychology* (pp. 3–33). NewYork: Wiley.

Thelen, E. (1996). Reply to Dalton. *American Psychologia, 51*, 552–553.

Thelen, E. (2000). Grounded in the world: Developmental origins of the embodied mind. *Infancy, 1*, 3–28.

Thelen, E. (2001). Dynamic mechanisms of change in early perceptual-motor development. In J. L. McCleland & R. S. Siegler (Eds.), *Mechanisms of cognitive development: Behavioral and neural perspectives* (pp. 161–184). Mahwah, NJ: Lawrence Erlbaum Associates.

Thelen, E., & Smith, L. B. (1998). Dynamic systems theories. In R. Lerner (Ed.), *Handbook of child psychology* (Vol. 1., pp. 563–634). New York: Wiley.

Thesen, T., Vibell, J. F., & Calvert, G. A. (2004). Neuroimaging of multisensory processing in vision, audition, touch and olfaction. *Cognitive Processes, 5*, 84–93.

Toichi, M., Kamio, Y., Okada, T., Sakihama, M., Youngstrom, E. A., Findling, R. L., & Yamamoto, K. (2002). A lack of self-consciousness in autism. *American Journal of Psychiatry, 159*, 1422–1424.

Tomlin, D., Kayali, M. A., King-Casa, B., Anen, C., Camerer, C. F., Quartz, S. R., & Montague, R. (2006). Agent-specific responses in the cingulate cortex during economic exchanges. *Science, 312*, 1047–1050.

Tononi, G., & Edelman, G. (1998). Consciousness and complexity. *Science, 282*, 1846–1851.

Tononi, G., Edelman, G. M. & Sporns, O. (1998). Compexity and coherency: Integrating information in the brain. *Trends in Cognitive Sciences, 2*, 474–478.

Toplak, M. E., Dockstader, C., & Tannock, R. (2006). Temporal information processing in ADHD: Findings to date and new methods. *Journal of Neuroscience Methods, 151*, 15–29.

Touwen, B. C. L. (1976). Neurological development in infancy. *Clinics in Developmental Medicine, No. 58*. London: Heinemann Medical Books.

Touwen, B. C. L. (1995). Epilogue: A neurologist's "homage." In T. C. Dalton & V. W. Bergenn (Eds.), *Beyond heredity and environment: Myrtle McGraw and the maturation controversy* (pp. 271–283). Boulder, CO: Westview.

Touwen, B. C. L. (1998). The brain and the development of function. *Developmental Review, 18*, 504–526.

Trevarthen, C. (2001). The neurobiology of early communication: Intersubjective regulations in human brain development. In A. F. Kalverboer & A. Gramsbergen (Eds.), *Handbook of brain and behavior in human development* (pp. 841–882). Dordrecht, Netherlands: Kluwer.

Ungerleider, L. F. (1995). Functional brain imaging studies of cortical mechanisms of memory. *Science, 270*, 769–775.

Van Geert, P., & Steenbeek, H. (2005). Explaining after by before: Basic aspects of a dynamic systems approach to the study of development. *Developmental Review, 25*, 408–444.

Van Heteren, C. F., Boekkooi, P. F., Jongsma, W., & Nijhuis, J. G. (2001). Fetal habituation to vibroacoustic stimulation in relation to fetal states and fetal heart rate parameters. *Early Human Development, 61*, 135–145.

Vohr, B. R., Wright, L., et al. (2000). Neurodevelopmental and functional outcomes of extremely low birth weight infants in the National Institute of Child Health and Human Development Neonatal Research Network, 1993–1994. *Pediatrics, 105*, 1216–1226.

Volterra, V., Caselli, M. C., Capirici, O., & Pizzuto, E. (2005). Gesture and the emergence and development of language. In M. Tomasello & D. I. Slobin (Eds.), *Beyond nature-nurture: Essays in honor of Elizabeth Bates* (pp. 3–40). Mahwah, NJ: Lawrence Erlbaum Associates.

Voronin, L. L., & Cherubini, E. (2003). "Presynaptic silence" may be golden. *Neuropharmacology, 45,* 439–449.

Wade, N. (1995). *Psychologists in word and image.* Cambridge, MA: MIT Press.

Wassenberg, R., Feron, J. M., Kessels, G. H., et al. (2005). Relation between cognitive and motor performance in 5- to 6- year old children: Results from a large scale cross-sectional study. *Child Development, 76,* 1092–1103.

Weinbach, A. P. (1937). Some physiological phenomena fitted to growth equations: I. Moro reflex. *Human Biology, 9,* 549–555.

Weinbach, A. P (1938a). Some physiological phenomena fitted to growth equations: II. Brain potentials. *Human Biology, 10,* 145–150.

Weinbach, A. P. (1938b). Some physiological phenomena fitted to growth equations: III. Rate of growth of brain potentials (alpha frequency) compared with rate of growth of the brain. *Growth, 2,* 247–251.

Weinbach, A. P. (1938c). Some physiological phenomena fitted to growth equations: IV. Time and power relations for a human infant climbing inclines of various slopes. *Growth, 4,* 123–134.

Weiss, P. (1965). Research in retrospect. In G. Gabbiani (Ed.), *Reflections on biologic research* (pp. 237–244). St. Louis: Warren H. Green.

Weizman, Z. O., & Snow, E. E. (2001). Lexical input as related to children's vocabulary acquisition: Effects of sophisticated exposure and support for meaning. *Developmental Psychology, 37,* 265–279.

Wellman, H. O. (1990). *The child's theory of mind.* Cambridge, MA: Cambridge University Press.

Westermann, G., & Miranda, E. R. (2004). A new model of sensorimotor coupling in the development of speech. *Brain and Language, 89,* 393–400.

Wexler, M., & Boxtel, J. J. A. (2005). Depth perception by the active observer. *Trends in Cognitive Sciences, 9,* 431–438.

Wimmer, H., & Perner, J. (1983). Beliefs about beliefs—representation and constraining function of wrong beliefs in young children's understanding of deception. *Cognition, 13,* 103–128.

Windle, W. F. (1979). *The pioneering role of Clarence Luther Herrick in American Neuroscience. Hicksville,* NY: Exposition Press.

Woodward, A. L. (1998). Infants selectively encode the goal object of an actor's reach. *Cognition, 69,* 1–34.

Woodward, A. L. (1999). Infant's ability to distinguish between purposeful and nonpurposeful behaviors. *Infant Behavior and Development, 22,* 145–160.

Woollacott, M. H. P., Burtner, P., Jensen, J., Jasiewicz, J. N., Roncesvalles, N., & Sveistrup, H. (1998). Development of postural responses during standing in healthy children and children with spasticity. *Neuroscience & Biobehavioral Reviews, 22,* 583–589.

Wunderlich, K., Schneider, K. A., & Kastner, S. (2005). Neural correlates of binocular rivalry in the human lateral geniculate nucleus. *Nature Neuroscience, 8,* 1595–1602.

Zelazo, P. D. (2000). Self-reflection and the development of consciously controlled processing. In P. Mitchell & K. Riggs (Eds.), *Children's reasoning and the mind* (pp. 169–189). New York: Psychology Press.

Zelazo, P. D., & Sommerville, J. A. (2001). Levels of consciousness of the self in time. In C. Moore & K. Lemmon (Eds.), *The self in time* (pp. 229–252). Mahwah, NJ: Lawrence Erlbaum Associates.

Zelazo, P. R. (1997). Infant-toddler information processing treatment of children with pervasive developmental disorder and autism: Part I. *Infants and Young Children, 10*, 1–14.

Zelazo, P. R. (1998). McGraw and the development of unaided walking. *Developmental Review, 18*, 449–471.

Zelazo, P. R. (2001). A developmental perspective on early autism: Affective, behavioral and cognitive factors. In J. A. Burack, T. Charman, N. Yirmiya, & P. D. Zelazo (Eds.), *The development of autism: Perspectives from theory and research* (pp. 39–60). Mahwah: NJ: Lawrence Erlbaum Associates.

Zelazo, P. R., & Zelazo, P. D. (1998). The emergence of consciousness. In H. Jasper, L. Descarries, V. Castellucci, & S. Rossignol (Eds.), *Consciousness* (pp. 149–165). Philadelphia: Lippencott-Raven.

Zigler, E., & Meunchow, S. (1999). *Head Start: The inside story of America's most successful educational experiment.* New York: Basic Books.

Zwaigenbaum L., Bryson, S., Rogers, T., Roberts, W., Brian, J., & Szatmari, P. (2005). Behavioral manifestations of autism in the first year of life. *Journal of Developmental Neuroscience, 23*, 143–152.

Author Index

Subject Index

A

acetylcholine (ACh) receptors,
  presynaptic, 89
AChE levels, 113
active attention *versus*
  passive reception, 113
allocentric perspectives, 79
alpha rhythm, 19, 93
ambiguity, 38–39
amodal relationships, 15
amygdale, 68, 132
anterior cingulate gyrus, 201
attention, 63–67
  active, *versus* passive reception, 113
  behavioral states and, 63–67
    bimodal stimulation,
      discrimination through, 66–67
    early sensory development,
      sequence of, 63–64
    stimulation, effect on
      prenatal state, 64–66
  focused, 125
  joint, 178–179
  looking behavior and, 123–126
  neurodynamics of, 173–177
  selective, 96, 113, 137, 154
  in temperament and
    emotional state, 132–134
  valuable difference of, 151–158
attention deficit hyperactivity disorder
  (ADHD), 133–134
attention deficits
  ADHD, 133–134
  temporal and multimodal
    basis of, 134–135
attitudes, 139–143
  in autism, control of, 142–143
  balance in, 139–141
  defined, 139
  effort and, 201–202

energy in, conservation of, 141–142
gravity, balance, and
  self-awareness in, 139–141
attunement theory (Trevarthen), 12–13
auditory input, 26, 154, 155, 160
auditory receptive fields, 26, 201
auditory stimulation, 67, 102, 153
autism
  as motion-dependent perceptual
    disorder, 130–131
  gaze and, 179
  learning, attitudes as a
    constraint to, 142–143
  sensory processing
    disorders in, 73, 157
  onset of, predicting, 151
awareness, conscious, 121, 123, 139, 151
axonal sprouting, 21

B

Babinski reflex, 19
balance
  in attitude control, 139–141
  in infants, maintaining
    upright sitting
    position, 124, 125
basal ganglia, 44, 69, 76, 124,
  134, 152, 175
behavioral states, 58–60
  attention and, 63–67
  bimodal stimulation, discrimination
    through, 66–67
  early sensory development,
    sequence of, 63–64
  stimulation, effect
    on prenatal state, 64–66
  temperament and, 67–69
    cortical development and, 67
    regulatory control, fetal
      state concordance and, 67–69
behaviorism (Watson), 4, 97